T0184060

Lecture Notes in Computer Science 11602

Commenced Publication in 1973
Founding and Former Series Editors:
Gerhard Goos, Juris Hartmanis, and Jan van Leeuwen

Editorial Board Members

David Hutchison
  Lancaster University, Lancaster, UK
Takeo Kanade
  Carnegie Mellon University, Pittsburgh, PA, USA
Josef Kittler
  University of Surrey, Guildford, UK
Jon M. Kleinberg
  Cornell University, Ithaca, NY, USA
Friedemann Mattern
  ETH Zurich, Zurich, Switzerland
John C. Mitchell
  Stanford University, Stanford, CA, USA
Moni Naor
  Weizmann Institute of Science, Rehovot, Israel
C. Pandu Rangan
  Indian Institute of Technology Madras, Chennai, India
Bernhard Steffen
  TU Dortmund University, Dortmund, Germany
Demetri Terzopoulos
  University of California, Los Angeles, CA, USA
Doug Tygar
  University of California, Berkeley, CA, USA

More information about this series at http://www.springer.com/series/7408

Xin Peng · Apostolos Ampatzoglou ·
Tanmay Bhowmik (Eds.)

Reuse in the Big Data Era

18th International Conference on Software
and Systems Reuse, ICSR 2019
Cincinnati, OH, USA, June 26–28, 2019
Proceedings

 Springer

Editors
Xin Peng
Fudan University
Shanghai, China

Apostolos Ampatzoglou
University of Macedonia
Thessaloniki, Greece

Tanmay Bhowmik
Mississippi State University
Mississippi State, MS, USA

ISSN 0302-9743 ISSN 1611-3349 (electronic)
Lecture Notes in Computer Science
ISBN 978-3-030-22887-3 ISBN 978-3-030-22888-0 (eBook)
https://doi.org/10.1007/978-3-030-22888-0

LNCS Sublibrary: SL2 – Programming and Software Engineering

© Springer Nature Switzerland AG 2019
This work is subject to copyright. All rights are reserved by the Publisher, whether the whole or part of the material is concerned, specifically the rights of translation, reprinting, reuse of illustrations, recitation, broadcasting, reproduction on microfilms or in any other physical way, and transmission or information storage and retrieval, electronic adaptation, computer software, or by similar or dissimilar methodology now known or hereafter developed.
The use of general descriptive names, registered names, trademarks, service marks, etc. in this publication does not imply, even in the absence of a specific statement, that such names are exempt from the relevant protective laws and regulations and therefore free for general use.
The publisher, the authors and the editors are safe to assume that the advice and information in this book are believed to be true and accurate at the date of publication. Neither the publisher nor the authors or the editors give a warranty, expressed or implied, with respect to the material contained herein or for any errors or omissions that may have been made. The publisher remains neutral with regard to jurisdictional claims in published maps and institutional affiliations.

This Springer imprint is published by the registered company Springer Nature Switzerland AG
The registered company address is: Gewerbestrasse 11, 6330 Cham, Switzerland

Preface

This volume contains the proceedings of the International Conference on Software and Systems Reuse (ICSR 2019) held during June 26–28, 2019, in Cincinnati, Ohio, USA.

The International Conference on Software and Systems Reuse is the premier international event in the software reuse community, and starting from this year, "Systems" was added to the name of the conference to emphasize the role of systems engineering in reuse and to highlight the relevance of reuse to cyber physical systems, sociotechnical systems, autonomous systems, intelligent systems, embedded systems, Internet of Things, systems of systems, and other Industry 4.0 applications. The main goal of ICSR is to present the most recent advances and breakthroughs in the area of software and systems reuse and to promote an intensive and continuous exchange among researchers and practitioners.

The conference featured three keynotes from industry, government, and academia, namely, Juha Savolainen from Danfoss, Michelle Simon from the U.S. Environmental Protection Agency, and Yang Liu from Nanyang Technological University. We received 32 submissions (excluding withdrawn submissions). Each submission was reviewed by three Program Committee members. The Program Committee decided to accept 13 papers, resulting in an acceptance rate of 40.1%. This conference was a collaborative work that could only be realized through many dedicated efforts. We would like to thank all the colleagues who made possible the success of ICSR 2019: Florine Postell, Xin Peng, Apostolos Ampatzoglou, Clemente Izurieta, Alexander Chatzigeorgiou, Areti Ampatzoglou, Tanmay Bhowmik, Wentao Wang, and Nan Niu. We also thank the ICSR Steering Committee for the approval to organize this edition in Cincinnati. Finally, we thank the sponsorship of Danfoss and the College of Engineering and Applied Science (CEAS) at the University of Cincinnati.

May 2019

Xin Peng
Apostolos Ampatzoglou
Tanmay Bhowmik

Organization

Conference Chair

Nan Niu   University of Cincinnati, USA

Local Chair

Florine Postell   University of Cincinnati, USA

Program Co-chairs

Xin Peng   Fudan University, China
Apostolos Ampatzoglou   University of Macedonia, Greece/University
                of Groningen, The Netherlands

Industry Innovation Co-chairs

Clemente Izurieta   Montana State University, USA
Alexander Chatzigeorgiou   University of Macedonia, Greece

Publicity Chair

Areti Ampatzoglou   University of Groningen, The Netherlands

Proceedings Chair

Tanmay Bhowmik   Mississippi State University, USA

Student Volunteer Chair

Wentao Wang   University of Cincinnati, USA

Program Committee

Eduardo Almeida   Federal University of Bahia, Brazil
Elvira-Maria Arvanitou   University of Macedonia, Greece
Paris Avgeriou   University of Groningen, The Netherlands
Rami Bahsoon   University of Birmingham, UK
Tanmay Bhowmik   Mississippi State University, USA
Stamatia Bibi   University of Western Macedonia, Greece
Jan Bosch   Chalmers University of Technology, Sweden
Yuanfang Cai   Drexel University, USA

Ann Campbell	SonarSource, Switzerland
Rafael Capilla	King Juan Carlos University, Spain
Bihuan Chen	Fudan University, China
Zadia Codabux	Colby College, USA
Eleni Constantinou	University of Mons, Belgium
Wei Dong	National University of Defense Technology, China
John Favaro	Intecs, Italy
Shinpei Hayashi	Tokyo Institute of Technology, Japan
He Jiang	Dalian University of Technology, China
Georgia Kapitsaki	University of Cyprus, Cyprus
David Kitchen	Johnson & Johnson, USA
Takashi Kobayashi	Tokyo Institute of Technology, Japan
Boris Kontsevoi	Intetics Inc., USA
Jaejoon Lee	Lancaster University, UK
Ge Li	Peking University, China
Hui Liu	Beijing Institute of Technology, China
Ting Liu	Xi'an Jiaotong University, China
Yang Liu	Nanyang Technological University, Singapore
Xiaoxing Ma	Nanjing University, China
Antonio Martini	University of Oslo, Norway
Klaus Schmid	University of Hildesheim, Germany
Ioannis Stamelos	Aristotle University of Thessaloniki, Greece
Hailong Sun	Beihang University, China
Jun Sun	Singapore University of Technology and Design, Singapore
Linzhang Wang	Nanjing University, China
Jun Wei	Chinese Academy of Sciences, China
Xin Xia	Monash University, Australia
Bing Xie	Peking University, China
Zhenchang Xing	Australian National University, Australia
Gang Yin	National University of Defense Technology, China
Shi Ying	Wuhan University, China
Yijun Yu	The Open University, UK
Uwe Zdun	University of Vienna, Austria
Hongyu Zhang	The University of Newcastle, Australia
Wei Zhang	Peking University, China
Jianjun Zhao	Kyushu University, Japan
Tom Zimmerman	Microsoft Research, USA

Contents

Software Reuse Practice

Software Product Line and Requirements Reuse

Reuse and Design and Evolution

Intelligent Software Reuse

Domain-Specific Software Development

Post Papers

Software Reuse Practice

A Flexible and Efficient
Approach to Component Test
in Time-Critical Scenarios

Xiaojing Bao$^{(\boxtimes)}$, Zhenxing Wang$^{(\boxtimes)}$, and Xiao Chen$^{(\boxtimes)}$

CFETS Information Technology (Shanghai) Co., Ltd., Building 6, No. 1388,
Zhangdong Rd., Pudong, Shanghai, China
{baoxiaojing,wangzhenxing,chenxiao_zh}@chinamoney.com.cn

Abstract. The quality of software components will greatly impact the quality of software end-products built from them. The traditional static and dynamic methods in software test have their limits and need to improve in component test area. The static test method has high runtime performance but low development productivity and is normally used for component interface test for its simplicity. The dynamic test method has high development productivity but low runtime performance and is normally used for business scenario test for its flexibility. While in time-critical applications, for example a financial trading system, the performance test of various business scenarios might produce high development cost due to low productivity of the static method. To solve this problem, this paper proposes a flexible and efficient approach to component test in time-critical scenarios. Inspired by the respective advantages of two traditional methods, runtime performance and development productivity are both achieved in this approach by rapid creation of test suites in a simple domain specific language and instant execution of them in a web-based service. A pilot project has successfully validated this approach in an inter-bank trading component test.

Keywords: Component test · Time-critical scenarios ·
Domain Specific Language · Test service

1 Introduction

As a first-class citizen of many modern software theories (e.g. CBSE [1], ABSD [2], SPLE [3], MSA [4]), software component [5] is a basic building block of software reuse [6] which has been proven to be an effective solution to the so-called "Software Crisis" [7]. Because of its importance in software development, the quality of software components will greatly impact the quality of software end-products built from them. Component test as the last step before component release plays a significant role in component quality assurance.

Component test has not only the commonalities of general software test (e.g. checking its conformance to function and performance requirements) but also the

© Springer Nature Switzerland AG 2019
X. Peng et al. (Eds.): ICSR 2019, LNCS 11602, pp. 3–13, 2019.
https://doi.org/10.1007/978-3-030-22888-0_1

specialties of software component (e.g. overcoming the difficulties from numerous work environments and complex external dependencies). The variety of potential applications and complexity of unpredictable dependencies in component test finally need more effort to increase test coverage and guarantee component quality.

Two traditional methods can be applied to test various scenarios in component test. The static method creates test scenarios by directly invoking component interface and organizing test workflow in a programming language, which will run in compiled version and have high runtime performance but low development productivity. The dynamic method creates test scenarios by wrapping component interface in an intermediate format if needed and orchestrating test workflow in a workflow engine, which will run in engine directly and have high development productivity but low runtime performance. Therefore, the static method is normally used in unit test and simple integration test for its simplicity, and the dynamic method is normally used in complex integration test and system test for its flexibility.

In the context of time-critical applications (e.g. financial trading systems), many components are released in library format for its minimum performance loss in system integration. Because of low runtime performance of the dynamic method, the static method is usually selected to accurately evaluate runtime performance of time-critical scenarios. But low productivity of the static method will also greatly limit the test coverage and finally impair the component quality and application prospect.

To meet the test requirements of accurate performance result and wide scenario coverage in time-critical applications, this paper proposes an approach to easily orchestrate test workflow as flexible as the dynamic method and automatically generate test code as efficient as the static method. A pilot project for a financial trading component has proven the productivity increase compared to the traditional methods.

2 Integrated Solution

The lifecycle of software test is relatively stable from the traditional waterfall model [8] to the modern agile model [9]. Component test follows the lifecycle illustrated in Fig. 1 [10].

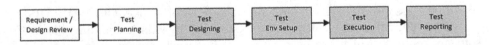

Fig. 1. The lifecycle of component test

This paper proposes a suite of automated component test methods, which introduce full or half automation in the gray phases in Fig. 1, which can be split into more detailed steps shown in Fig. 2.

Fig. 2. The main steps covered in our solution

Our solution focuses on three aspects to improve traditional methods. First aspect is higher abstraction which helps test team focus on business issues and eliminate technical varieties. Second aspect is more automation which helps test team avoid non-creative part of manual work. Third aspect is tighter integration which helps test team shorten test cycle. To be more detailed, several simple DSLs (i.e. Domain Specific Languages [11]) will be introduced to define language-independent test suites, and a series of automation tools will be created to convert test suites into test programs in some platform and language combinations. The former simple DSLs achieve flexibility as traditional dynamic method and the latter automation tools achieve performance as traditional static method. Finally, an integrated web-based service will be deployed to accept tests in HTTP requests, dynamically execute them and return reports in HTTP responses all in a few seconds. The simplified workflow of our approach is shown in Fig. 3. The "Test Suite" is a test definition written in TDL (i.e. Test Definition Language) based on standardized interface names from the "Component Definition" written in CDL (i.e. Component Definition Language), which will be sent to the web-based "Execution Service" by a HTTP request and executed for some specified "Test Env"s (i.e. some language and environment combinations). The "Execution Service" will generate binary "Test Program"s with the help of various templates and tools, then deploy each "Test Program" into the corresponding "Test Env". The "Test Input" and "Test Output" will be fed into and retrieved from each "Test Program" in its "Test Env" to generate a set of final "Test Report"s in a format provided by a "Report Template" and returned in a single HTTP response. All the work in the "Execution Service" is fully automated without any manual intervention.

Below, some important concepts in our approach will be described. We describe abstract definition of test components in Sect. 2.1, abstract definition of test suites in Sect. 2.2, and instant execution of test suites in Sect. 2.3.

2.1 Component Definition

As we mentioned before, component test has its specialties different from general software test. For example, the work environment in which a test component will run and external components on which a test component will depend are theoretically unpredictable. This variety of its future applications is the inherent value of a component which we can't eliminate. Traditionally, we have to program in different platforms or languages to test a single scenario, which will greatly limit test coverage due to available resources and budget.

Our solution to this difficulty is abstraction which is always a powerful weapon against this kind of problems. We developed a simple DSL called CDL

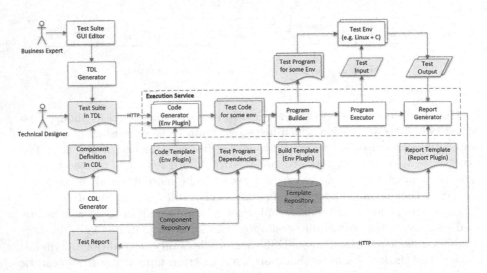

Fig. 3. The simplified workflow of our approach

(i.e. Component Definition Language) to define a component interface at business level. Then all references to a component in a test scenario will be defined in CDL format without any language dependency.

Figure 4 shows a demo structure of CDL. The "basic" section defines basic information of a component, which is required by the test suite to identify this component. The "query" section defines search conditions, which is required by an application designer to search for a suitable component. The "interfaces" and "ports" sections define the business behaviors, which is required by a business expert or technical designer to reference component operations or events in a test suite. In this demo structure, component interfaces are designed in a layered pattern [12] to represent different levels of abstraction.

When a test environment is determined, all references to components in a test suite will be translated into the target language by a code generator which handles the conversion from CDL to the target language. By introducing CDL, the requirement for different resources in different test environments is greatly decreased. Both the quality and productivity are increased accordingly.

However, some key points must be addressed here for CDL. First, a component is normally released in a specific format (e.g. a C library or Java JAR). That means there is no available CDL version of a component definition and an application developed in a different language could not visit this component directly. For the former problem, a series of CDL generators must be developed to extract CDL from components released in different formats. For the latter problem, a series of adapter generators must be developed to create language adapters for applications developed in different languages. Both of them are the inevitable one-off investment we must pay to test components in different environments. Second, the names of public operations and events have to be manually

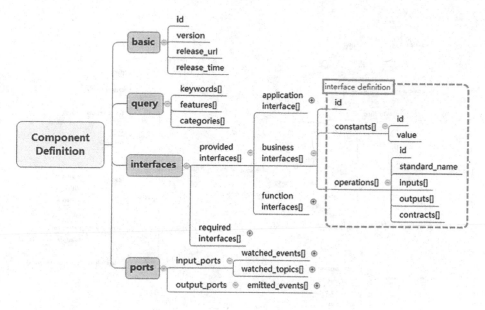

Fig. 4. A demo structure of CDL

standardized to generate test code from test workflow definitions. Because the consensus on the names of all business operations must be reached first, which must be defined in a language-independent standard.

2.2 Test Definition

In order to define a language-independent test suite in business level, we similarly developed a simple DSL called TDL (i.e. Test Definition Language) for this purpose. Then all scenarios and cases in a test suite will be defined in a TDL format without any language dependency, from which test code can be generated automatically.

Figure 5 shows a demo structure of TDL. There are 4 sections in "Request" definition. The "basic" section defines basic information of a test suite, which is required by execution service (described in Sect. 2.3) to identify the test suite and test component. The "options" section defines test scope, which is required by execution service to determine how many test environments to test for this component. The "config" section defines test scenarios, which will be translated into test programs for this test. The "data" section defines test cases, which are independent from test programs and will be fed into test programs as input and compared to output as expected result. There are also 4 sections in "Response" definition. The "basic" section repeats the same section in "Request" definition to match which request this response is for. The "error" section exists whenever an error happens to help test team fix problems. The "result" section records all test results and gives a simple test summary. The "report" section creates an optional report generated from the report template designated in "Request" definition.

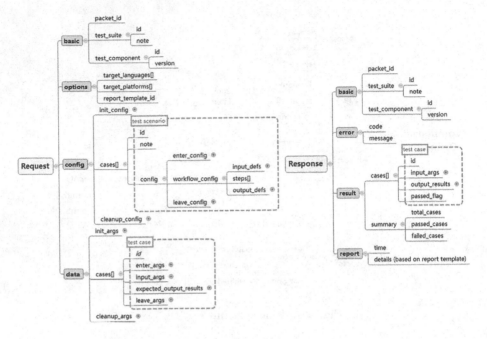

Fig. 5. A demo structure of TDL

Similarly, some key points must be addressed here for TDL. First, TDL is a little complex for a business expert to define test scenarios. A GUI editor is suggested to flat the learning curve and increase productivity. A third-party workflow editor can be utilized for this purpose but an extra DSL convertor must be developed to bridge the grammar difference between the third-party editor and TDL. A self-developed workflow editor is also an option if an integrated test platform is in development plan. Second, a language-independent workflow grammar is a core part of TDL. For an experienced technical designer, coding in text editor is more efficient than drawing in graph editor. We suggest to develop a simple and familiar workflow grammar for internal use (e.g. a simple C or Java like grammar with very few keywords). Third, TDL of a complicated test might become very large. We suggest a JSON or XML format for both TDL and CDL to help direct edit in a rich set of available editors.

2.3   Execution Service

Based on achieved flexibility and performance, an integrated execution service is proposed to boost productivity further more. A web-based service can instantly execute a test suite in HTTP request and return the result report in HTTP response, which chains all the needed automation tools and release test team from low-efficient and error-prone manual work. The simplified workflow of this web-based execution service is shown in Fig. 6.

When a test suite in TDL format is ready in "Test Suite Repository", it can be manually executed at once or scheduled for future execution periodically. Different from other available systems for test automation, this execution service accepts a test suite not in binary executable format but in textual TDL format, which means all the work from request analysis to report generation will be done transparently. To achieve this kind of high automation, some necessary templates must be provided in advance (e.g. code and build templates for different environments, report templates for different requirements). With execution service, a test designer can change a test scenario or case and get feedback immediately by a mouse click on a button in GUI.

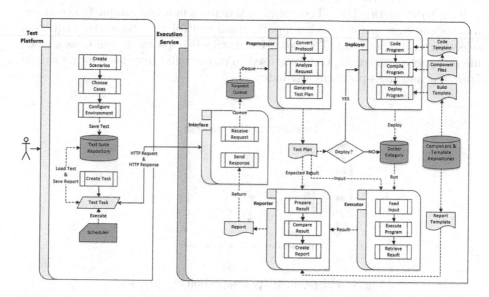

Fig. 6. The simplified workflow of execution service

Again, some key points must be addressed here for execution service. First, support for different test environments can be achieved by cross-host operations between local execution service and remote test environments. Second, support for test separation can be achieved by docker container directives embedded in build templates. Third, test input feed and test result retrieval can be achieved by named-pipe or socket communication code embedded in code templates. Last, any change to test scenarios will rebuild test programs which costs a few seconds, but any change to test cases will run immediately without rebuild.

This integrated automation of component test based on web-based service and DSL tools can link up different test steps and automate most of non-creative work done by hand before, which has a high feasibility in practice based on necessary manual support and available technical resources.

3 Engineering Practice

To validate this proposed solution for component test in time-critical scenarios, we launched a pilot project to check its feasibility. A business component called ODM for order matching in an inter-bank trading system is selected as the test component, which is written in C language and released as a shared library on Linux platform.

We defined CDL in JSON format and extracted them from referenced components by a CDL generator for C language. Similarly, we defined TDL in JSON format for request and response packages, which stands for the communication protocol between the test designer and the execution service. All pilot code is written based on this DSL. The workflow is defined in a very simple C-like grammar as the start point, which supports basic control structures (i.e. sequence, selection, and repetition). The execution service is implemented in C as a module in Apache web server. CMake is used to create build templates for its simple grammar and cross-platform attribute.

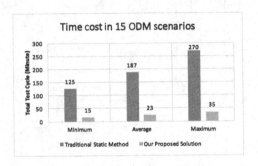

Fig. 7. The productivity comparison in ODM test

We linked up test steps by various spawned shell scripts and sub-processes, which will not be a performance issue for the limited invocations and relative long test time. In our pilot project, the time cost in a small test scenario with 3 business operations is about 2 s at first run and less than 100 ms in consequent runs for the successful cache mechanism. In our ODM experiment, the time cost in a test scenario is about 15 to 35 min by our automated approach compared to about 2 to 4.5 h by the traditional static method. We ran 15 ODM test scenarios and the statistics of time cost is shown in Fig. 7. Of course, the time saved in component test is achieved by the price of the investment in automation solution. The more scenarios covered in a component test, the more benefit will be achieved in a total calculation.

4   Related Work

Improving the efficiency of software test in a practical way has great economical attraction to every software development organization. A large number of theoretical and engineering studies have been invested to increase the test productivity in various aspects.

Go further into test automation [13] area, two main areas are GUI test automation and API test automation. An automation framework for GUI test generates UI events (e.g. key-strokes and mouse-clicks) to automate the manual operations. Memon et al. [14], Clarke [15], Amalfitano et al. [16], Vieira et al. [17] and many other works contributed in this area, a list of current available GUI test tools can also be found at [18]. Our approach can be integrated with GUI test which is not our focus however. An automation framework for API test uses a programming interface to validate expected behaviors without any user interaction. Our approach is mainly based on API test automation and covers several test phases.

In coding phase, many automatic code generation methods have been proposed. Rutherford et al. [19] argued the importance of test code generation in model driven development. Xu [20] presented a tool for automated test generation and execution by using high-level Petri nets as finite state test models. Sturmer et al. [21] described the design of a test suite for code generators, and introduced a new test approach for code generator transformations. We don't find any code generation method for component test targeted to various application environments in different languages and platforms. The basic idea of generating test code starting from language-independent component interface is also not found.

In testing phase, Saff et al. [22] introduced their productive method of continuous testing, and Diego [23] investigated the popular test automation tools nowadays. Again we don't find a fully automated solution from compilation to execution based on a web-based service.

5   Conclusion and Future Work

Software component is a basic building block in software reuse. The large potential application of a software component brings a big challenge to component test. We proposes an automated solution based on an integrated web-based service to respond this challenge. The key points in our solution are: (1) generate language-independent component interfaces automatically from components released in a specific language; (2) generate test code automatically from test suites written in a language-independent DSL; (3) compile, deploy, execute and report a component test automatically and dynamically in an integrated web-based execution service. We largely depends on DSL tools to accomplish above goals in each step. A pilot project has validated the feasibility of our approach for component test which is especially valuable for time-critical scenarios.

Facing an era in which big data, cloud computation and artificial intelligence technologies are more and more widely used, we are planning to make further test automation in "Create Test Scenario" and "Choose Test Cases" steps in Fig. 2 by mining regular business patterns and operation data from production data available in many industrial systems.

References

1. Crnkovic, I.: Component-based software engineering–new challenges in software development. Softw. Focus **2**(4), 127–133 (2001)
2. Medvidovic, N., Taylor, R.N.: Software architecture: foundations, theory, and practice. In: Proceedings of the 32nd ACM/IEEE International Conference on Software Engineering, vol. 2. ACM (2010)
3. Pohl, K., Böckle, G., van Der Linden, F.J.: Software Product Line Engineering: Foundations, Principles and Techniques. Springer, Berlin (2005). https://doi.org/10.1007/3-540-28901-1
4. Nadareishvili, I., et al.: Microservice Architecture: Aligning Principles, Practices, and Culture. O'Reilly Media Inc., Newton (2016)
5. McIlroy, M.D., et al.: Mass-produced software components. In: Proceedings of the 1st International Conference on Software Engineering, Garmisch Pattenkirchen, Germany (1968)
6. Griss, M.L.: Software reuse: architecture, process and organization for business success. In: Tools. IEEE (1998)
7. Randell, B.: The 1968/69 NATO software engineering reports. In: History of Software Engineering, p. 37 (1996)
8. Royce, W.W.: Managing the development of large software systems: concepts and techniques. In: Proceedings of the 9th International Conference on Software Engineering. IEEE Computer Society Press (1987)
9. Abrahamsson, P., et al.: Agile software development methods: review and analysis. In: Proceedings of the Espoo, pp. 3–107 (2002)
10. Software Testing Life Cycle (STLC), Software Testing Fundamentals. http://softwaretestingfundamentals.com/software-testing-life-cycle/
11. Fowler, M.: Domain-Specific Languages. Pearson Education, London (2010)
12. Fowler, M.: Patterns of Enterprise Application Architecture. Addison-Wesley Longman Publishing Co., Inc., Boston (2002)
13. Fewster, M., Graham, D.: Software Test Automation: Effective Use of Test Execution Tools. ACM Press/Addison-Wesley Publishing Co., New York (1999)
14. Memon, A.M., Pollack, M.E., Soffa, M.L.: Using a goal-driven approach to generate test cases for GUIs. In: Proceedings of the 1999 International Conference on Software Engineering. IEEE (1999)
15. Clarke, J.M.: Automated test generation from a behavioral model. In: Proceedings of Pacific Northwest Software Quality Conference. IEEE Press (1998)
16. Amalfitano, D., et al.: Using GUI ripping for automated testing of Android applications. In: Proceedings of the 27th IEEE/ACM International Conference on Automated Software Engineering. ACM (2012)
17. Vieira, M., et al.: Automation of GUI testing using a model-driven approach. In: Proceedings of the 2006 International Workshop on Automation of Software Test. ACM (2006)
18. Wikipedia: Comparison of GUI testing tools. https://en.wikipedia.org/wiki/Comparison_of_GUI_testing_tools

19. Rutherford, M.J., Wolf, A.L.: A case for test-code generation in model-driven systems. In: Pfenning, F., Smaragdakis, Y. (eds.) GPCE 2003. LNCS, vol. 2830, pp. 377–396. Springer, Heidelberg (2003). https://doi.org/10.1007/978-3-540-39815-8_23

20. Xu, D.: A tool for automated test code generation from high-level petri nets. In: Kristensen, L.M., Petrucci, L. (eds.) PETRI NETS 2011. LNCS, vol. 6709, pp. 308–317. Springer, Heidelberg (2011). https://doi.org/10.1007/978-3-642-21834-7_17

21. Sturmer, I., Conrad, M.: Test suite design for code generation tools. In: 2003 Proceedings of the 18th IEEE International Conference on Automated Software Engineering. IEEE (2003)

22. Saff, D., Ernst, M.D.: Reducing wasted development time via continuous testing. In: International Symposium on Software Reliability Engineering. IEEE (2003)

23. Giudice, D.L.: The Forrester Wave™: Modern Application Functional Test Automation Tools, Q4 2016. Gartner, 5 December 2016

Software Product Line and Requirements Reuse

Extending FragOP Domain Reusable Components to Support Product Customization in the Context of Software Product Lines

Daniel Correa[1](✉), Raúl Mazo[2,3], and Gloria Lucia Giraldo[1]

[1] Universidad Nacional de Colombia, Medellín, Colombia
{dcorreab, glgiraldog}@unal.edu.co
[2] Université Panthéon Sorbonne - CRI, Paris, France
raul.mazo@univ-paris1.fr
[3] Universidad Eafit, GiDITIC, Medellín, Colombia

Abstract. Software product lines (SPL) have become an efficient paradigm for systematic reuse. SPL engineering is about the planned reuse of common assets for the rapid production of a software systems family. In SPL, an effective product derivation process is key to ensure that the effort required to develop the common assets will be lower than the benefits achieved through their use. While several approaches and tools are available on SPL engineering activities such as, variability management, component assembling, and product testing; most of the existing approaches do not present detailed information on the strategies for product customization (which affects the product derivation effectiveness). In a previous work, we introduced fragment-oriented programming (FragOP), which is a framework used to design, implement, and reuse domain components. In this paper, we enhanced the FragOP approach through the use of customization points and customization files to support the product customization activity. In order to gain preliminary insights into how VariaMos (the tool in which the approach is implemented) supports the FragOP approach, we designed a usability test by following the ISO/IEC 25062:2006 Common Industry Format for usability tests. Eight graduate students from the Universidad Nacional de Colombia took part and were asked to carry out a series of modifications to an e-commerce SPL. The usability test reported high subject performance results; however, we found some usability flaws that should be addressed.

Keywords: Software product lines · Usability tool test · Fragment-oriented programming · Product customization

1 Introduction

A software product line (SPL) is a collection of software systems that satisfy the specific needs of a particular market segment, and that are developed from a common set of core assets in a prescribed way [1]. Many software and systems product line (SPL) implementation approaches, such as CIDE, DeltaJ, Munge, Antenna, AspectJ, and AHEAD emerged during recent years [2]. These approaches focus on an effective

© Springer Nature Switzerland AG 2019
X. Peng et al. (Eds.): ICSR 2019, LNCS 11602, pp. 17–33, 2019.
https://doi.org/10.1007/978-3-030-22888-0_2

SPL component assembling (constructing and assembling a software product from the reusable SPL assets). However, existing approaches do not present detailed information on the strategies for product customization [3]. For example, de Souza *et al.*, [3] reported that much of the resources and effort of the product derivation process is spent on product customization. They analyzed some companies in which between 10% and 30% of each product instantiated from their platforms needs to be customized. Even, Montavillo *et al.*, [4] which developed a visualization tool to estimate the customization effort, deduced that less than 50% of an SPL example product code was reused as-is from the core-assets. The main difference between a component assembling and a product customization is that the first one reuses and assembles pre-developed core-assets to generate a new product. The second one is carried-out after the component assembling and it is commonly done manually, because each product customization is unique, so there are not pre-developed customized core-assets.

In previous work, we developed an SPL implementation approach called Fragment-oriented programming (FragOP) [5]. FragOP is a framework used to design, implement and reuse domain components in the context of an SPL. FragOP is a mix between SPL compositional and annotative approaches. In the original formulation of FragOP [5], it consisted on the definition of (i) domain components, (ii) fragmentations points, which are annotations over the domain components code; and (iii) fragments, a new type of file which alters the domain components code. In this paper, this approach is enhanced to support the SPL product customization. This enhancement was included as a new capability of the VariaMos tool [6], which is a software tool that supports the FragOP approach. Therefore, to gain insights into how VariaMos supports the enhanced FragOP approach, we decided to develop a usability test. Usability is defined by the International Standard Organization [7] as "the extent to which a product can be used by specified users to achieve specific goals with effectiveness, efficiency, and satisfaction in a specified context of use". That means that if a product (a software tool in our case) does not provide effectiveness, efficiency, and satisfaction to its users, it is not usable, and therefore will probably not be used. The rest of this paper is structured as follows. In Sect. 2, we present the FragOP approach including its enhanced metamodel and process; therefore, we present the enhanced VariaMos tool. In Sect. 3, we discuss the FragOP main two capabilities (assembling and customization) with a real SPL example. In Sect. 4, we present a usability test of VariaMos. In Sect. 5, we discuss the related work and finally Sect. 6 summarizes the contributions and presents future research directions.

2   Fragment-Oriented Programming

In this section, we recall the notion of FragOP as described in [5] and present the FragOP enhancement and its implementation in VariaMos. Fragment-oriented programming (FragOP) is a framework used to design, implement and reuse domain components in the context of an SPL. FragOP is based on the definition of six fundamental elements: (i) domain components, (ii) domain files, (iii) fragmentations points, (iv) fragments, (v) customization points, and (vi) customization files. The fragments act as composable units (compositional approach) and the fragmentation points act as annotations (annotative approach). This mix of compositional and annotative approaches allows the FragOP to support multiple assets implemented over different languages, such as PHP, Java, JSP, CSS, HTML, and JavaScript, among others. The role of each FragOP element, their relationships, how are made up, and the information they store, it can be seen in the FragOP metamodel (see Fig. 1). Following, we present an overview of the FragOP metamodel elements:

SPL represents the software product line and contains an ID that represents the name of the corresponding SPL. **Domain requirements** represent SPL domain requirements (such as features and goals). **Domain components** represent SPL reusable domain components and contain an ID that represents a folder in which the component is stored. A **domain file** is a basic element of which most software components are made up; for instance, HTML, CSS, JavaScript, Java, and JSP files. A **fragment** is a special type of file which alters the application code. A **fragmentation point** is an annotation (a very simple mark) that specifies a "point" in which a domain file can be altered. A **customization file** is a file which specifies the domain files (for the current domain component) that should be customized. **Customization points** are annotations (very simple marks) that specify the "points" in which a domain file should be customized. **Product** represents a folder in which a new SPL product is derived. **Application files** are copies of domain files which are generated when a new product is derived. These files can be also modified by the fragments.

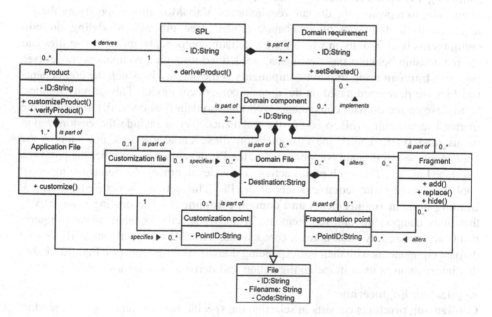

Fig. 1. FragOP metamodel (UML class diagram)

The FragOP metamodel presents the elements that must be used and understood in an SPL that implements a FragOP approach. However, it does not describe how to implement the SPL. That is the objective of the **FragOP process**. Following, we summarize the eight FragOP process activities (cf. Figure 2) including an example of its implementation within VariaMos (cf. Figure 3).

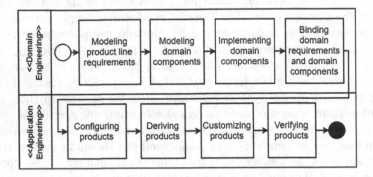

Fig. 2. FragOP process (UML activity diagram)

Domain Engineering
Modeling PL requirements is the activity in which variability models are used to graphically to represent the domain requirements. VariaMos allows specifying the PL requirements in the form of a "Feature model" (see Fig. 3a). **Modeling domain components** is an activity in which the PL domain components, their domain files and the relationship between these elements, are defined through a component model (see Fig. 3b). **Implementing domain components** is the activity in which the components and files are developed based on the domain component model. This activity implies: (i) to develop the domain components with their domain files code, (ii) to include the fragmentation points, (iii) to codify the fragments, (iv) to include the customization points, and (v) to codify the customization files. VariaMos does not support the implementation of domain components, so, the PL developer can use her/his preferred IDE (see Fig. 3c). The result of this activity is the development of a domain component pool that includes the reusable assets of the PL. This activity is detailed in Sect. 3. **Binding domain requirements and domain components**. The binding is an activity that links components and requirements; it allows specifying what domain requirements are realized by what domain components. VariaMos currently supports linking domain components with their corresponding domain requirements (see Fig. 3d). Later, this information is used in the configuration and derivation activities.

Application Engineering
Configuring products consists in selecting the specific features that a specific product will contain based on the stakeholder requirements. VariaMos permits configuring a product by selecting the specific leaf features that the SPL product will contain (see Fig. 3e). **Deriving products** consists in generating specific software products based on

the configured variability model (see Fig. 3f), the derivation activity is detailed in Sect. 3.1. **Customizing products** consists in modifying the derived products based on the customer's needs. For example, to parameterize configuration files or variables, to modify dummy texts, and to include specific customer requirements, among others (see Fig. 3g). The customization activity is detailed in Sect. 3.2. **Verifying products** is the last activity in the application engineering process. Due to the fact that FragOP allows injecting and modifying component file codes (through the use of fragments), it becomes relevant to verify the resulting products. VariaMos implemented ANTLR 4.7.1 and uses a series of parsers and lexers for languages, such as PHP, Java, CSS, MySQL, among others. Based on the derived application file extension, VariaMos analyses the grammar of each application file and generates alerts if errors are found (see Fig. 3h).

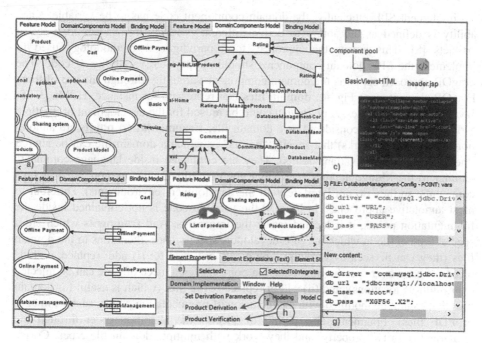

Fig. 3. FragOP process implemented with VariaMos

3   VariaMos (FragOP) Main Capabilities

In order to show the VariaMos (FragOP) main capabilities, and to describe the new FragOP elements, we took an existing e-commerce SPL called ClothingStores [5]. ClothingStores was improved to include the new FragOP elements: customization files and customization points. ClothingStores consists of 25 features and was developed covering most of the problems that SPL developers face when implementing an SPL; such as, **Crosscutting concerns** such as the Login component, that in case of being part of a final product, it must be integrated transversally over multiple other product files. **Fine-grained extensions** such as, modify the header menu, modify specific parts of the product views, and SQL files, among others. **Coarse-grained extensions** such as, replace a validation method over the admin classes, and include class methods, among others. **Product customization** such as the database configuration variables, the name of each derived web store, and some default texts inside the product views must be customized. **Managing multiple language files**, it was designed as a real e-commerce web system which included domain files types, such as SQL, images (.jpg and .png), JavaScript, HTML, JSP, Java, and CSS.

Following, we will describe the two FragOP main capabilities (assembling and customization) with the use of the ClothingStores example.

3.1   Assembling Capability

To implement SPL efficiently, the domain component code has to be variable. Variability is defined as the ability to derive different products from a common set of artifacts [8]. This means the approach, tool, paradigm or methodology used to implement the SPL domain components should support the variability of code. The FragOP approach supports the domain component variability through the use of three FragOP elements (see Fig. 4): **domain files** that represent, for instance, HTML, CSS, JavaScript and Java files. Any file that could be reused for the development of multiple SPL products can be considered as a domain file. **Fragmentation points** are annotations (very simple marks) that specify "points" in which a domain file can be altered (they can be seen as variant points). They are contained inside language comments (similar to the Munge approach, in which the conditional tags are contained in Java comments, so they do not interfere with the development environments). Different to most annotative approaches, in FragOP the variable code is not contained inside the fragmentation points, it is located inside the fragments. And **fragments** which are a special type of file in which the SPL developers specify code alterations to the domain files (they can be seen as variants). Fragments are used to: (i) add, replace, or hide pieces of code over specific fragmentation points (even a piece of code can be injected over multiple locations); and (ii) add or replace entire files (which is useful for domain files that cannot be modified with the inclusion of fragmentation points, such as images or PDF files). Fragments also permit to specify the alteration order through the "fragment priority" property, and they work with multiple domain file types. Correa *et al.* [5] present the complete structure of fragments and fragmentation points.

The VariaMos (FragOP) assembling capability is carried out at application level through the Fig. 3f option. The product derivation consists of generating specific software products based on the configured variability model. The selected features and the variability model are taken as an input. Then, the binding is resolved to show what components should be assembled based on the selected features; and the components are assembled over a product folder (the output). In this activity, VariaMos executes the fragments which modify the product application file code. For example, in Fig. 4 a domain file (header.jsp) supports the code variability through the inclusion of a fragmentation point (menu-modificator). Additionally, a fragment (alterHeader.frag) specifies a code alteration (to include a new header menu element) in the previous fragmentation point of the previous domain file. Once the product is derived, a copy of the header.jsp is included in the product folder (application file), and the alterHeader. frag injects the new menu element over the derived application file.

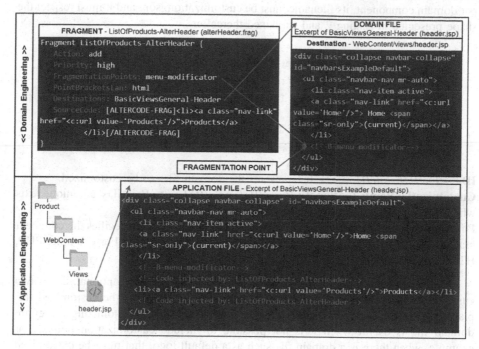

Fig. 4. An assembling scenario with the use of VariaMos (FragOP)

3.2 Customization Capability

Even when SPL products are derived based on the customer's needs, it is very common that these products require customization. For example, to parameterize configuration files or variables, to modify dummy texts, and to include specific customer requirements, among others. FragOP takes advantage of the customization points and customization files and facilitates the customization activity (see Fig. 5).

```
LanguageCommentBlock<BCP>-<PointID>LanguageCommentBlock
LanguageCommentBlock<ECP>-<PointID>LanguageCommentBlock
```
Listing. 1. Customization point shape.

Customization points are annotations that specify "points" in which a domain file should be customized. The customization points shape is similar to the fragmentation points shape, the main difference is that a customization point should contain a beginning part (BCP) and an ending part (ECP). Listing 1 shows the customization point shape. The code to be customized (at the application level) should be placed in the middle of both BCP and ECP parts. We use annotations because we want to support the customization of most kinds of files, and we know that most product customizations are unique.

A **customization file** is a file which specifies the domain files (for the current domain component) that should be customized. Only one customization file is allowed per domain component, its filename must be customization.json, and it must respect the shape presented in Listing 2 and explained thereafter.

```
{
    "IDs": ["FileID1", "FileID2", "..."],
    "CustomizationPoints": ["PointID1", "PointID2", "..."],
    "PointBracketsLans": ["language1", "language2", "..."]
}
```

Listing. 2. Customization point shape.

IDs: *<FileID1, FileID2, ...>*. It represents the domain files to be customized.
CustomizationPoints (optional): *<pointID1, pointID2, ...>*. PointIDs are unique texts which serve to identify customization points.
PointBracketsLans (optional): *<language1, language2, ...>*. It specifies the comment bracket languages in which the customization points are defined. For example, PHP, HTML and Java.

The customization points and the point brackets languages are optional; this way a customization file is able to specify entire domain files that must be customized (replaced) or specify customization points to be customized. Customizing an entire domain file is useful when it is not possible to include customization points. For example, when there is a domain file such as a default logo, that must be customized with the real client company logo.

The VariaMos (FragOP) customization capability is carried out at application level through a VariaMos option called "product customization". Using this option, a popup shows (i) the customization points of the derived application files, and the SPL developer manually customizes the application file codes; and (ii) the derived application files that should be entirely customized (replaced), and the SPL developer uploads the customized files. For instance, the ClothingStores SPL contained a domain file (Config.java) that specified four variables which allow the communication with the database engine. As a domain file, these variables present sample values; however, for a final product, the value of each variable must be customized. As a consequence, we included a customization point ("vars") inside the Config.java domain file (see Fig. 5). After the product assembling, the SPL developer customizes the Config.java file with real variable values, which generates the final application files. The content of these files is later verified through Fig. 3h VariaMos option.

VariaMos does not automatically customize the application files because this activity is customer-dependent. However, the activity is streamlined because without the use of customization points and customization files, the SPL developers should manually review each derived application file, trying to figure out what pieces of code and files should be customized. It is important to highlight that customization files and customization points are very useful for simple customizations, such as parametrizing variables, changing a default text or replacing an image file; nevertheless, complex customization such as creating new components must be applied manually by developers.

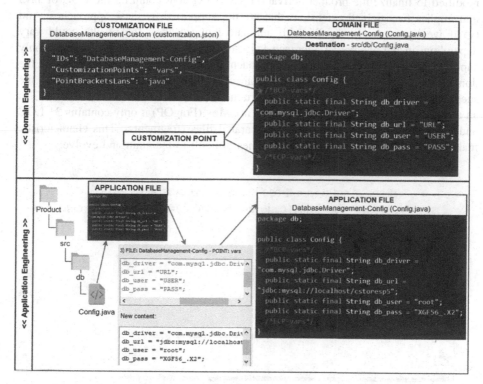

Fig. 5. A customization scenario with the use of VariaMos (FragOP)

3.3 Derivation Results

After following the FragOP process (see Fig. 2), we completed the derivation of the five ClothingStores products. We used the Koscielny *et al.*, [9] DeltaJ 1.5 case study (which presented a SimpleTextEditor SPL as the subject system) as the base to present the ClothingStores results. In comparison, the SimpleTextEditor consisted of 11 features, while the ClothingStores consists of 25 features. The results show that VariaMos (FragOP) is expressive enough to implement a real-world, variant-rich multi-language software system. An inspection of the product code shows that (see Fig. 6): (i) multiple assets of different types were automatically assembled and deployed in the respective project folder structure. (ii) Between 21 and 50 lines of code were manually customized (supported by the VariaMos tool) to complete each product finalization. Even, the database queries were automatically generated. (iii) Several LOC were derived and automatically injected. For instance, 27.72% of the P5 LOC were automatically injected. This means that a P5 product derivation carried manually without the use of VariaMos will require to manually modify 560 LOC. (iv) If we try to derive the P5 with a compositional approach that is attached to a host language like Java (such as AspectJ, DeltaJ, AHEAD), 26 files must be manually included in the product folder structure, and a minimum of 284 LOC (14% of the total product LOC) must be manually modified to finalize the product derivation. Even, without counting the LOC of Java that implies fine-grained extensions that are not supported by these approaches. And (v) if we try to derive the P5 with annotative approaches, the results could vary depending on the annotative approach language support (for instance, Antenna only supports Java); however, annotative approaches inject all code variations inside the domain files, which is not the case in VariaMos (FragOP). It means that a domain file such as ListOfProducts-OneProduct (oneproduct.jsp) will contain at least 104 LOC in an annotative approach. Nevertheless, in VariaMos (FragOP) it only contains 31 LOC and the code variations are located in separated files (fragments). This characteristic makes domain files of annotative approaches difficult to maintain and evolve.

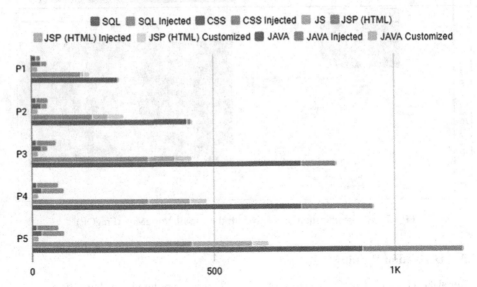

Fig. 6. LOC reused, automatically injected and customized of each derived ClothingStores product by file type

4   Usability Evaluation

This section presents a usability test of VariaMos (version 1.1.0.1). The main idea is to test the VariaMos usability to support the FragOP approach, and thus to gain insight into how easy or difficult it is to follow and understand the FragOP approach. To guide the usability test, we defined the next research question.

RQ: *Is VariaMos a usable tool that supports the FragOP approach?*

In this evaluation, we decided to develop and conduct a usability test by using the ISO/IEC Common Industry Format (CIF) for usability tests [10]. We also applied three evaluation techniques: (i) one for the definition of the experimental tasks, (ii) another for evaluating user satisfaction by gathering their opinion through a survey, and finally (iii) a semi-structured interview to enrich this usability test. The complete usability format result can be found online [11]. The following subsections present: (i) the procedure, (ii) the metrics, (iii) the results and (iv) threats to validity.

4.1 Procedure

The usability test was designed as a process with nine activities (see Fig. 7), which is described next.

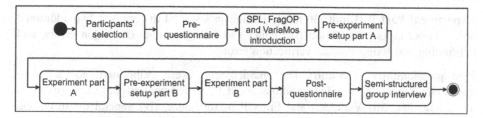

Fig. 7. Usability test process (UML activity diagram)

Participants' Selection. Eight graduate students from the *Universidad Nacional de Colombia* participated in this testing. Participants attended a postgraduate course in software modeling. The usability test was designed in two four-hour sessions. These participants are classified as "software developers who are interested in adopting an SPL methodology" which is one of the VariaMos user target population.

Pre-questionnaire (15 min). We requested the participants to complete a pre-questionnaire related to their background and software experience. The pre-questionnaire was designed using a Likert scale, which had a five-point format: (1) strongly disagree, (2) somewhat disagree, (3) neither agree nor disagree, (4) somewhat agree, and (5) strongly agree. The intention was to collect information about the participants' background and experience, and to confirm the participants' lack of knowledge with FragOP and VariaMos. The pre-questionnaire also showed the participants presented an average of 4 years of experience in software development.

SPL, FragOP and VariaMos Introduction (3 h). We designed a magistral class about the main concepts of SPL, FragOP, and VariaMos, and we developed a very small example of the use of FragOP and VariaMos. This introduction was important because the participants did not have knowledge of SPL, so, we introduced topics, such as software product lines, feature modeling, and product derivation.

Pre-experiment Setup Part A (30 min). The second session started with the "pre-experiment setup part A". Here, the participants were introduced to a document which presented a series of steps to set up an SPL project with the use of VariaMos.

Experiment Part A (Limit: 90 min). We shared with the participants a Google Drive folder with the experiment part A. Then, they were requested to complete five tasks. Therefore, two test administrators were observing and attending the participants' questions. The experiment part A tasks were about: (i) derivation and customization of a new SPL product, (ii) questions about the previous derived product, (iii) modification of a domain file, (iv) modification of the SPL which includes creating a feature, component, binding element, a fragment, and a fragmentation point. And (v) derivation of an additional SPL product.

Pre-experiment Setup Part B (15 min). The participants were introduced to a document which presented a series of steps to set up another SPL project.

Experiment Part B (Limit: 30 min). Participants started to complete two additional tasks. These tasks were about: (i) finding and fixing product derivation errors, and (ii) finding and fixing product verification errors.

Post-questionnaire (15 min). The participants were submitted to a post-questionnaire, which included questions about (i) experiment environment, (ii) overall satisfaction, (iii) VariaMos and FragOP performance, (iv) general question, and (v) specific questions about the VariaMos and FragOP theory.

Semi-structured Group Interview (25 min). We asked the participants four open questions about the tool usability, and we recorded the participants' answers. The questions were: (i) What did you like? (ii) What did you dislike/What should be improved? (iii) What are the opportunities when using this tool in daily business? and (iv) What are the risks when using this tool in daily business?

4.2 Metrics

We defined three usability metrics that tools must provide: effectiveness, efficiency, and satisfaction to its users. For the **effectiveness**, we recorded (i) completion rate (including assisted and unassisted completion), (ii) errors (defined as a task completed wrongly or not completed), and (iii) assists (defined as verbal help given by the test administrators to guide the participants to the next step in completing the task). For the **efficiency**, we recorded (i) task time (the amount of time to complete each task), and (ii) completion rate efficiency (mean completion task rate/mean task time). For the **satisfaction**, we used the post-questionnaire results and measured the participant's perception of ease of use, ease of learning, ease of remembering, and subjective satisfaction. Therefore, we take advantage of the semi-structured group interview results.

4.3 Results

Performance Results. All eight participants completed all of the seven tasks (see Table 1). Three of the participants completed all seven tasks without assistances.

A total of seven assistances were given to the participants, five of these assistances were requested to Task 4 – Part A, which was the most the complex task (participants spent a mean of 31 min to complete this task; see Fig. 8). Figure 8 also shows that the participants spend little time in the development of Task 5 – Part A and Task 2 – Part B. Task 5 – Part A was about a new product derivation, which took on average approximately 4 min; Task 2 – Part B focused on finding validation errors, we included a syntax error over a domain file and on average the participants only spent approximately 4 min in finding and fixing the error. The mean total time to complete all the seven tasks was approximately 72 min. Therefore, there were not errors because all the participants completed all the tasks properly.

Table 1. Participants' performance result summary

	Assisted task completion rate	Unassisted task completion rate	Total task time	Errors	Assistances	Mean task time	Efficiency
Mean	100.000	100.000	72.125	0.000	0.875	10.304	9.982
Standard dev	0.000	0.000	12.654	0.000	0.835	1.808	1.826
Standard error	0.000	0.000	4.474	0.000	0.295	0.639	0.646

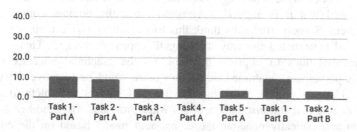

Fig. 8. Participants' average time (minutes) to complete each task

Finally, it is important to highlight that all participants were novice SPL developers and FragOP novice developers. So, the results in this test provide preliminary evidence that VariaMos *is a usable tool that properly supports the FragOP approach* (RQ). All of the participants completed all the tasks (effectiveness), and the mean task time was approximately 10 min (efficiency). The tool also provides errors notifications; which can help developers to easily find fragment errors or domain component errors.

Satisfaction Results. The satisfaction results were obtained from two sources. First, we analyzed 21 of the 26 post-questionnaire questions. Scores for the 21 questions were given for each participant, based on four usability attributes: ease of use, ease of learning, ease of remembering and subjective satisfaction. It is important to realize that usability is not a single, one-dimensional property of a user interface. Usability has multiple components and is traditionally associated with different usability attributes.

Second, we analyzed the semi-structured interview results which will be presented at the end of this section. Finally, the other five post-questionnaire questions results are used in Sect. 4.4 as a source of information for the validation threads. The summary for the 21 questions results can be seen in Fig. 9. The highest satisfaction result was about the "ease of use" of VariaMos with a mean of 4.153 (see Fig. 9a). Therefore, in average the participants had 4.6 correct answers of a total of 6 when asked about VariaMos and FragOP functionalities (see Fig. 9b).

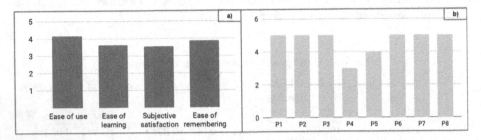

Fig. 9. Participants' satisfaction question average results - Participants' correct answers about VariaMos and FragOP

Finally, the semi-structured interview showed that in general the participants liked the software application and saw the potential of this tool and the FragOP approach. They mentioned that it is a good strategy to reuse the domain components and assembled them. Some participants think this tool could improve their work at their companies and appreciated the way the FragOP approach worked. There were also some recommendations to improve the tool: (i) the graphical interface could be improved. A participant mentioned that future work could be to move the graphical interface into a web project. Allowing the use cell phones or tablets to open the application or to avoid the installation of software programs. (ii) Another participant suggested to automatically generate the component model based on the component pool folder information, which will save time.

4.4 Threats to Validity

Participants sample. The number of subjects may seem relatively small. However, the ISO/IEC CIF for usability tests states "eight or more subjects are recommended" [10]. **Conclusion validity.** There is a threat that many of the results are not based on statistical relationships but on qualitative data. However, given that main aim of the study was to study the behavior and opinions of users of a tool, qualitative research methods are well suited. The analysis of the collected data still depends on our interpretation. The work was performed by a single researcher, but the result was carefully checked by two other researchers. **Project size.** We selected a basic SPL project due to target users that participated in this usability test; however, we have shown in previous sections that the tool also works with complex SPL projects. **Insufficient skills to execute the tasks.** This threat was discarded by the participants' pre-questionnaire results. **External factors and lack of documentation.** They were discarded by the results of five post-questionnaire questions. Finally, rigorous experiments with complex SPL projects and SPL industry users should be developed in future work.

5 Related Work

There are many SPL implementation approaches that support the SPL component assembling, such as CIDE, DeltaJ, Munge, Antenna, AspectJ, and AHEAD, among others [2]. However, most of these approaches do not provide a product customization capability. Literature presents some customization strategies. Kim *et al.*, [12] propose three strategies: selection, plug-in, and external profile technique. However, these strategies only work with interface classes and are not applied in SPL scenarios. Rabiser *et al.*, [13] propose a decision-oriented software product line approach to support the end user personalization of a system based on its needs. However, the personalization is limited to what the decision model supports. Pleuss *et al.*, [14] propose the use of abstract UI models to bridge the gap between automated, traceable product derivation and customized, high-quality user interfaces. However, it requires to create abstract UI models with all possible scenarios, and this is only applied to user interfaces. Other strategies include inheritance, overloading, dynamic class loading, but not all assets are object-oriented. Finally, Montalvillo *et al.*, [4] developed CUSTOMS, a visualization utility for FeatureHouse that helps to estimate the product customization effort, broken down by product and core-asset.

In the usability testing field, Rabiser *et al.*, [15] presented an implementation of the capabilities in a configuration tool called DOPLER CW. They performed a qualitative investigation on the usefulness of the tool's capabilities for user guidance in product configuration by involving nine business-oriented experts of two industry partners from the domain of industrial automation. They also presented general implications for tool developers. Therefore, Teruel *et al.*, [16], presented a usability evaluation of the CSRML tool 2012; which is a Requirements Engineering CASE tool for the goal-oriented Collaborative Systems Requirements Modeling Language (CSRML). They involved 28 fourth-year Computer Science students in the evaluation, which was reported by following the ISO/IEC 25062:2006 Common Industry Format for usability tests. They obtained high usability levels, but they also revealed some usability flaws. We took as a base these reports to elaborate the VariaMos usability test.

6 Conclusions

This paper presents an enhanced version of FragOP, a framework used to design, implement and reuse domain components in the context of an SPL; which is a mix between a compositional and an annotative approach. The enhanced version supports the SPL product customization. Therefore, we improved an SPL tool called VariaMos to support the FragOP approach. We also included a usability test of VariaMos to gain insights into how VariaMos supports this approach. The key contributions of this paper are (i) the FragOP and VariaMos enhancements, including an improved FragOP metamodel, FragOP process, and a new customization capability through the use of customization points and customization files. (ii) An SPL implementation through the use of the ClothingStores example; which included the derivation of five different products and an analysis of the derivation results. And (iii) the development of analysis of a usability test for the VariaMos tool. The test results provided preliminary evidence that VariaMos is a usable tool that properly supports the FragOP approach. All participants completed all of the tasks, and the mean task time was approximately 10 min. However, we found the VariaMos UI presented some minor issues (related to responsive design). In the short term, we plan to improve VariaMos to support complex binding relationships, support other variability models such as Orthogonal Variability Model (OVM), and improve the VariaMos UI. Finally, as a future work, we plan to develop more rigorous experiments: (i) to validate the approach benefits, (ii) to compare the different approaches to design and implement the domain components, and (ii) to develop an industrial case to provide valuable evidence about the benefits and limitations of VariaMos (FragOP).

References

1. Clements, P., Northrop, L.: Software Product Lines: Practices and Patterns. Addison-Wesley, Boston (2001)
2. Thüm, T., Kästner, C., Benduhn, F., Meinicke, J., Saake, G., Leich, T.: FeatureIDE: an extensible framework for feature-oriented software development. Sci. Comput. Program. **79**, 70–85 (2014)
3. de Souza, L.O., O'Leary, P., de Almeida, E.S., de Lemos Meira, S.R.: Product derivation in practice. Inf. Softw. Technol. **58**, 319–337 (2015)
4. Montalvillo, L., Díaz, O., Azanza, M.: Visualizing product customization efforts for spotting SPL reuse opportunities. In: SPLC, pp. 73–80. ACM (2017)
5. Correa, D., Mazo, R., Goméz-Giraldo, G.L.: Fragment-oriented programming: a framework to design and implement software product line domain components. Dyna **85**(207), 74–83 (2018)
6. Mazo, R., Muñoz-Fernández, J.C., Rincón, L., Salinesi, C., Tamura, G.: VariaMos: an extensible tool for engineering (dynamic) product lines. In: SPLC, pp. 374–379. ACM (2015)
7. ISO 9241-11:1998: Ergonomic Requirements for Office Work with Visual Display Terminal (VDTs) – Part 11: Guidance on Usability (1998)
8. Apel, S., Batory, D., Kästner, C., Saake, G.: Feature-Oriented Software Product Lines. Springer, Berlin (2013)
9. Koscielny, J., Holthusen, S., Schaefer, I., Schulze, S., Bettini, L., Damiani, F.: DeltaJ 1.5: delta-oriented programming for Java 1.5. In: PPPJ, pp. 63–74. ACM (2014)
10. ISO/IEC 25062, Software engineering—Software product Quality Requirements and Evaluation (SQuaRE) - Common Industry Format (CIF) for usability test reports (2006)
11. FragOP-Thesis GitHub repository. https://github.com/danielgara/FragOP-thesis. Accessed 21 Jan 2019
12. Kim, S.D., Min, H.G., Rhew, S.Y.: Variability design and customization mechanisms for COTS components. In: Gervasi, O., et al. (eds.) ICCSA 2005. LNCS, vol. 3480, pp. 57–66. Springer, Heidelberg (2005). https://doi.org/10.1007/11424758_7

13. Rabiser, R., Wolfinger, R., Grunbacher, P.: Three-level customization of software products using a product line approach. In: HICSS, pp. 1–10. IEEE (2009)
14. Pleuss, A., Hauptmann, B., Dhungana, D., Botterweck, G.: User interface engineering for software product lines: the dilemma between automation and usability. In: symposium on Engineering Interactive Computing Systems, pp. 25–34. ACM (2012)
15. Rabiser, R., Grünbacher, P., Lehofer, M.: A qualitative study on user guidance capabilities in product configuration tools. In: ASE, pp. 110–119. ACM (2012)
16. Teruel, M.A., Navarro, E., López-Jaquero, V., Montero, F., González, P.: A CSCW requirements engineering CASE tool: development and usability evaluation. Inf. Softw. Technol. **56**(8), 922–949 (2014)

Towards a Software System for Facilitating the Reuse of Business Processes

Konstantinos Athanasopoulos[(⊠)], Georgios Theodoridis,
Christos Darisaplis, and Ioannis Stamelos

School of Informatics, Aristotle University of Thessaloniki,
54623 Thessaloniki, Greece
{kathanasop, ttgeorgios, chridari, stamelos}@csd.auth.gr

Abstract. Business processes are the driving force of organizations regardless of their size, type or age. There are some processes that are explicit, formal and well documented and others that are in tacit and informal form. Processes are usually complex and require deep knowledge to understand them. For this reason, Business Process Management is a priority for organizations worldwide. Domain Specific Languages are programming languages that are designed to be implemented in specific fields. This paper introduces an open source toolset that will facilitate the reuse of processes in both the public and private sector through a Domain Specific Language and an Integrated Development Environment with a dedicated graphical tool for users that have no previous experience in modeling processes.

Keywords: Business Process Management · Domain Specific Language · Domain specific modeling · Business Process · Open source · e-Government

1 Introduction

Smart Entrepreneurship and e-Government are the modern concepts that describe the digital transformation of Private and Public Sector organizations in a highly evolving technological environment and a globalized competitive economy. The digital transformation of an organization is a fundamental prerequisite for its continuous internal and external functional adaptation to modern reality, which should be done in terms of redesigning and optimizing the processes that provide value to its customers, citizens and businesses [1, 2].

Today, the number of organizations adopting Business Process Management Systems (BPMS) to model and digitize their processes is growing dramatically [3]. By automating workflow processes, the benefits for the organization are significant, but an optimal result is not always guaranteed [4].

The European Union, recognizing the need to reduce or simplify bureaucratic procedures, is promoting ISA^2 (Interoperability solutions for public administrations, businesses and citizens), in which researchers contribute to the development of open source tools. With ISA^2, the joinup platform allows the diffusion and reuse of open source tools for the implementation of long-term public sector solutions [5]. One of

© Springer Nature Switzerland AG 2019
X. Peng et al. (Eds.): ICSR 2019, LNCS 11602, pp. 34–46, 2019.
https://doi.org/10.1007/978-3-030-22888-0_3

these tools is the CPSV-AP, which focuses on the development of a common vocabulary describing the public services of its Member States [6].

This paper introduces an experimental toolset (Fig. 1.) aimed to support administrative and business processes in both public and private sectors. During its development, it will take advantage of CPSV-AP, documented processes and online repositories, namely diadikasies.gr [7], that are used to describe a process while emphasizing on the importance of reusing the models.

Its individual tools concern:

- The development of a Domain Specific Language (DSL) to describe the processes of a Public Sector with an extension to the appropriate business areas of the Private Sector (e.g. Banking, Insurance)
- The development of an Integrated Development Environment (IDE) to help record and model processes in a structured way without the need of prior programming knowledge.

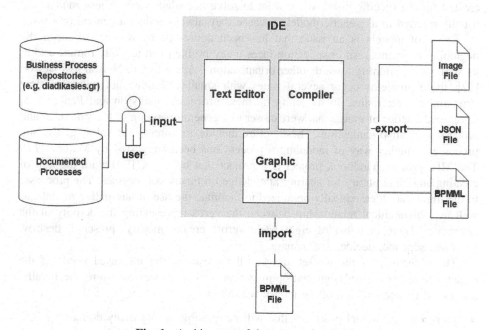

Fig. 1. Architecture of the proposed toolset

The necessity of developing the toolset arrived once we were tasked to help the employees of the Municipality of Kalamaria record, model and optimize their tasks and processes in 2017 [8]. Through this experience, we learnt that Public Administrations across Greece are not trained to properly record or understand the concept of a process. Even though employees in the same position are obliged to follow the same legislation for a process, their interpretations vastly vary and, as no written process or model match each other, reusability has not yet been achieved. Past research and studies have confirmed our findings by providing further insight to this phenomenon [9, 10].

The remainder of the paper is structured as follows: Sect. 2 provides background information in the concept of process reuse and the proposed toolset's objectives. Section 3 delves into the development of the toolset and Sect. 4 concludes the paper.

2 Domain Analysis and Toolset's Objectives

The concept of reuse is applied in practice by many professionals in the field of process modeling due to the complexity and difficulty encountered in recording and modeling the processes. Oberweis [11] pointed out that there are two key candidate strategies for the development of large and realistic modeling processes. The first is a gradual development of the model with continuous updating, evaluation and formalization of individual processes. This can be achieved by using existing processes that will make up a larger one. The second strategy is to adapt already existing models that were not created for the specific problem we want to solve but adapt them. These models are usually referred to as generic models because they always reflect a general process.

Reuse of models is an issue that has been addressed by researchers since the beginning of science. An organization faces many problems in its daily routine and in its strategic positioning towards other organizations. According to Nelson and Nelson [12], these problems occur several times with small variations but with the same structural characteristics. In modeling business processes, Eriksson and Penker [13] developed a series of motifs that were closer to a general mapping of the structures and processes of an organization. These series include resources and rules, goals, and processes. Another way of modeling a process has been suggested by Malone [14]. The MIT process handbook project is a project that began in 1991 with the aim of creating an online library for sharing knowledge on business processes. The processes in the library are hierarchically organized to facilitate the use of alternative models, as well as a hierarchical relationship between the verbs representing the activity of the enterprise. There is a list of eight basic verbs: create, modify, preserve, destroy, combine, separate, decide, and manage.

The objectives of the toolset aim to fill the gap in the increased needs of the organizations for the redesign and optimization of their processes. More specifically, successful implementation of the toolset will allow:

- To record and model processes that will be reusable across many domains
- To integrate the DSL in a stand-alone IDE environment, which can work with existing BPMS open source tools and require no past programming or process modeling experience
- The acquisition of new innovative knowledge and skills for the organizations that will adopt it
- The optimization of existing processes based on their operating cost.

The toolset's DSL and IDE will provide all the necessary linguistic elements and structures that will allow a user to easily and quickly articulate the actions and processes of the private and public sector, hence, amplifying the importance of reuse.

3 Development of the Toolset

3.1 Introducing BPMML

BPMML (Business Process Markup and Modeling Language) is the name of our proposed DSL. It is a markup and modeling language that can be used to create and visualize a process that also conforms to the Business Process Model and Notation (BPMN) standard. It focuses on simplicity and learnability, without sacrificing efficiency and potential, as the average user will most likely not be familiar with programming terms and structures. Nonetheless, we aim to provide useful tools for advanced users and developers to build on the language and create their own graphs or graphical environments.

BPMML is built on Python 3. We use Lark as our parsing library; it is in active development and can simplify the parsing process while focusing on readability.

Since reuse and compatibility are our focus, advanced users will be provided with the tools to build and expand our toolset. One of the outputs is a JSON (JavaScript Object Notation) file in a standardized format that will enable developers to build their own designing software and potentially develop an online graph designing tool. A DOT (graph description language) file can be used to design a graph, so that advanced users may alter the way a graph is displayed without changing the BPMML compiler itself.

Lexical Overview. A summary of the current BPMML's lexical analysis is provided below:

- **start:** defines the start of our code and must always be present
- **end:** defines the end of any multiline structure/block including *start*
- **basic commands:** there is a list of basic commands/tasks to be used in a graph. For the time being, they are only displayed on the graph in a basic box shape, but they can be stylized accordingly in the future (especially in a fully developed GUI). We restrict the user to specific commands so that there is a common standard of modelled processes that will be reused
- **process:** used to define a process. A process is defined as a collection of steps, grouped together under a process name. The process named "main" will initiate the execution of the code. Processes can be nested to one another, defining them as subprocesses. Nested (or *called*) processes that have a name which starts with "_" are not defined as subprocesses but simply as grouped steps, a property that is useful for reducing the repetition of same steps
- **users:** used to define the users related to a process
- **basic divisions, departments and positions:** as with the basic commands, there is a list of possible divisions, departments and positions a user may have
- **change users:** defines a structure that allows additions and removals of users within it (for the current process)
- **add:** is a step within the *change users* structure. It adds the corresponding user to the current list of users in the current process
- **remove:** is a step within the *change users* structure. It removes the corresponding user from the current list of users in the current process

- **parallel:** used to parallel steps. All steps within it will display their content parallel to one another. To keep some steps linear, we group them as a *process* (by creating a subprocess or a process with a name starting with "_")
- **try:** is a part of the conditional structure and groups the steps the *retry* command will loop back to. Its steps are executed and displayed normally when reached in the code
- **check:** is a part of the conditional structure and defines the condition to be displayed within BPMN's diamond shape
- **yes:** is a part of the conditional structure and groups the steps in the affirmative edge of the structure
- **no:** is a part of the conditional structure and groups the steps in the negative edge of the structure
- **retry:** is an optional step within *yes/no* of the conditional structure. It commands the graph to display a loopback edge to the beginning of the *try* step, making loopbacks possible in our graph.
- **abort:** is an optional step within *yes/no* of the conditional structure. It commands the graph to display an edge leading to an end/failure node
- **continue:** used as an empty step and exists to better visualize an empty step instead of leaving it blank
- **call:** used to reference an existing *process* by name. It basically inserts the called process into the graph as a subprocess of the current running process
- **import file** function and **global arguments**: Their aim is to increase BPMML's reusability and allow the use of preconditions that will enable localization to different domains, countries and legislation. They currently under development.

Detailed usage and grammar analysis will be explained in the following sections.

Grammar Analysis. With the aid of coding examples, each command and structure currently used in BPMML will be analyzed.

Start Structure. The *start* structure is used to wrap the code. It fundamentally corresponds to the starting and ending nodes of a BPMN graph.

```
Start
...
end
```

For the time being, there are no other usages or initialization variables that the start structure accepts but we could potentially define a graph type of our choice, the language to be used and other global settings like those within it.

Basic Commands. The *basic* commands, which is still under development and careful consideration, is a list of tasks available in BPMML. The acceptable syntax is displayed below, with <string> meaning any phrase with alphanumeric characters plus "_".

```
command <string>
```

Assuming a task list contains *verify* and *sign* as valid tasks, BPMML consequently categorizes them as valid basic commands. A document can be verified and then signed. Code would look like this:

```
verify document
sign document
```

Process Structure. The *process* structure is used to categorize and group the code in different blocks. All code must be a part of a process, excluding the start structure. Every process can have a name defined in a string variable. The process "main" must always exist and it defines the starting point of our code compilation.

```
process <string = name of process>
...
end
```

Below is an example based on the previous verify and sign document process:

```
start
   process main
      verify document
      sign document
   end
end
```

Processes can be nested to one another creating a subprocess. Subprocesses are important to organize tasks and beautify our code. Below follows an example of a subprocess, entitled "Document Handling", that can be easily reused:

```
start
  process main
    process Document Handling
       verify document
       sign document
    end
  end
end
```

The examples above created a local subprocess to the "main" process as they are directly nested within it. Local processes are not held in memory; once they are executed they have no future usage and so, they can share names. Global processes are processes that are not nested to any other process, making them directly nested to the start structure. For example, the "main" process is a global process. Global processes must have unique names and can be executed by using the call command.

```
call <string = global process name>
```

We do not wish to create a subprocess every time we call a global process but simply reuse tasks. The code bellow showcases an example of reusability:

```
start
   process Document Handling
      verify document
      sign document
   end
   process main
      call Document Handling
   end
end
```

Users Structure. The *users* structure creates a block, in which we can define any number of users for the current process. It is an optional structure and if defined, it must exist directly under the process definition. A user is defined in a top down fashion, starting with their division then department, position and lastly their name.

```
process main
   users
      division department position <string=name>
      ...
   end
end
```

Example:

```
process main
  users
    Marketing Division Sales Department Manager John
    Smith
    Marketing Division Advertising Department Manager
    Matt Johnson
  end
end
```

Change Users Structure. Like the *users* structure, the *change users* structure defines users. It can add and remove users within a process, defining a change of the personnel responsible for the upcoming tasks.

```
                    change users
                        add <user>
                        remove <user>
                    end
```

Here is an example of a complete process, in which John Smith and Smith Johnson verify the document, but Alice Wonder signs it.

```
start
  process Document Handling
    users
        Marketing Division Sales Department Manager John
Smith
        Marketing Division Advertising Department Manager
Smith Johnson
    end

    verify document
    change users
        remove Marketing Division Sales Department Manager
John Smith
        remove Marketing Division Advertising Department
      Manager Smith Johnson
        add Marketing Division General Department Manager
      Alice Wonder
    end
    sign document
  end

process main
    call Document Handling
end
```

For the time being, the full user description must be used for removal as homonymous personnel may exist.

Parallel Structure. The *parallel* structure is responsible for paralleling tasks. Any task inside its block will be parallel to the rest.

```
                    parallel
                        ...
                    end
```

In most cases, we want to parallel multiple series of linear tasks to one another. That is possible by grouping them to processes. In this way, we "force" the user to use processes while paralleling multiple tasks which by extent "forces" them to keep the code organized. This enforcement is a positive property, especially for casual users as we want the code to be both easily writable and readable from them. Below is an example of paralleling two document handling processes:

```
process main
  parallel
    process Document Handling
      verify document
      sign document
    end
    process _Document Handling
      verify another document
      sign another document
    end
  end
end
```

Conditional Structure. The conditional structure is responsible for the conditional statements.

```
try
  .
  .
  check <string>
    yes
      .
      .
    end
    no
      .
      .
    end
end
```

For the moment, we will ignore the *try* block and focus on the rest. The *check* command is accompanied by a string containing the condition and/or question. Then, two blocks follow within it, the yes and no blocks. These are the two possible routes a process may have; it contains the tasks for the condition being true or false accordingly.

Bellow follows an example based on the document handling process. The code will check if the verification was completed successfully and proceed to sign the document or else reject it:

```
try
  verify document
check Is the document verified?
  yes
    sign document
  end
  no
    reject document
  end
end
```

The "verify document" is included in the *try* block. The reason is not yet clear; we could have left the *try* block empty (or use *continue*) while writing the task of verification right above the conditional structure. For the time being, any tasks that are closely related to the condition we want to check should be in the *try* block to keep the code organized.

With the introduction of the *retry* command, the *try* block can be explained. Based on the previous example, we will not reject but instead, correct the document in the event of a false verification. Once corrected, the new version will need to be verified again. Below is the above code with the addition of the *retry* command:

```
try
  verify document
check Is the document verified?
  yes
    sign document
  end
  no
    correct document
    retry
  end
end
```

The *retry* command creates a loopback and connects the current node to the tasks in the *try* block. Basically, the *try* block exists so that loopback is possible without goto and similar archaic programming commands.

There is also the abort command that signifies termination of the process:

```
try
  verify document
check Is the document verified?
  yes
     sign document
  end
  no
     abort
     end
end
```

3.2   Developing the IDE and BPMML's Graphical Tool

Our proposed IDE aims to provide a user-friendly experience. It currently comprises a text editor, BPMML's compiler and a graphical tool to model the processes. It is an open source project written in Java, under the MIT license.

To achieve efficient and intuitive modeling abilities, the graphical tool makes use of PICTURE's block-based method [15]. In summary, the fundamental modeling construct is the so-called process building block. A process building block represents a certain set of activities within a process. Processes are represented as a linear, sequential flow of building blocks, which guide the user. These building blocks are the only way to describe a process.

The graphical tool will offer a list of semantically fixed building blocks to model a process, accomplishing not only syntactic but also semantic cohesion. Common conflicts are avoided, and additional characteristics of the processes can be presented with the help of process attributes, assigned to the building blocks by the user. To model forks in procedures and describe specific parts in greater detail, the graphical tool will offer the ability to create subprocesses that allow the user to split the model in different, visually distinct parts (Fig. 2). Once the preconditions and global arguments are implemented in the BPMML compiler, the graphical tool will offer additional forks through different scenarios.

The building blocks can be customized to a specific organization's needs with different semantics. The tool also supports input and output from files, being able to read the BPMML from a JSON file and render the corresponding model. It can export an image file of the model's diagram or a JSON file written in BPMML.

Incorporating a clear, minimalistic workspace, the tool simplifies the user's work to plain intuitive operations. For example, a new block can be added to a process/subprocess by simply dragging it from the building blocks list to the relevant rectangle. By picking up an already existing block inside a process/sub-process, the user can change their order or modify their attributes. This way it can be used by people with little prior knowledge on the field.

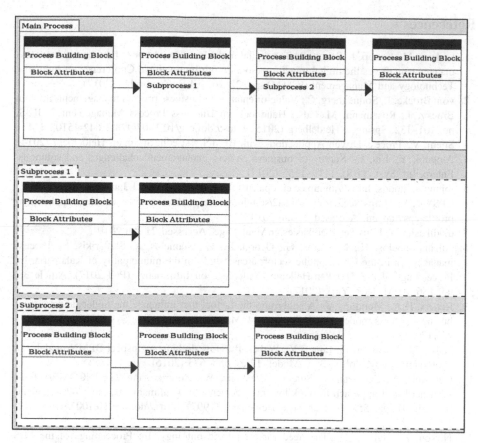

Fig. 2. Part of the workspace panel with process and subprocess building blocks

4 Challenges and Future Work

The development of the toolset will provide a new approach to record, model and reuse business processes. Both the language and the graphical interface aim to enhance the user experience through simple, readable code and models that are easy to manipulate, expand and optimize. The main challenges for successfully deploying it include:

- Designing a DSL that will cover the tasks of an organization and allow them to be reused in similar domains following a set of preconditions
- Integrating them into an IDE which, in addition to recording and modeling, will allow the "translation" of processes into more programming languages or markup code (e.g. Java, XML, e.tc)
- Pilot testing and validating through user testing and diadikasies.gr.

Once fully tested, the toolset will be translated to other languages, localized appropriately for each country and further expanded with new functions that will enhance the process models and secure their interoperability with other established BPMS.

References

1. Lederer, M., Knapp, J., Schott, P.: The digital future has many names - how business process management drives the digital transformation. In: 6th International Conference on Industrial Technology and Management (ICITM), pp. 22–26. IEEE, Cambridge (2017)
2. vom Brocke, J., Sonnenberg, C.: Value-orientation in business process management. In: vom Brocke, J., Rosemann, M. (eds.) Handbook on Business Process Management 2. IHIS, pp. 101–132. Springer, Heidelberg (2015). https://doi.org/10.1007/978-3-642-45103-4_4
3. Stiehl, V.: Process-Driven Applications with BPMN, 1st edn. Springer, Heidelberg (2014)
4. Alotaibi, Y., Liu, F.: Survey of business process management: challenges and solutions. Enterp. Inf. Syst. **11**(8), 1119–1153 (2017)
5. joinup solutions. https://joinup.ec.europa.eu/solutions. Accessed 21 Jan 2019
6. CPSV-AP. https://ec.europa.eu/isa2/solutions/core-public-service-vocabulary-application-profile-cpsv-ap_en. Accessed 21 Jan 2019
7. diadikasies.gr. https://en.diadikasies.gr/Main_Page. Accessed 21 Jan 2019
8. Athanasopoulos, K., Nikoletos, G., Georgiadis, G., Stamelos, I., Skolarikis, S.: Process management in the Greek public sector: a case study in the municipality of Kalamaria. In: Proceedings of the 21st Pan-Hellenic Conference on Informatics (PCI 2017), Article 38, pp. 1–6. ACM, New York (2017)
9. Reijers, H.A., Mendling, J.: A study into the factors that influence the understandability of business process models. IEEE Trans. Syst. Man Cybern. - Part A: Syst. Hum. **41**(3), 449–462 (2011)
10. Haisjackl, C., Soffer, P., Lim, S.Y., Weber, B.: How do humans inspect BPMN models: an exploratory study. Softw. Syst. Model. **17**(2), 655–673 (2016)
11. Oberweis, A., Schätzle, R., Stucky, W., Weitz, W., Zimmermann, G.: INCOME/WF—a Petri net-based approach to workflow management. In: Krallmann, H. (ed.) Wirtschaftsinformatik'97, pp. 557–580. Physica, Heidelberg (1997). https://doi.org/10.1007/978-3-642-57737-6_32
12. Nelson, K., Nelson, H.: The need for a strategic ontology. In: Proceedings of the MIS (Management Information Systems) Quarterly Special Issue Workshop on Standard Making: A Critical Research Frontier for Information Systems, pp. 12–14 (2003)
13. Eriksson, H.E., Penker, M.: Business Modeling with UML, 1st edn. Wiley, New York (1998)
14. Malone, T.W., Crowston, K., Herman, G.A.: Organizing Business Knowledge: The MIT Process Handbook. MIT Press, Cambridge (2003)
15. Becker, J., Pfeiffer, D., Räckers, M.: Domain specific process modelling in public administrations – the PICTURE-approach. In: Wimmer, Maria A., Scholl, J., Grönlund, Å. (eds.) EGOV 2007. LNCS, vol. 4656, pp. 68–79. Springer, Heidelberg (2007). https://doi.org/10.1007/978-3-540-74444-3_7

Automated Support to Capture Creative Requirements via Requirements Reuse

Quoc Anh Do[✉], Surendra Raju Chekuri, and Tanmay Bhowmik

Mississippi State University, Mississippi State, MS 39762, USA
{aqd14,src463,tb394}@msstate.edu

Abstract. Increasingly competitive software industry, where multiple systems serve the same application domain and compete for customers, favors software with creative features. To promote software creativity, research has proposed multi-day workshops with experienced facilitators, and semi-automated tools to provide a limited support for creative thinking. Such approach is either time-consuming and demands substantial involvement from analysts with creative abilities, or useful only for existing large-scale software with a rich issue tracking system. In this paper, we present a novel framework, useful for both new and existing systems, providing an end-to-end automation to support creativity. In particular, the framework reuses freely available requirements for similar software, leverages state-of-the-art natural language processing and machine learning techniques, and generates candidate creative requirements. We apply the framework on three application domains: Antivirus, Web Browser, and File Sharing, and further report a human subject evaluation. The results demonstrate our framework's ability to generate creative features and provoke innovative thinking among developers with various experience levels.

Keywords: Requirements engineering · Requirements reuse · Creativity · Natural language processing · Language model · Requirement boilerplate

1 Introduction

Software requirements, often written in natural language, describe the services a software system should provide in order to fulfill stakeholders' needs and desires [30]. Requirements engineering (RE) is the process of identification and documentation of such requirements for further analysis, communication, and subsequent implementation [30]. Much of traditional RE is built upon the notion that requirements exist in the stakeholders' minds in an implicit manner [20], and has focused on models and techniques to aid the identification and documentation activities of such requirements. However, with the advance of internet and the rapid growth of software market, we see an ever increasing competition where multiple software systems serve the same application domain and compete for customers. Consequently, modern software market favors software that

© Springer Nature Switzerland AG 2019
X. Peng et al. (Eds.): ICSR 2019, LNCS 11602, pp. 47–63, 2019.
https://doi.org/10.1007/978-3-030-22888-0_4

provides novel and useful features [24]. Therefore present-day requirements engineers need to create innovative requirements in order to equip the software with competitive advantage. To that end, RE, recently framed as a creative problem solving process, plays a key role in capturing more useful and novel requirements, thereby improving a software system's sustainability [24].

Creativity, a multidisciplinary research field, is widely considered as "the ability to produce work that is both novel (i.e., original and unexpected) and appropriate (i.e., useful and adaptive to task constraints)" [35]. Creativity in RE is the capture of requirements that are new to the project stakeholders but may not be historically new [24]. Research suggests that creative requirements for a software system could be obtained by *exploring, combining,* or *transforming* existing ideas in the conceptual domain [8,24] (known as exploratory, combinational, and transformational creativity, respectively [24]). A common approach to improve software creativity employs intensive multi-day workshops where ideas for requirements are manually generated with guidance from experienced human facilitators [23,25]. Although considered to be successful in promoting creativity, the considerable costs stemming from economic, time, and geographical pressures make the widespread adoption of such intensive processes less feasible [16]. Researchers have also investigated semi-automated techniques [10,29], frameworks [6,7,12], and tools [36] to support creative thinking. Such approach, however, is still time consuming [29], demands substantial involvement from analysts with creative abilities [10,12,36], and useful only for existing large-scale software with a rich issue tracking system [6,7].

In this paper, we propose a novel framework that reuses freely available requirements of other software in the application domain and automatically generate candidate creative requirements leveraging state-of-the-art natural language processing (NLP) and machine learning (ML) techniques. In particular, our framework starts with collecting existing requirements from online product listings (e.g., Softpedia[1]). Then, it applies ML techniques, including the doc2vec algorithm [18], to retrieve distributed vector representations of the requirements, which are further clustered leveraging BIRCH, an efficient clustering algorithm for ML with high-dimensional data [37]. Next, the framework applies simple heuristics to requirements selected from the clusters in order to extract valuable attributes, including process, objects, and additional details about objects. Finally, these attributes are supplied to Rupp's boilerplate [31], a popular reusable sentence structure widely used in RE, to formulate new requirements. We apply our framework on three popular software domains on Softpedia: Antivirus, Web Browser, and File Sharing. We further conduct a human subject evaluation with 30 participants and the results indicate promising implications of our framework for developers, with various experience levels, seeking creative software features.

The contributions of our work lie in developing a framework to automatically generate concise but potentially creative requirements leveraging state-of-the-art NLP and ML techniques. Furthermore, the framework provides an automated

---

[1] https://www.softpedia.com.

support with limited human intervention that facilitates creative practice in the RE process for both new and existing software systems. The rest of the paper is organized as follows. Section 2 covers some background information on the techniques we use. Section 3 introduces our framework with concrete demonstrations. Section 4 details the human subject evaluation followed by Sect. 5 presenting further discussion and limitations of the work, Sect. 6 highlights some related work. Finally, Sect. 7 concludes the paper with an outline for our future work.

2   Background

This section presents an overview on some key techniques leveraged in our automated framework, aiming to make the approach more generalizable. Hereafter, we consider requirements analysts, referring to stakeholders who capture and elaborate software requirements, synonymous to requirements engineers. In addition, the terms <u>requirement</u> and <u>feature</u> are used interchangeably in this paper.

2.1   Requirement Boilerplate

Natural language (NL), which is inherently informal in nature, has been the dominated medium for documenting requirements. Such informality in NL often leads to many issues including ambiguity and unnecessary complexity. In order to alleviate this problem, researchers have proposed boilerplates [31], i.e., reusable templates with placeholders that can be replaced by actual attributes to formulate structured requirement statements. Since generating such statements is one of the major goals of this work, boilerplates play a pivotal role in our framework. Two widely referenced boilerplates in RE literature include Rupp's boilerplate [31] and the EARS boilerplate [27]. Compared to EARS, however, the former is more compact yet highly effective. Aiming to generate straightforward and directly usable requirements, in this work, we adopt a simplified form of Rupp's boilerplate [31], which is as follows.

Rupp's boilerplate.

> **\<system name\>**shall provide <u>user</u> with the ability to **\<process\>**
> **\<object\>**[additional details about object]

Example.

$$\overbrace{\textbf{Antivirus system}}^{\text{system}}\text{shall provide user with the ability to }\overbrace{\textbf{fast scan}}^{\text{process}}\overbrace{\textbf{files}}^{\text{object}}$$

$$\underbrace{\text{depending on}\textbf{the computer specification}}_{\text{additional details}}$$

As the boilerplate indicates, this work focuses on finding 3-tuples (process, object, additional details) of related words/phrases to complete the missing slots in Rupp's boilerplate [31], thereby improving the generated requirements' meaningfulness. Items in the 3-tuple are defined as follows [31].

Process: A verb or verb phrase describing an action or functionality users can use to fulfill a certain task.

Object: A noun or noun phrase describing an item the process acts upon.

Additional details: A noun phrase containing more context for the feature.

In what follows, we present an overview on some NLP techniques we deploy to extract the verbs, objects, and additional details from existing requirements scraped from online resources (i.e., Softpedia in this paper).

2.2 NLP Techniques

RE research has extensively applied NLP techniques to extract important information hidden among software artifacts including software requirement specifications, source code, and bug reports [3,6]. Here, we highlight two of those NLP techniques, Part-of-Speech (POS) Tagging and Text Chunking, which are playing a critical role in our framework.

POS Tagging is the process of assigning corresponding part of speech (i.e., noun, verb, adjective, etc.) to individual units in a sequence of string called tokens, most commonly identified as words. A good POS tagger is often trained on a very large, pre-labeled corpus (usually contain at least few millions of words such as the Penn Tree Bank dataset [26]). Figure 1 shows an example of a tagged requirement. A word's tag is determined based on its neighbors and the surrounding context. POS tagging often acts as an essential building block for more advanced and complex NLP techniques.

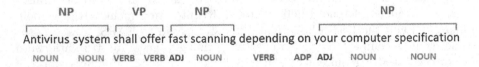

Fig. 1. Part-of-speech and text chunking example.

Text Chunking is defined as the procedure of splitting the text into non-overlapping segments of syntactically related words, called chunks [5]. It can help identify important keywords and ideas in the long text, therefore, reduce processing time. Examples of text chunks are noun phrase (NP), verb phrase (VP), and prepositional phrase (PP). Figure 1, presents a sample requirement that has been annotated with text chunks. Here, for example, *Antivirus system* is a noun phrase constructed from two individual nouns: antivirus and system.

2.3 Language Model

In our case, capturing the 3-tuples (cf. Sect. 2.1) involve predicting probable next-words based on the preceding ones by processing a large amount of textual data. Traditional count-based language models, e.g., n-gram, could be used for such predictions. However, as the amount of data increases, the run time and space complexity for count-based models increase exponentially due to "the curse of dimensionality" [4]. Therefore, we need to find a more advanced approach for our framework to extract the 3-tuples and we choose doc2vec [18], a generalization of the popular word embedding method word2vec [28]. It is an unsupervised machine learning algorithm, developed by Le and Mikolov [18], to capture the fixed-length vector representations of variable-length text inputs such as sentences and paragraphs. Unlike count-based methods representing words as discrete values, doc2vec encodes text documents in continuous-numbered vectors, thereby reduces the complexity of the model while capturing the syntactic and semantic relationships among documents in a satisfactory manner [18].

3 Our Framework

Figure 2 provides an overview of our framework that generates creative software requirements reusing existing requirements. The framework follows a sequential process starting with a web scraper collecting requirements from software libraries, e.g., Softpedia. The collected requirements go through several phases including filtering and clustering. Furthermore, similarity analysis, POS tagging, and text chunking are used to extract requirement attributes that will be used to complete Rupp's boilerplate [31], thereby generating candidate requirements. At this point, a requirement analyst can evaluate and further elaborate the candidates to meet his or her needs[2]. In the rest of this section, we discuss each phase of our framework in detail.

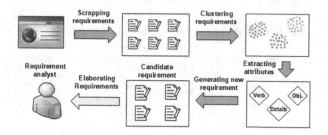

Fig. 2. A framework for requirement creation.

3.1 Collecting Requirements

Domain Selection: In order to test our framework, we collect existing requirements from apps of three popular software domains: Antivirus, Web Browser, and File Sharing. We choose these domains as our subjects for several reasons.

---

[2] The source code is available at http://tinyurl.com/y6pgqn2f.

First, they top the chart with most apps listed, therefore, expected to enrich our requirement dataset. Second, as they are widely used, created requirements for these domains can be beneficial to a large number of users. Finally, highly familiar domains will enable participants in our human subject study (cf. Sect. 4) to critically evaluate the creativity aspects of the generated features.

Data Cleaning: Data quality is crucial in solving data-oriented problems. As the collected requirements come from various sources and are written by many people, they are expected to be somewhat messy. Therefore, we need to prepare a clean, high-quality set of requirements before further processing. To that end, we apply the following steps.

1. Discard features that are either too short or too long. [Based on our data, we consider only the features with number of words between 5 and 15 as the rest either directly state a functionality (e.g., browse websites) or include many unrelated words, making them not a good fit for Rupp's boilerplate in our case.]
2. Remove all non-English words and non-alphabetical characters. Our manual investigation suggests that non-English words are often technical term or typos from writers and are unlikely to be good fits for boilerplate attributes.
3. Convert all words to their original form with lemmatization (e.g., scanned, scans ⇒ scan) to reduce inflectional forms and computational resources.

Table 1 represents the demography of our collected requirements.

Table 1. Overview of the collected requirements.

Domain	Number of systems	Number of features		Vocabulary (# of words)
		Initial	Filtered	
Antivirus	221	1,087	901	3,214
Web Browser	168	1,286	884	2,853
File Sharing	182	474	342	1,714

3.2 Clustering Requirements

This phase involves grouping collected requirements into clusters where each cluster contains highly related features. We assume that, although developers try to distinguish their apps over others in the same domain by introducing more and more innovative features, the common functionalities in the application domain are fundamentally similar. Therefore, clustering requirements play an important role to aid combinational creativity, where new ideas are formed by combining familiar ideas [8].

Clustering algorithms, such as k-means [22] and k-nearest neighbors [2], are widely used. In this paper, however, we use BIRCH [37], a more efficient and scalable clustering algorithm for very large datasets. This allows us to easily extend our framework to work with larger-scale data in the future. The clustering process is twofold. First, we use doc2vec [18] to train the requirement dataset. The output will be real-valued vectors where each vector represents a requirement and similar requirements tend to have similar vector values. Next, these requirement vectors will be used for the BIRCH algorithm to produce requirement clusters. Detailed discussion on these two steps are given below.

Training Doc2Vec Model: We train our model with gensim[3], a widely-used open-source framework for NLP. For each domain, we first tokenize each feature into a list of individual words and treat them as input data for our training model. We separately train each domain with the following parameters. [The values are chosen based on our heuristic experiments with data.]

1. **vector_size = 200.** The fixed-length size of continuous-valued vector representing each feature. Suggested vector size is between 100 and 300 [18,28]. As our dataset contains a fairly small vocabulary, we choose vector size equal to 200 to reduce computational complexity while maintaining satisfactory performance.
2. **min_count = 2.** The minimum number of occurrences of a word in the corpus to be included in the training. We discard all words with only one occurrence as they are unlikely to contribute in building semantic similarity model for the set of features.
3. **epochs = 25.** The number of iteration for all training instances. Le and Mikolov [18] suggest to use 10 to 20 iterations for a very large corpus (i.e., containing millions of words). However, for smaller dataset that we obtained, training with more iterations can help achieve better distributed representation (i.e., similar features tend to be represented by similar vectors).

The output is a matrix $M_{n \times 200}$ where n is the number of requirements for the trained domain and each requirement is mapped to an unique row in M. If two requirements are semantically similar, their corresponding vector representations should be comparable. This characteristic is used to cluster requirements, detailed in next section.

Obtaining Requirement Clusters: We apply the BIRCH algorithm [37], implemented in scikit-learn[4], to cluster requirements. In order to identify the optimized number of clusters, we calculate Silhouette values ranging from -1 to $+1$ where higher value indicates that the points in one cluster are highly correlated to its own cluster and poorly correlated to others [32]. For each domain, we start the clustering process with $k = 2$ and continue to increase k until the

---

[3] https://radimrehurek.com/gensim/.
[4] https://scikit-learn.org.

Silhouette values start decreasing. To that end, the ideal number of clusters for Antivirus, Web Browser, and File Sharing we obtained are 5, 4, and 5 with Silhouette values of 0.468, 0.424, and 0.376, respectively.

3.3 Generating Requirements

This phase aims to create new requirements utilizing Rupp's boilerplate (cf. Sect. 2.1). Here, we discuss the strategy used to sample requirements from clusters, followed by the techniques leveraged to extract boilerplate's attributes to form new requirements.

Sampling Requirements: To examine the performance of our framework in generating innovative requirements, for each domain, we follow stratified sampling strategy [11], where the data is sampled from disjoint requirement clusters. Following [11], this approach is expected to provide samples that better represent the requirement population. To that end, we randomly select a pool of 100 requirements from all clusters within same domain. The number of requirements that each cluster contributes will be proportional to the number of requirements in that cluster.

Creating New Requirements: We now proceed to constructing new candidate requirements from the sampled requirements. To extract the boilerplate's attributes, we use **spacy**[5] for POS tagging and text chunking activities. We first locate the process as a verb/verb phrase from a tagged requirement, then continue to find subsequent attributes including object as noun/noun phrase and additional details as another noun phrase. Existing requirements may have more than one group of attributes. For each group of three requirements in the pool, we alternatively combine their set of attributes to make new requirements. Assuming that we obtain three attributes out of each requirement, we can form up to 3 verbs × 2 objects × 1 additional details = 6 new requirements.

3.4 Selecting Candidate Requirements

To promote creativity, we follow Bhowmik *et al.* [6] to retrieve least-familiar requirements, which are expected to be more innovative. To that end, we calculate the TF-IDF similarity score between each generated requirement and existing requirements in the same domain. Requirements with lower scores are less common in the domain. We select requirements lying at the bottom 10% of the similarity score chart and then randomly select 5 final candidate requirements (cf. Table 2). Such randomization strengthens the human-subject evaluation of our framework detailed in Sect. 4. In addition, we posit 5 requirements from each domain to be a manageable number for our study participants.

---

[5] https://spacy.io.

Table 2. Generated requirements. (Each requirement starts with: **The system shall provide user with ability to ...**)

Antivirus	AV1	... get any background illegal sniffer hacker
	AV2	... suspend password protection shield
	AV3	... build advanced heuristic analysis malicious program
	AV4	... switch antivirus vulnerability
	AV5	... prevent emergency situation any recovery tool
Web Browser	WB1	... export microsoft internet explorer a file
	WB2	... drop search button to the top
	WB3	... keep any user intervention recent web page
	WB4	... display functionality description
	WB5	... make file easy mouse gesture
File Sharing	FS1	... customize the files
	FS2	... set icon every downloading file
	FS3	... highlight the network user
	FS4	... save traffic download speed
	FS5	... share the client firewall

4 Human Subject Evaluation

4.1 Research Questions

This part of our research focuses on assessing the overall performance of our framework in creative requirements generation. A major objective of this human subject study is to evaluate the creative merits of the automated requirements for Antivirus, Web Browser, and File Sharing applications. To that end, we ask the research question: RQ_1 – *How creative the requirements generated by our framework are?*

Here, we would like to reiterate that automated text generation is inherently complicated and still limited to a certain degree despite the development in modern NLP. Although several advanced-level Rupp's boilerplates [31] exist, in this work, we consider a preliminary version for its simplicity. Therefore, the generated statements may not always be properly complete or grammatically correct. Nevertheless, sometimes such statements or collection of terms might be interesting enough to act as creativity triggers [10] and invoke creative thinking among beholders. Therefore, we also want to evaluate such triggering aspects of our generated requirements asking the following research question: RQ_2 – *How helpful the generated requirements are in capturing new requirements?*

In small-to-medium-sized software firms, including startups, regular developers often act as requirements analysts performing activities of analyzing and clarifying requirements. As different developers undoubtedly possess different level of experience and skill sets, it would be interesting to explore how much our frameworks outcomes depend on the analyst's experience level. Thereby, we ask the following research question: RQ_3 – **Developers with what level of experience benefit from our automated framework?**

4.2 Study Setup

We recruited 30 developers, with diverse backgrounds and expertise in software development, from the pool of both undergraduate and graduate students and staff programmers at our institute. Confidentiality agreement was made with the participants to respect their anonymity. Following the creativity work by Murukannaiah *et al.*, we developed a questionnaire asking the participants to rate an automated requirement for three different attributes: **clarity**–unambiguous and provides an appropriate level of detail, **novelty**–original and unexpected, and **usefulness**–adaptive to the system and contains value or utility; on a 5-point Likert scale: 1 = very low, 2 = low, 3 = medium, 4 = high, 5 = very high. The questionnaire included 5 randomly selected requirements for each domain (cf. Table 2). Also, the participants were asked to justify their ratings and to voluntarily rewrite/elaborate the requirements if they found the idea to be interesting. Towards the end of the questionnaire, for each software domain, the participants also provided an overall rating on the helpfulness of the automated statements in capturing new requirements on a 5-point Likert scale: 1 = not at all helpful, 2 = slightly helpful, 3 = somewhat helpful, 4 = moderately helpful, 5 = extremely helpful. In addition, the questionnaire asked about the participant's level of familiarity with the domains and years of software development experience. Before the questionnaire started, the participants were provided with a short tutorial explaining the rating scales and the keywords: clarity, novelty, and usefulness. Each participant worked individually and spent approximately 1.5 h, on an average, to complete the activities.

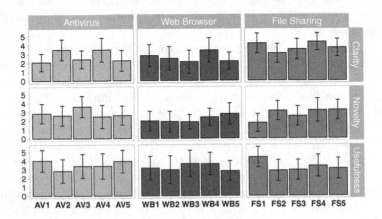

Fig. 3. Helpfulness of generated requirements.

4.3   Results and Analysis

*RQ₁. **How creative the requirements generated by our framework are?*** Figure 3 presents the average rating with standard error for each requirement on its clarity, novelty, and usefulness. We notice that the clarity scores are relatively better for file sharing (ranged from 3 to 4, i.e., medium to high). However, some mixed opinions are clearly noticeable for other domains with just 2 antivirus and 1 web browser requirements receiving above 3 average ratings. Since the requirements are neither always properly complete, nor they are grammatically correct, the ratings are probably not surprising. The novelty and usefulness ratings, on the other hand, are fairly consistent along the domains. We observe that the majority of file sharing and a couple of antivirus requirements receive close to medium or higher novelty ratings with all web browser requirements obtaining medium or lower. The average usefulness ratings are fairly consistent and intriguing as we find all the requirements (except one antivirus, AV2) receiving 3 or more (up to 4.5 for FS1). In retrospect, it is not feasible to expect every requirement generated by an automated mechanism to be perfect on clarity, novelty, and usefulness. Accordingly, the results suggest that our framework often generates requirements with medium to high level creativity. A post-hoc analysis provides further insight along this line which is detailed in Sect. 5.

*RQ₂. **How helpful the generated requirements are in capturing new requirements?*** With an option to voluntarily rewrite and elaborate a requirement, we notice 253 (56.2% out of 450 total possibilities; 30 participant × 15 requirements) instances of rewritten requirements. Given that is was an optional activity for our participants, we find it to be reasonably high. Furthermore, the average ratings from participants on the helpfulness of the automated statements in capturing new requirements are 3.75, 3.25, and 3.6 with the medians being 4, 3, and 4 for File Sharing, Web Browser, and Antivirus, respectively (cf. Fig. 4). The results indicate that our framework often generates moderately helpful requirements provoking creative thinking for further elaboration. We present more insights on this aspect, specially on Web Browser, in Sect. 5.

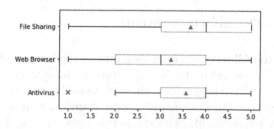

Fig. 4. Requirement usefulness ratings.

*RQ₃. **Developers with what level of experience benefit from our automated framework?*** In order to answer this question, we investigate if there is any association between developers' experience and the activity of rewriting the requirements (for each domain). Based on the professional experience, we divide the participants into three groups: **low experience** (<2 years), **average experience** (2 to 4 years), and **high experience** (>4 years). Thereby, we find 8, 12, and 10 participants with low, medium, and high experience, respectively. For each software domain, we count the total number of requirements rewritten by the developers in each experience group. Since rewriting the requirements was optional, we assume that each participant had an equal likelihood of either choosing or ignoring this option. As the groups are not balanced, we first normalize the counts (e.g., if 26 instances of requirements for Antivirus are elaborated by 8 participants, then how many are elaborated by 100 participants) and perform a chi-squared test [1], a widely used statistical tool to analyze categorical data. Table 3 presents the contingency table associated with this test. Although, we obtain a χ^2 value of 28.31 ($df = 4$ and $p = 0.000011$), a closer look into the contingency table indicates interesting implications. We notice that only the participants with low experience has a statistically significant negative association ($spr = -3.4$ and $p = .021$) with reformulating requirements for web browsers. The remaining 8 cells in the table, on the other hand, do not exhibit any statistically significant association. This analysis, to our surprise, mostly suggests that our framework is beneficial for developers with different experience levels.

Table 3. Relationship between developer experience and rewriting requirements

	Low			Medium			High			Total
	frequency	spr	p-value	frequency	spr	p-value	frequency	spr	p-value	
Antivirus	325	1.5	.714	258	−0.9	.926	330	−0.5	.992	913
Web Browser	212	−3.4	**.021**	283	2.5	.187	320	1.0	.920	815
File Sharing	275	1.9	.438	200	−1.6	.659	270	−0.4	.996	745
Total	812			741			920			2473

5   Discussion

5.1   Insights on Certain Observations

Mixed Ratings for Clarity. A closer look into the collected data suggests that the participants often picked on the incompleteness and syntax issues. For example, in case of AV3: "Antivirus system shall provide the user with the ability to build advanced heuristic analysis malicious program", a comment in the justification section reads "...looks like a good one but incomplete and awkward wording. Had to read a few times to actually get it". This participant further rewrites the requirement as "Antivirus system shall provide the user with the ability to generate an advanced heuristic analysis report on any malicious program". In fact, 60% participants (18 out of 30) elaborated this requirement incorporating their thoughts on malicious programs including malwares. We also notice that, despite low clarity, AV3 receive comparatively higher average ratings for novelty and usefulness, 3.75 and 3.5 respectively (cf. Fig. 3).

Lower Score for Novelty. According to Maiden *et al.* [24], creativity in RE is the capture of requirements that are new to project stakeholders but may not be historically new to humankind. Therefore, the system under consideration plays a role in the novelty aspect of a requirement. A feature can be novel for a specific software but might exist in some other system in a different form. In our study, the participants rate requirements for application domains (they know very well and regularly use), not exactly for a system. In our opinion, this aspect limits the level of surprise, especially in case of Web Browser, which is a very common software domain. As one of the participants puts for WB4, "...the browsers I know of display functionality description when I hover the mouse on an icon." We notice that sometimes the participants were conservative on their novelty and usefulness ratings even though they clearly got excited about the idea. For example, in case of FS5 "System shall provide the user with the ability to share the client firewall", some common comments include "useful in the right situation..., fairly novel, but not sure about the potential security risks.... would not rate very high". On a different note, such observation indicates that the automated requirements possess the ability to inspire critical thinking among the beholders.

Rewriting the Requirements. All 15 requirements received attention for further elaboration with some being attempted more often than the others. AV1, AV5, and WB2 are among those frequently elaborated requirements (rewritten by 24, 22, and 22 participants, respectively). A further analysis unveils an interesting trend. All three are ranked low on their clarity ($\approx$2) and novelty (between 2 and 2.9). In fact, WB2 "Browser shall provide the user with the ability to drop search button to the top" is one of the lowest rated requirements in our study (overall avg. $\approx$2.67). However, the participants still took time to brainstorm on this and some of the elaborated requirements look striking. One such intriguing example: "The browser shall include a permanent drop-down search bar so that users can easily search the internet at any given time." This requirement basically suggests an integrated panel on the browser with a search bar so that the user can search the net without moving away from the current website he or she is browsing. This feature practically provides the advantage of having double monitors. This observation brings forth some interesting questions: Is the framework indeed capable of promoting creativity for a highly matured application domain? Even if the novelty of some automated requirements is low, could they still act as a good starting point for more innovative features? In future, we want to conduct further investigations along these lines.

5.2   Limitations

This paper presents the development and demonstration of an automated framework as well as a human subject evaluation. In what follows, we discuss the limitations from both the framework and evaluation perspectives.

From the Framework Perspective. Our framework is heavily limited to the availability of a large number of clearly written feature descriptions. As we use Rupp's boilerplate [31] that needs additional contextual information for objects to formulate requirement statements, product highlights written in terms of some key words and discrete phrases (a common practice followed in Google Play) will not be useful for our framework. Furthermore, in order to handle the inherent complexity in automated text generation, our framework implements a rather simplified version of Rupp's boilerplate [31] which can actually accommodate up to six placeholders with highly customized options. This approach sometimes leads to incomplete and unstructured statements (e.g., AV5 and WB3), thereby affecting the clarity of the requirements. This is another major limitation of our framework, which, we posit, would be minimized by implementing a more enriched boilerplate. In addition, our underlying algorithm treats the frequently seen contextual text as the additional details for objects (cf. Sect. 2.1), thereby compromising the element of surprise to a certain extent. We made this call to improve the meaningfulness of our automated requirements. How this approach would perform on a dataset collected from heterogeneous application domains is yet unknown.

From the Evaluation Perspective. In order to evaluate different performance related aspects of our framework, we use a 5-point Likert scale, a commonly used approach for scaling opinion-based responses. However, the participants' level of familiarity with the application domain might pose a potential bias in the overall ratings for clarity, novelty, and usefulness. In order to mitigate this issue, we provided a tutorial, allowed access to the internet and discussion with the researcher conducting the study for further clarification. In addition, all three software domains are commonly used by our participants in their day-to-day lives. Although, a few participants reported low and medium level of familiarity with the technical aspects of Antivirus and File Sharing, respectively, we do not expect this to contribute serious bias in the overall findings.

6 Related Work

6.1 Creativity in Requirements Engineering

Earlier creativity research in RE mostly focused on intense multi-day workshops to promote creativity. For example, Maiden and Gizikis [23] conducted workshops encouraging brainstorming and creative thinking among the stakeholders during the requirements process. Maiden and colleagues [25] further proposed RESCUE, a scenario-driven RE process involving creativity workshops to elicit system requirements [25]. Creativity techniques incorporating such workshops require end-to-end human involvement [16] and depend heavily on the "creative muse" of the facilitators. Lately, some tools and frameworks are also proposed to support creative thinking for requirements. For instance, Zachos and Maiden [36] developed an algorithm that explored web services in domains analogous to a current requirements problem. In order to capture requirements from scenario and to help people think creatively while collecting information, Karlsen *et al.* [17] proposed an integrated software tool. Sakhnini *et al.* [34] applied the elementary pragmatic model (EPM) [19] to support creative requirements elicitation. Burnay *et al.* [10] recently examined creativity triggers as a technique for stimulating stakeholders' imagination. Murukannaiah and colleagues [29] proposed a sequential process of manually acquiring requirements from crowd [15]. The aforementioned tools and frameworks mostly provide partial support and still require substantial human involvement to generate new ideas.

6.2   Automated Creation of Software Requirements

So far, automated generation of creative requirements has received limited attention. Current literature provides few examples incorporating automation to a certain degree. Farfeleder *et al.* [14] implemented a semantic guidance system using domain ontology to support formulating new requirements based on manually defined attributes including concepts, relations, and axioms. In addition, recent research also focus on the automatic creation of requirements triggers to aid creativity aspect in requirements elicitation [13,33]. Recently, Bhowmik *et al.* [6] presented a framework to provide an automated support for creating new requirements applying topic modeling [21] and part-of-speech tagging [9] on the existing requirements of the *same* software system. This framework, however, is only applicable for a software with a long history over issue tracking system and needs to collect and process more complex data including requirements, identity of individual stakeholders, and their contributions in the form of posted comments and artifacts. Another effort of automation is reported by Do and Bhowmik [12] where they experimented with Hidden Markov Model to automatically generate requirements based on hidden creative attributes of existing requirements. However, the outcomes of this approach are extremely random as the generated statements are sequence of apparently unrelated words providing very limited understandability. In this paper, we propose an automated framework which is applicable for both new and existing systems and generates requirements with improved meanings compared to [12].

7   Conclusions

In this paper, we present a novel framework to provide an automated support for innovating requirements by reusing existing requirements from similar software systems. We also report a human subject evaluation of our framework and the results demonstrate its ability to generate creative software features. In addition, the framework provokes creative thinking among developers with various experience levels, thereby boosting the innovative aspects of refined requirements.

In future, we plan to improve our framework by realizing more complex structures for requirements. In addition, we aim to generate more complete requirements, thereby further minimizing the dependency on human analysts.

References

1. Agresti, A., Kateri, M.: Categorical Data Analysis. Springer, Berlin (2011)
2. Altman, N.S.: An introduction to kernel and nearest-neighbor nonparametric regression. Am. Stat. **46**(3), 175–185 (1992)
3. Arora, C., Sabetzadeh, M., Briand, L., Zimmer, F.: Automated extraction and clustering of requirements glossary terms. IEEE TSE **10**, 918–945 (2017)
4. Bengio, Y., Ducharme, R., Vincent, P., Jauvin, C.: A neural probabilistic language model. J. Mach. Learn. Res. **3**(Feb), 1137–1155 (2003)
5. Berwick, R.C., Abney, S.P., Tenny, C.: Principle-Based Parsing: Computation and Psycholinguistics, vol. 44. Springer, Heidelberg (1991). https://doi.org/10.1007/978-94-011-3474-3
6. Bhowmik, T., Niu, N., Mahmoud, A., Savolainen, J.: Automated support for combinational creativity in requirements engineering. In: RE, pp. 243–252 (2014)
7. Bhowmik, T., Niu, N., Savolainen, J., Mahmoud, A.: Leveraging topic modeling and part-of-speech tagging to support combinational creativity in requirements engineering. Requirements Eng. **20**(3), 253–280 (2015)
8. Boden, M.A.: The Creative Mind: Myths and Mechanisms. Routledge, Abingdon (2003)
9. Brill, E.: A simple rule-based part of speech tagger. In: Proceedings of the Workshop on Speech and Natural Language, pp. 112–116 (1992)
10. Burnay, C., Horkoff, J., Maiden, N.: Stimulating Stakeholders' imagination: new creativity triggers for eliciting novel requirements, In: RE, pp. 36–45. IEEE (2016)
11. Diez, D.M., Barr, C.D., Cetinkaya-Rundel, M.: OpenIntro Statistics, vol. 12. CreateSpace, Scotts Valley (2012)
12. Do, Q.A., Bhowmik, T.: Automated generation of creative software requirements: a data-driven approach. In: WASPI, pp. 9–12. ACM (2018)
13. El-Sharkawy, S., Schmid, K.: A heuristic approach for supporting product innovation in requirements engineering: a controlled experiment. In: Berry, D., Franch, X. (eds.) REFSQ 2011. LNCS, vol. 6606, pp. 78–93. Springer, Heidelberg (2011). https://doi.org/10.1007/978-3-642-19858-8_10
14. Farfeleder, S., Moser, T., Krall, A., Stålhane, T., Omoronyia, I., Zojer, H.: Ontology-driven guidance for requirements elicitation. In: Antoniou, G., Grobelnik, M., Simperl, E., Parsia, B., Plexousakis, D., De Leenheer, P., Pan, J. (eds.) ESWC 2011. LNCS, vol. 6644, pp. 212–226. Springer, Heidelberg (2011). https://doi.org/10.1007/978-3-642-21064-8_15
15. Groen, E.C., Doerr, J., Adam, S.: Towards crowd-based requirements engineering a research preview. In: Fricker, S.A., Schneider, K. (eds.) REFSQ 2015. LNCS, vol. 9013, pp. 247–253. Springer, Cham (2015). https://doi.org/10.1007/978-3-319-16101-3_16
16. Horkoff, J., Maiden, N.A.: Creativity and conceptual modeling for requirements engineering. In: REFSQ Workshops, pp. 62–68 (2015)
17. Karlsen, I.K., Maiden, N., Kerne, A.: Inventing requirements with creativity support tools. In: Glinz, M., Heymans, P. (eds.) REFSQ 2009. LNCS, vol. 5512, pp. 162–174. Springer, Heidelberg (2009). https://doi.org/10.1007/978-3-642-02050-6_14
18. Le, Q., Mikolov, T.: Distributed representations of sentences and documents. In: International Conference on Machine Learning, pp. 1188–1196 (2014)
19. Lefons, E., Pazienza, M., Silvestri, A., Tangorra, F., Corfiati, L., De Giacomo, P.: An algebraic model for systems of psychically interacting subjects. IFAC Proc. Volumes **10**(12), 155–163 (1977)

20. Lemos, J., Alves, C., Duboc, L., Rodrigues, G.N.: A systematic mapping study on creativity in requirements engineering. In: SAC, pp. 1083–1088 (2012)
21. Linstead, E., Lopes, C., Baldi, P.: An application of latent Dirichlet allocation to analyzing software evolution. In: ICMLA, pp. 813–818 (2008)
22. Lloyd, S.: Least squares quantization in PCM. IEEE Trans. Inf. Theor. **28**(2), 129–137 (1982)
23. Maiden, N., Gizikis, A., Robertson, S.: Provoking creativity: imagine what your requirements could be like. IEEE Softw. **21**(5), 68–75 (2004)
24. Maiden, N., Jones, S., Karlsen, I.K., Neill, R., Zachos, K., Milne, A.: Requirements engineering as creative problem solving: a research agenda for idea finding. In: RE, pp. 57–66 (2010)
25. Maiden, N., Manning, S., Robertson, S., Greenwood, J.: Integrating creativity workshops into structured requirements processes. In: Proceedings of the ACM Conference on Designing Interactive Systems: Processes, Practices, Methods, and Techniques, pp. 113–122 (2004)
26. Marcus, M.P., Marcinkiewicz, M.A., Santorini, B.: Building a large annotated corpus of English: the penn treebank. Comput. Linguist. **19**(2), 313–330 (1993)
27. Mavin, A., Wilkinson, P., Harwood, A., Novak, M.: Easy approach to requirements syntax (EARS). In: RE, pp. 317–322. IEEE (2009)
28. Mikolov, T., Sutskever, I., Chen, K., Corrado, G.S., Dean, J.: Distributed representations of words and phrases and their compositionality. In: Advances in Neural Information Processing Systems, pp. 3111–3119 (2013)
29. Murukannaiah, P.K., Ajmeri, N., Singh, M.P.: Acquiring creative requirements from the crowd: understanding the influences of personality and creative potential in crowd RE. In: RE, pp. 176–185. IEEE (2016)
30. Nuseibeh, B., Easterbrook, S.: Requirements engineering: a roadmap. In: Proceedings of the Conference on the Future of Software Engineering, pp. 35–46 (2000)
31. Pohl, K.: Requirements Engineering: Fundamentals, Principles, and Techniques. Springer Publishing Company, Incorporated (2010)
32. Rousseeuw, P.J.: Silhouettes: a graphical aid to the interpretation and validation of cluster analysis. JCAM **20**, 53–65 (1987)
33. Sakhnini, V., Berry, D.M., Mich, L.: Validation of the effectiveness of an optimized EPMcreate as an aid for creative requirements elicitation. In: Wieringa, R., Persson, A. (eds.) REFSQ 2010. LNCS, vol. 6182, pp. 91–105. Springer, Heidelberg (2010). https://doi.org/10.1007/978-3-642-14192-8_11
34. Sakhnini, V., Mich, L., Berry, D.M.: The effectiveness of an optimized epmcreate as a creativity enhancement technique for web site requirements elicitation. Requirements Eng. **17**(3), 171–186 (2012)
35. Sternberg, R.J., Sternberg, R.J.: Handbook of Creativity. Cambridge University Press, Cambridge (1999)
36. Zachos, K., Maiden, N.: Inventing requirements from software: an empirical investigation with web services. In: RE, pp. 145–154 (2008)
37. Zhang, T., Ramakrishnan, R., Livny, M.: Birch: an efficient data clustering method for very large databases. ACM SIGMOD Record. **25**, 103–114 (1996)

A Comparative Analysis of Game Engines to Develop Core Assets for a Software Product Line of Mini-Games

Martín Sierra[1], María Constanza Pabón[1]([envelope]), Luisa Rincón[1,2],
Andres Navarro-Newball[1], and Diego Linares[1]

[1] Pontificia Universidad Javeriana, Cali, Colombia
{mvsierra,mcpabon,lfrincon,anavarro,dlinares}@javerianacali.edu.co
[2] Centre de Recherche en Informatique, Université Panthéon Sorbonne, Paris, France
http://www.javerianacali.edu.co

Abstract. The selection of a video game engine to develop core assets of a Software Product Line (SPL) of mini games could be highly influenced by the requisites of the SPL, differentiating it from the usual selection criteria applied when building complex video games. This article presents a comparative analysis between two video game engines, *unity* and *P5*. The purpose of this analysis was to select the most appropriate option to implement the SPL core assets. Taking into account the requirements of the products to be generated from the SPL, we found that the option initially proposed as the most appropriate did not meet the most relevant requirements of the SPL.

Keywords: Core assets development · Game engines · Comparative analysis · Software product line · Software reuse

1 Introduction

The central idea behind creating a Software Product Line (SPL) is to systematically exploit commonalities and variabilities across a set of related products through systematic reuse [13]. The SPL defines a software architecture shared by the products that are part of the product line and a set of reusable assets, also named *core assets*, that enables the rapid construction of particular products. Creating an SPL requires two phases. The first one, the *Domain Engineering*, deals with the development of the core assets, which are reused in the different products of the product line. The second one, the *Application Engineering*, is responsible for implementing the unique parts of each product, if any, as well as selecting and assembling the core assets previously created in the domain engineering, in order to generate a product [3].

One of the fundamental decisions in the development of an SPL is the selection of the technology that will be used to implement the core assets. The core assets must not only meet the requirements of the products, but they must also

© Springer Nature Switzerland AG 2019
X. Peng et al. (Eds.): ICSR 2019, LNCS 11602, pp. 64–74, 2019.
https://doi.org/10.1007/978-3-030-22888-0_5

capture the variability among products, providing common functionality, and providing a way for easily instantiate them to the target applications [7].

As reported in previous articles [10,14], a few years ago we initiated a real-world interdisciplinary project to create an SPL of mini-games to support speech therapies for children with hearing impairment. The industry experience reported in this paper is linked to that project and presents a comparison between two video game engines (Unity and P5) to create core assets within the context of the SPL of mini-games. The comparison of the video game engines was carried out in two stages. In the first stage, the general characteristics of three engines were studied: Unity, P5, and PyGame. In the second stage, Unity and P5 were selected to make a proof of concept on how to implement variability and commonality for a product line of mini-games. The comparison considers the performance, learning curve, and license terms of both engines as additional criteria to decide which engine to use.

The comparison of these engines might facilitate practitioners in deciding which engine(s) can best serve their needs in other SPL implementations. Developing the project that motivated this study, we found that requirements imposed by the development of an SPL change the selection criteria to choose the tools to build core assets. In particular, the selection of a game engine follows different criteria from those generally taken into account for the development of video games, as shown in Sect. 3.

The rest of this article is as follows: Sect. 2 describes the main requirements of the SPL that influenced the selection of the game engine. Later, Sect. 3 presents the three game engines that were reviewed, the criteria used in the comparison and the obtained results. The Lessons learned during this comparison with both engines are presented in Sect. 4. Finally, the article presents the conclusions and future work in Sect. 6.

2   Context

The *Instituto para Niños Ciegos y Sordos del Valle del Cauca (INCS)* is a Colombian organization that offers, among other services, speech development therapy for hearing impaired children. For these children, therapy sessions are held in the institute's facilities and the children must repeat the exercises at home until the next therapy session.

Motivated by the INCS' desire to make the exercises more appealing to children, an SPL is being developed to create custom-made mini-games. Due to space limitations, no further details of this product line are shown, but more information is available at [10]. These mini-games are therapeutic activities previously designed by an interdisciplinary team that includes speech therapists and psychologists. The purpose of the custom-made mini-games is innovative, as therapists will configure and generate particular activities to assign to each patient, according to his/her current needs, which is something uncommon in previous work (Sect. 5). The activities are intended to provide support in the training of basic concepts of the Spanish language following a well-structured process of language development.

(a) Configuration form

(b) Customized *Dominó* activity

Fig. 1. Screen-shots: configuration form and resulting custom-made mini-game.

Through the implementation of the SPL, the therapist will have the possibility to configure and generate, trough an automatic assembly process, custom-made mini-games for each patient. For example, Fig. 1 shows a screen-shot of the configuration form (part a) and the resulting mini-game (part b) for a domino activity (the images are in Spanish since the system is oriented to Spanish speakers). These mini-games could be used during the therapy session at the INCS and also, playing the mini-games, the children could do their homework.

A game engine is a software development environment designed for building video games [17]. The selection of the video game engine is important because it defines the implementation technology for the core assets, which is the basis to obtain custom-made mini-games from the product line. However, the game engine does not affect the user interface or the user experience of the configuration process that the therapist performs to generate the mini-games. The following requirements of the SPL of mini-games impact the engine selection:

R1. The process of assembly and deliver custom-made mini-games must be fast and fully automated. Therapists will customize and generate the mini-games during the therapy session. Therefore, it should be possible to create them automatically in less than one minute. Furthermore, since these users have no knowledge of software development, the SPL must generate ready to use mini-games, and no adjustment or customization at the development level is possible. This restricts the time in which the products' features are bound, that is, the binding time [13]. Thus the core assets should support *dynamic binding*.

R2. The mini-games must be a web executable file. The importance of the web environment lies in offering portability to the mini-games obtained from the product line as users can access a web application on different devices such as computers or tablets.

R3. Games must have 2-D graphics only. Since the games are aimed at very young children whose cognitive development is in the process of development, the proposed mini-games should be simple, in terms of graphics, concepts, and forms of interaction.

R4. Capacity for growth. The SPL is expected to continue growing in the number of mini-games, and it is very likely that different developers implement those mini-games.

R5. No license fees. The SPL will be used by the INCS which is a non-profit organization; thus there are limited economic resources for the operation of the platform.

3   Comparison Among Video Game Engines

In the video game industry, several engines have been proposed for the production of video games. Pygame, P5, and Unity are three of these engines. Pygame and P5 are well known for their 2D support and Unity is widely used to develop different types of video games.

Pygame[1] is a Python module focused on the development of 2D video games that is characterized by its versatility and ease of learning. Python natively supports object-oriented programming, allowing this paradigm to be used in the development of software artifacts.

Unity[2] is a popular multi-platform game engine available for Windows, Mac OS and Linux. It supports 2D and 3D games development and has an integrated user interface that allows the rapid creation of reusable components, called *prefabs*, made by code and graphics. Unity 2D uses a plane view from the 3D world.

P5[3] is a Javascript library that has a set of tools and functions focused on drawing in the web page canvas. The Javascript language supports objects, and since the ES6 revision, it allows to write code following an object-oriented notation.

Despite the advantages of Pygame, we have not gone further with this engine in the comparison. The reason is that Pygame does not have the option to generate executable files that run in web environments, which was necessary to meet the R2 requirement described in Sect. 2. Instead, video games produced on this engine can only run as stand-alone applications.

The comparison was made using five evaluation criteria: *reuse, automatic assembly, performance, learning curve* and *license*. Table 1 summarizes the results and provides a comparative view. The following sections present details of the information given in this table. *Reuse* was chosen because it is the basis for the development of any product line [7]. *Automatic assembly* points to the fulfillment of requirement R1. *Performance* was included because the resulting SPL must be able to produce mini-games to be used immediately during the therapy session (see R1). Thus, the speed at which the product is generated is an important limitation for the case that motivates the SPL. Since different developers would be involved in growing the SPL (see R4), the *learning curve* is a significant factor in the choice of the game engine. Finally, *license fees* were also included to fulfill the R5. Requirements R2 and R3 were taken as the first criteria for the selection of the engines that were compared.

---

[1] https://www.pygame.org/wiki/about.

[2] https://unity3d.com/es.

[3] https://p5js.org/.

Table 1. Comparison results among Unity and P5

Criterion	Unity	P5
Reuse	Inheritance with Prefabs, parameters	Inheritance with classes, parameters
Automatic assembly	Creating and compiling project	Creating project
Performance:		
- Generation time in Windows	25–30 min	1–2 s
- Generation time in Linux	6–7 min	1–2 s
Learning curve	6 months	2 weeks
License	Annual fee	Free use

3.1 Reuse

The benefits promised by product line engineering are based on the construction of core assets that can be reused to build many products from the product line [4]. In the SPL that motivates this comparison between game engines, for example, a therapist could assign to a patient a mini-game in the form of a *Dominó* activity intended to reinforce pet-related nouns, while the therapist wishes to assign to another patient the same mini-game but intended to teach wild animals actions. In this example, there are common and variable elements. The main common point between both cases is the game mechanic, which is in the example the logic of the domino game. Features such as punctuation, audio of the mini-game, or visual structure of the domino card are also common. On the other hand, variable features are the semantic category, for one child is pets while for the other child is wild animals, as well as, the syntactic structure to practice: nouns in the first case and verbs in the second. Figure 1(b) shows a screen shot of a *Dominó* activity.

There are several ways to manage variability and commonality on an SPL, among them, conditional compilation, aggregation, delegation, inheritance, and parameterization [16]. Therefore, to evaluate the reuse capability on both engines, we developed the reusable components required to build the *Dominó* activity previously depicted. We found that inheritance and parameterization are adequate techniques to implement commonality and variability in both engines.

Inheritance is an OOP feature that allows the definition of classes that reuse and extend the state and behavior from other classes. As an example, in the *Dominó* activity, the *DominoCard* inherits the properties and behavior from the class *Card* which has a general definition shared by all kind of cards. Then, the *DominoCard* establishes specific characteristics and behaviors, such as the card width and height, the type and speed of the card movement, or the mirror rotation. In order to generate a *Dominó* activity, both card classes, the parent and the corresponding child, are included.

Parameterization is a mechanism that allows modifying the behavior of a component by changing the values of some of its attributes. In both environments, the parameterization was implemented using a JSON file written when the SPL generates the activity. This file includes dynamic images' location URLs (to use different images in different activities), and tags related to the activity to produce. When the activity is executed, it gathers the data of the JSON file and adapts its behavior and visual presentation accordingly. In this way, dynamic binding is implemented in the SPL.

Conceptually speaking, both, parameterization and inheritance, were implemented in the same way in *Unity* and *P5*; however, the technical details of the inheritance implementation are different, as shown below.

Inheritance in Unity. All Unity elements are GameObjects. The form and behavior of these objects are defined by adding properties or smaller components such as scripts that manage physics, audio controllers, sprite images or animations. However, every time a GameObject is reused it is necessary to rebuild it, slowing down the process. Unity prefabs solve this problem since the same or different projects could use them without rebuilding them from scratch. Prefabs are therefore reusable artifacts that an SPL could use to implement core assets. A prefab contains a GameObject with all its components, including definitions of classes, images, audios, and scripts to manage the physics (ex. collision detection) or other elements. Then, through the use of prefabs, inheritance could be implemented.

Inheritance in P5. Since the ES6 revision, Javascript includes OOP-style notation. Thus, the reuse of code in P5 could be done using classes as core assets. These classes include the visual design as an attribute, and other logic, as the collision detection. This kind of logic was written from scratch because P5 does not provides such add-ons, as does the Unity IDE. Although this characteristic could give the advantage of giving the developer better control over the behavior of the components, it has as a disadvantage, that it may require larger development times.

3.2 Automatic Assembly

Regardless of the underlying game engine, When a therapist configures one activity and launches its generation, the assembly process creates a project with a particular directory structure. The structure corresponds to the underlying game engine. There is a *core-assets* directory containing all the SPL's assets. The assembly process picks from this directory the components needed to assemble the activity and copies them to the project directory.

Assembly in Unity. When working with Unity, the core-assets directory includes the activities prefabs. Using the no-graphics parameter to avoid opening the Unity IDE, Unity is executed in batch to compile the project created.

Assembly in P5. On this context, to generate an activity, the assembly process creates the game directory and an *index.html* file. This file has the commands to import the classes required to build the product. Once the game directory ready, it is moved to the user's public directory where a web portal can take and run it.

3.3 Performance

Although video game performance often refers to execution response times, the critical measure for the SPL that led to this comparison is the time needed to generate the mini-games. Performance in execution was not considered as relevant given that these are simple 2D games; therefore they are not expected to consume resources significantly.

In Unity, as shown in Table 1, the generation of the *Dominó* activity (presented in Sect. 2) took between 25 and 30 min in Windows, and between 6 and 7 min in Linux. This amount of time may be due to the way Unity supports 2D. Probably, 2D applications could be overloaded by the complexity of the internal 3D space management over which the 2D is deployed. Another reason could be the transformation task performed, to produce an executable web file, because the development environment is multiplatform. However, investigating solutions to these possible bottlenecks is out of the scope of this project as we aim to use the tool within an SPL to produce mini-games in the least possible time and not enhancing the tool to do so.

In P5. The generation of a *Dominó* activity in P5 took between 1 and 2 seconds both in Windows and Linux. *P5* supports web and 2D space natively and does not need any conversion task.

3.4 Learning Curve

In Unity. Although Unity has extensive documentation, it is not very clear on aspects of great importance for the project like the use of requests or sockets for communication between application modules, or the command line compilation of projects. Additionally, the handling of the objects of the game is complex in comparison with the simplicity required in the mini-games (requirement R3), impacting the developers learning curve. The compilation time also affected the learning curve and efficiency in the mini-game development because developers had to wait a long time to test the changes they added to the applications.

In P5. Due to wide acceptance in the video game development community, *P5* has good tutorials. The implementation of the aspects mentioned before took two weeks, including the re-factoring tasks.

3.5 Licensing Terms

Each time the therapist assigns an activity to a child the game engine will generate a new game. Therefore, it is continuously required an engine license.

In Unity. Even though the institutions involved in the project are non-profit organizations, their level of income leads them to have to pay an annual license fee that results very costly for the project. However, there remains the possibility of applying for a Unity License Grant Program for educational institutions.

P5 and JS are open source tools.

4 Lessons Learned

Several lessons were learned from the implementation of the SPL core assets in *Unity* and *P5*. Among them, this section focuses on the differences of the criteria for selecting a game engine to implement an SPL of video games with the ones usually applied in traditional video game development.

To select a game engine to build complex games it is more common to use criteria such as the maturity and support of the engine, the diversity of assets available to facilitate visual and physical representation of objects, the response times during game execution, and the possibility of compiling the game for multiple platforms.

Unity has become an industry standard supported by most prominent names in technology. Indeed, Unity's official Public Relations web page[4] states that Unity is the most used real-time 3D development tool in the world. They claim that there is Unity in more than 3 billion devices and there are more than 28 billion solutions made with Unity.

With these impressive statistics in mind, Unity would be the platform to select because of the support available, its maturity, and the assets that ease the building of high complex games (such as camera and light management or objects physics). However, for the specific case of the product line which led to the comparison in the first place, there are unsolvable challenges that made P5 resulted selected: (1) As mentioned, one fundamental criterion of the project is the activity generation time. The generation times in *P5* and *Unity* were very different, Unity did not fit the desired times meanwhile, *P5* times were considerably lower. (2) A fast learning curve is essential because the SPL is expected to continue to grow in the number of mini-games. For this reason, it is also desirable to reduce the development time of the mini-games. In this case, the development times in Unity were much longer than in P5, possibly because Unity's robustness makes the development of simple video games more complex. Thus, in cases where the goal is the development of simple games, selecting a lightweight tool could be more appropriate. (3) Given the nature of the INCS, the use of free software is required.

5 Related Works

Video games have been widely used for helping students learn a language. For example, Tip Tap Tones [5] is a mobile game aimed at helping learners acquire

---

[4] https://unity3d.com/es/public-relations.

the tonal sound system of Mandarin Chinese. Kana Warrior [15] is a game aimed at helping Japanese students learn to read characters quickly. There are some examples of games aimed at learning sign languages; however, fewer games focus on communities such as the hearing impaired [6]. Another game [9] proposes a card game for learning how the English language is conveyed and interpreted between speaker and hearer in spoken discourse (pragmatics), however, this tool is focused on non-native speakers.

Regarding reuse and variability management in video games, ad-hoc techniques such as clone-and-own are commonly used to create new games making it hard to maintain and support [1, 8]. However, using SPL to implement video games started recently, for example, Nascimento et al. [12] abstract, through the study of the domains, the common and variable features of three video games focused on mobile devices in order to generate a fourth video game based from the SPL. In this same line, Vander Alves [2] uses mobile games applications to evaluate variability in J2ME games. Video games have also been useful for teaching concepts related to product line engineering as reported McGregor [11].

6   Conclusions and Future Work

This paper presented a comparative study of *Unity* and *P5* as engines to built core assets of a software product line of video games that support the oral and written rehabilitation therapies in children with hearing impairments. The differentiating factors of this SPL are: (1) The activities are mini-games focused on attending the particular needs of each child. (2) The generation of the mini-games must be fully automated: the SPL should generate them without any expert intervention. (3) Only 2-D games are needed.

In order to select the SPL development tools, we test two game engines, Unity and p5. Through the comparison was possible to verify that *Unity* and *P5* are suitable engines to develop core assets in the context of a product line of video games; however, using *P5*, we streamline both the development and the generation times. It should be noted that the results of this comparison are not generally applicable since it was made in a specific context. However, in the SPL context it could be concluded that the most robust tool may not be the most appropriate option; on the contrary, such selection depends mainly on the specific requirements. Also, we proved that the SPL paradigm and the reuse concept could be adapted, not only for business software but also in the development of serious games focused on health issues like rehabilitation.

Currently, the *Dominó* activity is in the web portals[5][6]. In the future, we will add to the SPL the components that, together with those already implemented, allow us to build and generate other mini-games, among them, *Secuencia* activity and *Ordenando mi casa* activity.

---

[5] http://pacientesat.javerianacali.edu.co.
[6] http://terapeutasat.javerianacali.edu.co.

Acknowledgments. This work is part of the project No. 125174455451, titled "Apoyo a la Terapia de Rehabilitación del Lenguaje Oral y Escrito en Niños con Discapacidad Auditiva". This project is funded by the Departamento Administrativo de Ciencia, Tecnología e Innovación de la República de Colombia (COLCIENCIAS).

References

1. Albassam, E., Gomaa, H.: Applying software product lines to multiplatform video games. In: Proceedings of the 3rd International Workshop on Games and Software Engineering: Engineering Computer Games to Enable Positive, Progressive Change. IEEE Press (2013)
2. Alves, V., Niu, N., Alves, C., Valença, G.: Requirements engineering for software product lines: a systematic literature review. Inf. Softw. Technol. **52**(8), 806–820 (2010)
3. Apel, S., Batory, D., Kästner, C., Saake, G.: Feature-Oriented Software Product Lines. Springer, Heidelberg (2013). https://doi.org/10.1007/978-3-642-37521-7
4. Clements, P., Northrop, L.M.: Software Product Lines: Practices and Patterns, 1st edn. Addison-Wesley Professional, Boston (2001)
5. Edge, D., Cheng, K.Y., Whitney, M., Qian, Y., Yan, Z., Soong, F.: Tip tap tones: mobile microtraining of mandarin sounds. In: Proceedings of the 14th International Conference on Human-computer Interaction with Mobile Devices and Services. ACM (2012)
6. Escudeiro, P., et al.: Serious game on sign language. In: Proceedings of the XV International Conference on Human Computer Interaction. ACM (2014)
7. Her, J.S., Kim, J.H., Oh, S.H., Rhew, S.Y., Kim, S.D.: A framework for evaluating reusability of core asset in product line engineering. Inf. Softw. Technol. **49**(7), 740–760 (2007)
8. Lima, C., do Carmo Machado, I., de Almeida, E.S., von Flach G. Chavez, C.: Recovering the product line architecture of the apo-games. In: Proceedings of the 22nd International Systems and Software Product Line Conference, vol. 1. ACM (2018)
9. Marquez, J.: Designing card games for learning the pragmatics of a second language. In: Proceedings of the 2018 Annual Symposium on Computer-Human Interaction in Play Companion Extended Abstracts. ACM (2018)
10. Martínez, J-C., et al.: Using software product lines to support language rehabilitation therapies: an experience report. In: 2018 ICAI Workshops (ICAIW). IEEE (2018)
11. McGregor, J.D.: Ten years of the arcade game maker pedagogical product line. In: Proceedings of the 18th International Software Product Line Conference: Companion Volume for Workshops, Demonstrations and Tools, vol. 2. ACM, New York (2014)
12. Nascimento, L., Santana de Almeida, E., de Lemos Meira, S.: A case study in software product lines - the case of the mobile game domain. In: 34th Euromicro Conference Software Engineering and Advanced Applications (2008)
13. Pohl, K., Böckle, G., van Der Linden, F.J.: Software Product Line Engineering: Foundations, Principles and Techniques. Springer, New York (2005). https://doi.org/10.1007/3-540-28901-1

14. Rincón, L., Martínez, J.-C., Pabón, M.C., Mogollón, J., Caballero, A.: Creating a software product line of mini-games to support language therapy. In: Serrano C., J.E., Martínez-Santos, J.C. (eds.) CCC 2018. CCIS, vol. 885, pp. 418–431. Springer, Cham (2018). https://doi.org/10.1007/978-3-319-98998-3_32

15. Stubbs, K.: Kana no senshi (kana warrior): a new interface for learning Japanese characters. In: CHI 2003 Extended Abstracts on Human Factors in Computing Systems. ACM, New York (2003)

16. Svahnberg, M., Bosch, J.: Issues concerning variability in software product lines. In: van der Linden, F. (ed.) IW-SAPF 2000. LNCS, vol. 1951, pp. 146–157. Springer, Heidelberg (2000). https://doi.org/10.1007/978-3-540-44542-5_17

17. Zerbst, S., Düvel, O.: 3D Game Engine Programming. Game Development Series. Premier Press (2004)

Reuse and Design and Evolution

Behavioral Evolution of Design Patterns: Understanding Software Reuse Through the Evolution of Pattern Behavior

Derek Reimanis$^{(\boxtimes)}$ and Clemente Izurieta

Montana State University, Bozeman, MT 59718, USA
derek.reimanis@msu.montana.edu, clemente.izurieta@montana.edu

Abstract. Design patterns represent a means of communicating reusable solutions to common problems, provided they are implemented and maintained correctly. However, many design pattern instances erode as they age, sacrificing qualities they once provided. Identifying instances of pattern decay, or pattern grime, is valuable because it allows for proactive attempts to extend the longevity and reuse of pattern components. Apart from structural decay, design patterns can exhibit symptoms of behavioral decay. We constructed a taxonomy that characterizes these negative behaviors and designed a case study wherein we measured structural and behavioral grime, as well as pattern quality and size, across pattern evolutions pertaining to four design pattern types. We evaluated the relationships between structural and behavioral grime and found statistically significant cases of strong correlations between specific types of structural and behavioral grime. We identified statistically significant relationships between behavioral grime and quality metrics, as well between behavioral grime and pattern size.

Keywords: Software evolution · Software quality assurance · Design patterns · Software reuse

1 Introduction

Software products have evolved rapidly over the last several decades. Increasingly complex software requirements from customers have prompted advances in software reuse and automation across all disciplines. These circumstances have helped create an ecosystem where the expectations of software products is significantly higher, and where once minor upgrades were sufficient, now fully-fledged, highly specialized, and entirely automated products are expected. To cope with higher expectations and complex requirements, software reuse is becoming a mainstream approach to meet those needs.

The deployment of complex products with multiple components does not come without its drawbacks, however. The expectation that multi-component complex systems are delivered on time and within budget, require the adoption of robust processes to accommodate all phases of the product's software

© Springer Nature Switzerland AG 2019
X. Peng et al. (Eds.): ICSR 2019, LNCS 11602, pp. 77–93, 2019.
https://doi.org/10.1007/978-3-030-22888-0_6

life-cycle. One such process is software quality assurance (QA); which seeks to measure and monitor all aspects of software quality over the entire lifetime of a software solution. Software design represents the vision of a software solution, considering current and potential future requirements. Designs must be flexible enough to accommodate change, facilitate extensibility, and promote the ease of interchangeable and reusable software components, while still maintaining a high level of quality. A common strategy employed to assist with this balance is the use of design patterns, which can act as reusable design-level and knowledge-share software components among developers [14].

Design patterns embody recurring and reusable solutions to common problems encountered in the software development process [7]. Design patterns capture experience reuse and represent decisions that are made in the design phase of a software life-cycle. They have the properties of being reusable, maintainable, and easy to extend in future versions. The choice to utilize design patterns in a project comes with the understanding of an important assumption– specifically that the initial implementation of a pattern instance may take longer than a non-pattern implementation, but future revisions and maintenance efforts will be faster and therefore cheaper if a pattern is present. This assumption holds true in a theoretical sense, yet is controversial in a practical sense. Historically, design pattern realizations have been found to deviate or drift from their initial and pure intent, thus eliminating many of the beneficial qualities the pattern offers in the first place. Such a deviation may occur if a new developer is unfamiliar with a code-base, or if pressure from management to ship a product requires 'quick-and-dirty' extensions of the pattern. The existence and extent of such deviations are not fully explored; for example, it is not known whether the presence of such a deviation within a design pattern provides more harm to a software product than choosing not to utilize a design pattern in the first place.

1.1 Research Problem

With the understanding that design patterns offer reusable solutions to common problems in software development [7], the importance of verifying correctness of design patterns is crucial. A design pattern instance that deviates from its specification loses many of its reusable qualities, meaning the pattern instance can no longer be applied as a reuse mechanism. Previous research efforts have both explored the existence and measured the effects of design pattern deviations only from a structural perspective. The structural perspective of a design pattern refers to the class members of the pattern, including the operations and attributes of the pattern's classes, as well as the relationships between class members. This research has found that such deviations do exist within a design pattern's evolution, and that these deviations have a negative effect on software quality. However, the structural perspective is one of many perspectives into a design pattern. Another perspective used to understand design patterns is the behavioral perspective, or the events that occur as a design pattern instance is operating at program run-time, which are not visible from a structural perspective. A behavioral perspective offers additional insights into a design pattern and its evolution, thus refining existing scientific models and taxonomies [8,19] that capture design pattern evolution.

1.2   Research Objective

The goal of this research is to expand the body of knowledge surrounding software reuse, as it pertains to design pattern evolution, from a behavioral perspective. Three specific activities aligned with our overarching goal are identified. First, the identification of design pattern deviations from a behavioral perspective. Second, the characterization of behavioral deviations into a structured organizational scheme, a taxonomy. Third, the evaluation of the effects of behavioral deviations on existing structural models as well as software quality. Meeting these objectives will complement existing structural approaches, and provide software stakeholders with more advanced techniques and tools to monitor software quality, so that important decisions surrounding a software product, specifically reuse of components, can be made with increased certainty.

1.3   Contributions

The contributions of this work are threefold:

- A taxonomy that captures behavioral grime in design pattern instances.
- Evaluation of the relationships between structural grime and behavioral grime.
- Evaluation of the relationships between behavioral grime and pattern quality.

2   Background and Related Work

In the following section we discuss relevant background and research, which can be broadly labeled as software quality assurance. We also provide definitions for key terms, and follow by detailing the process we employed to identify important research topics aligned with our goal.

2.1   Design Pattern Formalization

Design patterns can be formally specified using a combination of the Role-Based Meta-Modeling Language (RBML) [13] and the Object Constraint Language (OCL) [21]. RBML specializes the Unified Modeling Language (UML) [18] metamodel and captures key elements of a design pattern, based on specific roles that participants in that design pattern may take. A design pattern specification consists of two sub-specifications, the Structural Pattern Specification (SPS) and the Interaction Pattern Specification (IPS) [13]. An SPS characterizes the structural elements of a pattern, including the class members, attributes, operation signatures, and relationships. An IPS characterizes the behavioral elements of a pattern, referring to the flow of information that occurs as a design pattern is in operation, at program run-time. SPSes are analogous to UML class diagrams, whereas IPSes are analogous to UML sequence diagrams. Both SPSes and IPSes exist at a meta-level that describes design specifications, which is referred to as the M2 level [6]. A given pattern instance, as implemented in a software project, exists at the design level, which is referred to as the M1 level. The process of checking conformance for a pattern instance entails mapping the pattern's members that exist at its M1 level implementation to its corresponding pattern roles, captured with an SPS and IPS, at its respective M2 level pattern definition.

2.2 Design Pattern Decay

Software applications are used everyday, yet they do not 'wear out' over extended use periods in the classical sense, as physical objects would. Instead, software is subject to a different type of wear, related to the maintenance of the underlying design and code. Over time, many factors such as unforeseen changing requirements, developer turnover, legacy code dependencies, and others, will contribute to the degradation of software quality. This phenomenon is captured by the terms *software decay* and *code decay*. Software and code are deemed *decayed* if they are *harder to change than they should be* [3]. A specific form of software decay is *design pattern decay*. Design pattern decay refers to the addition of undesired elements or loss of desired elements in a design pattern pattern instance, over the lifetime of the design pattern [9,10]. Design pattern decay is considered a sub-domain of design decay, which is analogous to code decay with the exception that the decay occurs in the design level of a software project instead of the code level. Design pattern decay consists of two categories; *design pattern grime* and *design pattern rot* [9]. Design pattern grime, hereafter referred to as *grime*, is defined as the build-up of unintended artifacts over the lifetime of a design pattern instance. These artifacts do not contribute to the pattern's intended role in the overall software project, detracting away many of the beneficial qualities the pattern would otherwise provide. Previous work has shown that the presence of grime is associated with decreases in testability and adaptability, as well as the presence of anti-patterns [11]. Additionally, recent work has shown that the presence of grime is related to the depreciation of system correctness, system performance, and system security [4]. Furthermore, Feitosa et al. has found that grime has a tendency to accumulate linearly, suggesting the quality of a pattern worsens as the grime of that pattern increases [5]. Design pattern rot, hereafter referred to as *rot*, is defined as the removal of key elements of the pattern such that the pattern no longer retains its core elements. A pattern that has succumbed to rot no longer identifies as such; instances of rot in software projects has eluded researchers because of the difficulty in identifying it.

3 Research Approach

In an effort to expand on software reuse, as it pertains to design pattern evolution from a behavioral perspective, the strategy employed in this research has three-steps; first, the identification or detection of unintended behavioral items, as they appear in the code of design pattern instances. Second, the characterization of unintended behavioral items into categories that simplify the remediation effort. Third, the measurement of severity of unintended behavioral items so that remediation efforts can be prioritized.

3.1   GQM

We use Basili's Goal-Question-Metric (GQM) approach [1] as a guide for this research. The GQM approach provides an outline of high-level research goals (RG) supplemented with questions (RQ) and metrics (M) that guide the research. The GQM for this research is listed below:

RG1: *Investigate* design pattern instances *for the purpose of* identifying and characterizing behavioral deviations *with respect to* proper pattern behaviors as defined by the design pattern's specification *from the perspective of* the software system *in the context of* design patterns in open source software systems.

> **RQ1** How does the behavior of a design pattern instance deviate from the expected behavior of that pattern type?
> **RQ2** Is there evidence to suggest that behavioral grime is present in pattern instances of a single pattern type?
> **RQ3** Is there evidence to suggest that behavioral grime is present in pattern instances across different pattern types?
> **RQ4** To what extent can a pattern instance have both structural and behavioral grime?
> **RQ5** What is the relationship between structural and behavioral grime?

RG2: *Quantify* the impact of behavioral grime *for the purpose of* capturing the effect of behavioral grime on patterns *with respect to* proper pattern behavior as defined by the design pattern's specification *from the perspective of* the software system *in the context of* design patterns in open source software systems.

> **RQ6** What is the relationship between behavioral grime and design pattern quality, in terms of pattern integrity and pattern instability?
> **RQ7** Is the size of a design pattern instance related to the amount of behavioral grime in that pattern instance?

Metrics: Several metrics are outlined that aid in answering the questions, which are described in Table 1. Formulations for each metric are given, with respect to a pattern instance P.

3.2   Study Design

The study design for this research is depicted in Fig. 1. To begin, we selected several software projects to study according to the selection process presented in the paragraph below. From these software projects, we identified design pattern instances using the design pattern detection tool developed by Tsantalis

Table 1. Description of the metrics used in this study

Metric name	Description
Structural Conformance (**M1**)	The percentage of structural roles in P that conform to at least one structural role from P's SPS
Behavioral Conformance (**M2**)	The percentage of behavioral roles in P that conform to at least one behavioral role from P's IPS
Structural Grime Count (**M3**)	A count of the number of unique instances of structural pattern grime in P
Behavioral Grime Count (**M4**)	A count of the number of unique instances of behavioral pattern grime in P
Pattern Integrity (**M5**)	$\frac{M1+M2}{2}$
Pattern Instability (**M6**)	Adopted from Martin's Instability metric (I) [16], the efferent coupling of P divided by the sum of the efferent coupling of P and the afferent coupling of P $$\frac{C_e(P)}{C_e(P)+C_a(P)}$$
Pattern Size (**M7**)	Adopted from Li and Henry's Size2 metric ($size2$) [15], the sum of attributes and methods across all classes in P

et al. in [20]. We chose this tool because it is based on strong theory and provides evidence of little to no false positives in practice. Additionally, we used the tool SrcML [2] to assist in the source code parsing process. We chose this tool because it offers a translation from language-specific source code to standard format XML, meaning this process becomes language-agnostic. Following XML generation, we reverse-engineered the UML class and sequence diagrams of the entire software project. Once we had reverse-engineered the UML class and sequence diagrams, we generated a UML representation of the design pattern by combining the design pattern's detection with the corresponding UML diagrams. Next, we subjected each design pattern instance to a process of coalescence. The process of pattern coalescence involves identifying members of the design pattern not captured by the design pattern detection tool. Such members may be subclasses, super-classes, or pattern-methods within a pattern class that the design pattern detection tool may have missed. Following coalescence, we extracted the evolution of each pattern instance by tracking and connecting contributing roles of patterns across software versions. Once pattern instance evolutions were generated, we entered the evaluation stage wherein we evaluated pattern conformance, pattern grime, and pattern quality/size for each version (pattern instance) in the pattern instance evolution.

The process of selecting experimental units, or software projects, is as follows. In an effort to increase generalizability of results, we chose to analyze five projects in total. To ensure relevancy, projects were selected based on their popularity ranking on the online code repository GitHub[1]. Specifically, we ranked

---

[1] www.github.com.

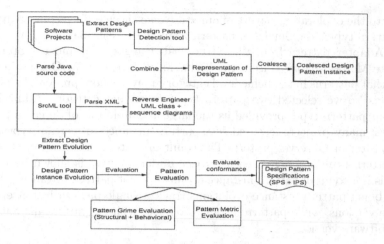

Fig. 1. Summary of study design. Design pattern instances are extracted from software projects, and the associated UML is reverse-engineered from source code. The evolution of each pattern instance is generated, and evaluations for conformance, grime, and metrics are found across each pattern instance evolution.

Table 2. Demographics of the projects under analysis

Project name	Domain	Releases (total releases)	Release dates
Selenium	Testing framework	3.0–3.141.59 (20)	Oct 2016–Nov 2018
RxJava	Asynchronous streaming	2.0–2.2.7 (20)	Oct 2016–Feb 2019
guava	Java libraries	9.0–27.1 (20)	Apr 2011–Mar 2019
spring-boot	Java packaging framework	1.0–2.1.3 (20)	Apr 2014–Feb 2019
Hystrix	Fault tolerance library	1.0.2–1.5.18 (20)	Nov 2012–Nov 2018

all projects according to their 'number of stars', which is synonymous with a favorite or bookmark, and selected the first five projects such that each project had at least 2,000 commits, 75 releases, and 100 unique contributors. In most cases, all projects had significantly more than the minimum required filters; for example the selenium project features 23,550 commits, 116 releases, and 424 contributors. From each project, we selected the 20 most recent minor releases evenly divided between most recent minor release and most recent major release, under the assumption that the project follows traditional notation for release numbers, which is: [major.minor.bug_fix]. If a project did not have at least 20 minor releases in major release window, we selected minor releases from the next-major release. We utilized this process to generate an even spread of data points between the most recent release and the last major release. The outcome from this project selection process is presented in Table 2, along with the release numbers and respective release dates.

Due to the exploratory nature of our study, we chose to focus our analysis on four pattern types; the Singleton pattern from the 'Creational' category [7], the Object-Adapter pattern from the 'Structural' category [7], and the State and Template Method patterns from the 'Behavioral' category [7]. Our initial intuition is that patterns in the behavioral category may be more prone to behavioral deviations, so we selected two pattern types from that category. Additionally, these four pattern types provided us the largest sample size of detected pattern instances; many projects featured zero pattern instances of certain types, such as the Visitor or Observer pattern. The count of pattern instance evolutions for each pattern type and across each project under analysis is shown in Table 3. Note this is a count of pattern instance evolutions, not pattern instances; the difference being pattern instance evolutions track a single pattern instance across multiple versions, while pattern instances refer to a single pattern instance at a single software version.

Table 3. Count of pattern instance evolutions for each of the projects under analysis

Project name	Singleton evolutions	Object-Adapter evolutions	State evolutions	Template method evolutions
Selenium	9	21	28	9
RxJava	5	27	124	11
guava	44	9	34	103
spring-boot	13	4	10	17
Hystrix	14	0	5	5
Total	85	61	201	145

4   Results

Behavioral evaluations of pattern grime have, to the best our knowledge, not been explored in the literature. This allows us to make use of exploratory techniques when reviewing our findings. We thus, utilize correlation analyses and linear regression approaches to identify potential relationships between variables, and will reserve causative analysis techniques for future experiments when research hypotheses are identified.

RQ1: To answer this research question, which is concerned with identifying how the behavior of a design pattern instance can deviate from the expected behavior of that pattern type, we performed an *in-vitro* experiment [12]. Specifically, we created an instance of the Observer pattern that perfectly aligns to its SPS and IPS. Such an instance might be impractical in the real-world, yet would mark a starting/calibration point for experiments. We injected code into this Observer pattern instance that constitutes modular structural grime, as presented by Schanz and Izurieta [19]. Modular structural grime is concerned with the relationships that pattern members may have with either other pattern members, or non-pattern members. Therefore, modular structural grime provides a constraint on all possible pattern behaviors. In other words, a given behavior, whether between pattern members or non-pattern members, cannot exist unless the two members share a structural relationship. To each injected modular grime instance, we applied the behavioral deviations as presented by Reimanis and Izurieta [17]. Specifically, these deviations are 'Improper Order of Sequences', in which expected behaviors occur in an incorrect order, and 'Excessive Actions' in which excessive actions hamper the run-time expectations of a pattern. For this work, we chose to focus on a subset of Excessive Actions, which we refer to as 'Repetitive Actions', or cases where the same behavior is performed within the same scope, or function call, of a pattern instance at run-time. After applying said behavioral deviations to the modular grime taxonomy, we generated a taxonomy of behavioral grime, which is shown in Fig. 2.

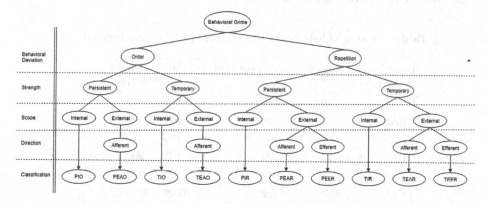

Fig. 2. Behavioral grime taxonomy. Dimensions of behavioral grime are listed on the left, and corresponding characterizations are shown in the taxonomy tree.

The dimensions for this taxonomy are mirrored from the modular grime taxonomy [19], which are explained as follows. Strength refers to the strength of a relationship between two UML members; Persistent Strength refers to a UML association while Temporary Strength refers to a UML use-dependency. Scope refers to the context of the relationship between two UML members; Internal Scope refers to a relationship between two pattern members, and External Scope refers to a relationship between one pattern member and one non-pattern member. Direction refers to the direction of the relationships. Afferent Direction refers to an incoming relationship while Efferent Direction referring to an outgoing relationship. In the taxonomy, the Classification row refers to the acronym that captures that type of behavioral grime; for example, the PIO classification is an acronym for 'Persistent-Internal-Order' grime. This behavioral grime taxonomy closely mirrors the modular grime taxonomy presented in [19], with two exceptions. First, we have incorporated the 'Behavioral Deviations' dimension, which corresponds to the type of behavioral grime (Order or Repetition). Second, one will notice that the taxonomy is not symmetrical across Order and Repetition sub-trees; specifically, the sub-tree pertaining to External Efferent Order (-EEO) type grime is non-existent. This is because this sub-tree represents an outgoing relationship from a pattern member to a non-pattern member can not be in an incorrect order; such relationships are not captured by the design pattern, and thus cannot be in an incorrect order.

RQ2, RQ3: **RQ2** and **RQ3** are concerned with identifying behavioral grime within and across multiple pattern instances. To answer these questions, consider Table 4, which summarizes the grime counts found from our analysis. Each cell in the table refers to a count of behavioral grime across all patterns instances of the corresponding pattern type. Note that no instances of Order grime were found across the entire analysis, and thus we will refrain from showing Order grime results. This does not imply that Order grime does not exist, but rather it means we failed to detect any in this study.

Table 4. Count of behavioral grime across each pattern instance

Behavioral grime type	Singleton	Object-Adapter	State	Template method
PIR	0	296	645	15
PEAR	0	2028	377	60
PEER	390	583	896	392
TIR	24	229	842	266
TEAR	0	4289	921	153
TEER	2088	6822	10320	3053

RQ4, RQ5: These research questions are concerned with identifying the potential relationship between structural and behavioral grime. To answer these questions, we began by generating a pairwise scatter-plot for each type of structural and behavioral grime, which is shown in Fig. 3. Structural grime is shown on the x-axis, and Repetition behavioral grime is shown on the y-axis. Points in the scatter-plot represent the count of modular grime and repetition grime for a single pattern instance.

RQ6: This research question is concerned with the relationship between behavioral grime and pattern quality, as measured by our surrogate quality-metrics, Pattern Instability (M5) and Pattern Integrity (M6). Similarly to **RQ4** and **RQ5**, we began by generating pairwise scatter-plots for these metrics for each behavioral grime type to visually assess trends. This scatter-plot is shown in Fig. 4.

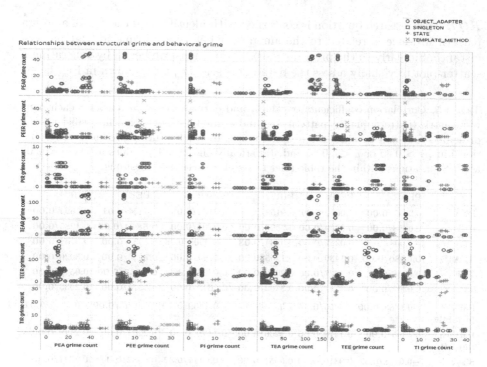

Fig. 3. Pairwise scatter-plots illustrating the relationships between structural grime, shown on the x-axis, and behavioral grime, shown on the y-axis.

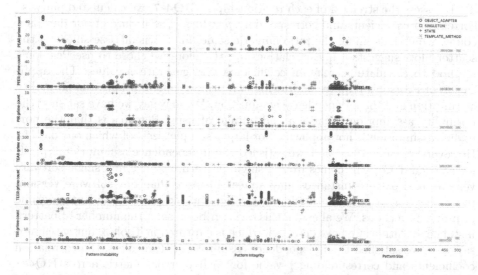

Fig. 4. Pairwise scatter-plots of pattern quality, measured via surrogate metrics Pattern Instability and Pattern Integrity, pattern size, and behavioral grime.

RQ7: This research question is concerned with identifying if the size of a design pattern instance is related to the amount of behavioral grime in that pattern instance. Similarly to the previous research questions, we began by generating a scatter-plot to visually assess the data. This scatter-plot is shown in Fig. 4.

Table 5. Correlation coefficients (r-values) and corresponding p-values for each pairwise metric (pattern quality, pattern size, and grime type). In each cell, coefficients are presented first and p-values are presented second. Bold values represent strong relationships, $r > 0.60$ or $r < -0.60$ and statistically significant p-values at the $\alpha < 0.05$ level. Separations within the table refer to separate research questions.

	PEAR	PEER	PIR	TEAR	TEER	TIR
PEA	0.2021/**0.00**	0.0002/0.99	0.0153/0.19	0.2132/**0.00**	0.0324/**0.01**	0.0694/**0.00**
PEE	0.0358/**0.00**	0.3339/**0.00**	0.2095/**0.00**	0.0704/**0.00**	**0.5814/0.00**	0.1285/**0.00**
PI	−0.0084/0.48	0.0352/**0.00**	0.0264/**0.03**	−0.0006/0.96	0.4053/**0.00**	0.0764/**0.00**
TEA	**0.6086/0.00**	0.1430/**0.00**	0.1355/**0.00**	0.5781/**0.00**	0.2050/**0.00**	0.3026/**0.00**
TEE	0.0006/0.96	0.2227/**0.00**	0.2018/**0.00**	0.0225/0.06	**0.6763/0.00**	0.0549/**0.00**
TI	0.0762/**0.00**	0.3547/**0.00**	0.3702/**0.00**	0.0612/**0.00**	0.5374/**0.00**	0.2633/**0.00**
Pattern Instability	−0.1888/**0.00**	0.0255/**0.03**	−0.0100/0.40	−0.1659/**0.00**	−0.0445/**0.00**	−0.0300/**0.01**
Pattern Integrity	0.1555/**0.00**	0.1470/**0.00**	0.2206/**0.00**	0.1179/**0.00**	0.2204/**0.00**	0.2119/**0.00**
Size2	−0.0118/0.32	0.0810/**0.00**	0.0951/**0.00**	−0.0117/0.32	0.0932/**0.00**	0.2341/**0.00**

To assess the strength of each relationship in **RQ4-7**, we calculated pairwise correlation coefficients and corresponding p-values. The nature of our data is a count, which falls under the ratio numeric scale, and a visual assessment of the scatter-plots suggests a linear relationship; therefore we chose to use Pearson's method to calculate correlation coefficients and generate p-values. The application of Pearson's requires addressing two primary assumptions; the normality assumption and the independence assumption. We may say we have satisfied the normality assumption because an advantage of using Person's is that the normality assumption is not applicable for larger sample sizes, of which our data is. However, we cannot say we have satisfied the independence assumption. Specifically, each data point comes from a single pattern instance in a single software version, and pattern instances may appear in more than one software version, meaning grime in a future version might be, and likely is, dependent on grime in previous versions. We alleviate this concern because of the number of pattern instance evolutions we have detected, which is captured in Table 3, but we cannot say we have satisfied the independence assumption. Regardless, the correlation coefficients and corresponding p-value for each pairwise metric across **RQ4-7** is listed in Table 5, with strong relationships ($r > 0.60$ or $r < -0.60$) and statistically significant p-values at the $\alpha < 0.05$ level shown in bold. Each p-value corresponds to the probability that the correlation coefficient we received was not due to chance, under the assumption that the true correlation coefficient is zero, which implies a very weak relationship.

5   Discussion

The following discussion points highlight the significance of design pattern research as knowledge communication artifacts in software reuse. We extend the body of knowledge by categorizing and evaluating behavioral grime through the exploration of selected pattern evolutions.

The first series of statistical tests focused on understanding the relationships between structural and behavioral grime. For nearly all pairwise comparisons between structural and behavioral grime, very low p-values were found, suggesting that the results we received were not due to chance, and that no relationship exists between structural and behavioral grime types. This is an interesting result, because comparing the correlation coefficients from Table 5 to the respective p-values in Table 5, many correlation coefficients are quite small, which would normally suggest a higher p-value. However, because our sample sizes were large, we found a correlation coefficient that, while being non-zero in many cases, was based upon enough data to supply a confident statistical estimate. This means that the correlation coefficient estimates we found may be close to the true value of the correlation coefficients, but more experiments need to be performed to confirm this position.

With respect to relationships between structural and behavioral grime, specifically of interest is the behavioral grime type TEER (Temporary External Efferent Repetition). Grime of this type manifests itself as non-pattern members that are used by a pattern, but only as a use-dependency (not an association). Such items constitute a deviation from a pattern's specification, which imply the pattern implementation is more difficult to reuse in the future. TEER grime was moderately correlated with two structural grime types (PI and TI), yet was also strongly correlated with two structural grime types (PEE and TEE). The correlations with PEE and TEE do not come as a surprise, considering the structural forms of that grime type dictate behavioral allowances. In other words, the presence of TEER grime cannot exist without the presence of one of either PEE or TEE. However, recall that TEER grime is specifically a *repetition* of behaviors. This means that while a pattern instance may have PEE and TEE structural grime, manifested as a relationship between pattern members and non-pattern members, the relationship is called upon more than once within the scope of a pattern's operation. Conceivably, these usages could originate from poorly constructed logical flows within code, in which the same logical call, or operation, might be performed at different points in a single operation. To assert this thought, we manually reviewed the code of one state pattern instance and discovered that the instance was setting the same state at multiple different places, all within the same operation. This practice is not strictly discussed in the State pattern's best practices, but certainly a cleaner and more reusable version of the pattern instance would be one in which the state would be set once per operation. While future research is required to reveal the true effects of such a practice, such revelations illustrate why behavioral deviations are an important topic to study.

The second series of statistical tests focused on capturing the relationships between behavioral grime and pattern quality, with respect to our surrogate metrics, Pattern Instability and Pattern Integrity. Nearly all pairwise p-values reported as very low, suggesting we reject the possibility that no relationship exists between behavioral grime types and pattern quality. Interestingly, the correlation coefficients for Pattern Instability are low and negative, hinting that a weak but present inverse relationship exists between Pattern Instability and behavioral grime. In other words, an increase in behavioral grime is associated with one, or both, of the following: A pattern instance's efferent coupling decreases while its afferent coupling does not decrease, or a pattern instance's afferent coupling increases faster than its efferent coupling. In most cases, the size of a pattern instance always increased over its evolution, suggesting that the second option holds true; that afferent coupling increases faster than efferent coupling. Put another way, as pattern instances aged and evolved, they tended to be used more by non-pattern members, not that they made use of more non-pattern members. In these cases, results suggest that behavioral grime increases as well; regardless, the increased coupling between non-pattern members and pattern members inhibits future pattern reuse.

Our results pertaining to Pattern Integrity are seemingly counter-intuitive; the results suggest that as Pattern Integrity increases, i.e., as a pattern instance more closely follows its specification, the amount of behavioral grime within that pattern instance increases as well. One would envision that behavioral grime would decreases as Pattern Integrity increases, because that would suggest a refactoring of said pattern instance, aligning it more closely with pattern standards. However, two likely explanations are plausible. First, the case could be that the pattern instance is evolving and new pattern members are being added that conform to the respective SPS and IPS, yet these new pattern members contain behavioral grime. Second, the case could be that refactorings are being performed that better align existing pattern members to their SPS and IPS, yet the refactorings introduce more behavioral grime. In either case, a more robust and extensive study is required to solve this conundrum.

The third series of statistical tests focused on finding the relationship between behavioral grime and pattern size. Our expectations were that as a pattern instance evolved and grew, it would also gain more behavioral grime. Behavioral grime types PEAR and TEAR reported relatively large p-values, suggesting that we are unable to assume that no relationship exists between PEAR/TEAR and pattern size. However, the other types of behavioral grime reported very small p-values, suggesting we can reject the null, and that evidence exists to support a relationship between behavioral grime and pattern size. Looking at the correlation coefficients, we see small positive coefficient values, strengthening our initial expectations. While these values are not as large as expected, we can claim that the evidence from this study suggests pattern instances gain behavioral grime as they get larger. While the increasing size of a pattern instance over its evolution is indicative that the pattern is being reused, the presence of behavioral grime may imply that the pattern's growth rates are slowing down. Future work will address this question, looking at the growth rates of behavioral grime as they pertain to pattern size.

6   Threats to Validity

There are several design and implementation considerations in this study that threaten the validity of the results. External validity is concerned with the generalization of results. In this study, we limited ourselves to 20 minor-release versions of five Java projects, chosen based on popularity from the online repository GitHub. While we attempted to systematically select projects so that our results would be generalizable, we can only claim that our results hold true for the projects under analysis. More case studies following this same process are necessary before more general claims can be made. Internal validity refers to the ability to reach causal conclusions based on the study design. Internal validity is minimal in this study because we make no causal claims, just correlations. Future studies will be directed at increasing this body of knowledge, thus we will explore causal links, yet for this study only correlations were used. Construct validity refers to the choice of independent and dependent variables, with respect to conclusion. Construct validity is threatened in our study because of our use of the Pattern Integrity and Pattern Instability metrics as surrogate metrics for pattern quality. Our rationale for choosing these two surrogate metrics comes from theory that suggests a very small value for Instability increases system stability, positively affecting quality, and that high values for Integrity correspond to more standard and robust implementations, also positively affecting quality.

7   Conclusion

Our research goals focused on the exploration and initial understandings of behavioral deviations, as they pertain to design pattern evolution and software reuse. To this end we have constructed a taxonomy that classifies behavioral grime types. Furthermore, we designed and implemented a case study wherein we measured counts of structural and behavioral grime, as well as quality and size, across pattern instance evolutions pertaining to four design pattern types, originating from 20 versions of five open source software projects. We evaluated the relationships between structural and behavioral grime and found statistically significant cases of strong correlations between specific types of structural and behavioral grime. We identified statistically significant relationships between behavioral grime and both choice quality metrics, as well as pattern size. Patterns are a means of knowledge communication through the reuse of common solutions, and these findings provide important directions that can help practitioners in reducing problems encountered through the evolution of software components.

References

1. Caldiera, V.R.B.G., Rombach, H.D.: The goal question metric approach. Encycl. Softw. Eng., 528–532 (1994)
2. Collard, M.L.: Addressing source code using SrcML. In: IEEE International Workshop on Program Comprehension Working Session: Textual Views of Source Code to Support Comprehension (IWPC 2005). Citeseer (2005)
3. Eick, S.G., Graves, T.L., Karr, A.F., Marron, J.S., Mockus, A.: Does code decay? Assessing the evidence from change management data. IEEE Trans. Softw. Eng. **27**(1), 1–12 (2001)
4. Feitosa, D., Ampatzoglou, A., Avgeriou, P., Nakagawa, E.Y.: Correlating pattern grime and quality attributes. IEEE Access **6**, 23065–23078 (2018)
5. Feitosa, D., Avgeriou, P., Ampatzoglou, A., Nakagawa, E.Y.: The evolution of design pattern grime: an industrial case study. In: Felderer, M., Méndez Fernández, D., Turhan, B., Kalinowski, M., Sarro, F., Winkler, D. (eds.) PROFES 2017. LNCS, vol. 10611, pp. 165–181. Springer, Cham (2017). https://doi.org/10.1007/978-3-319-69926-4_13
6. France, R., Kim, D., Song, E., Ghosh, S.: Metarole-based modeling language (RBML) specification v1. 0. Technical report 02-106, Computer Science Department, Colorado State (2002)
7. Gamma, E.: Design Patterns: Elements of Reusable Object-oriented Software. Pearson Education India, Noida (1995)
8. Griffith, I., Izurieta, C.: Design pattern decay: the case for class grime. In: Proceedings of the 8th ACM/IEEE International Symposium on Empirical Software Engineering and Measurement, p. 39. ACM (2014)
9. Izurieta, C.: Decay and Grime Buildup in Evolving Object Oriented Design Patterns. Colorado State University, Fort Collins (2009)
10. Izurieta, C., Bieman, J.M.: How software designs decay: a pilot study of pattern evolution. In: First International Symposium on Empirical Software Engineering and Measurement (ESEM 2007), pp. 449–451. IEEE (2007)
11. Izurieta, C., Bieman, J.M.: Testing consequences of grime buildup in object oriented design patterns. In: 2008 1st International Conference on Software Testing, Verification, and Validation, pp. 171–179. IEEE (2008)
12. Juristo, N., Moreno, A.M.: Basics of Software Engineering Experimentation. Springer, Heidelberg (2013)
13. Kim, D.K.: A meta-modeling approach to specifying patterns. Ph.D. thesis, Colorado State University. Libraries (2004)
14. Lajoie, R., Keller, R.K.: Design and reuse in object-oriented frameworks: patterns, contracts, and motifs in concert. In: Object-Oriented Technology for Database and Software Systems, pp. 295–312. World Scientific (1995)
15. Li, W., Henry, S.: Maintenance metrics for the object oriented paradigm. In: 1993 Proceedings First International Software Metrics Symposium, pp. 52–60. IEEE (1993)
16. Martin, R.C.: Agile Software Development: Principles, Patterns, and Practices. Prentice Hall, Upper Saddle River (2002)
17. Reimanis, D., Izurieta, C.: Towards assessing the technical debt of undesired software behaviors in design patterns. In: 2016 IEEE 8th International Workshop on Managing Technical Debt (MTD), pp. 24–27. IEEE (2016)
18. Rumbaugh, J., Jacobson, I., Booch, G.: Unified Modeling Language Reference Manual. Pearson Higher Education, New Delhi (2004)

19. Schanz, T., Izurieta, C.: Object oriented design pattern decay: a taxonomy. In: Proceedings of the 2010 ACM-IEEE International Symposium on Empirical Software Engineering and Measurement, p. 7. ACM (2010)
20. Tsantalis, N., Chatzigeorgiou, A., Stephanides, G., Halkidis, S.T.: Design pattern detection using similarity scoring. IEEE Trans. Softw. Eng. **32**(11), 896–909 (2006)
21. Warmer, J.B., Kleppe, A.G.: The Object Constraint Language: Precise Modeling with UML. Addison-Wesley Object Technology Series (1998)

Developing a Flexible Simulation-Optimization Framework to Facilitate Sustainable Urban Drainage Systems Designs Through Software Reuse

Yang Yang and Ting Fong May Chui[✉]

Department of Civil Engineering, The University of Hong Kong, Pokfulam,
Hong Kong SAR, China
yyang90@connect.hku.hk, maychui@hku.hk

Abstract. In stormwater management, increasing attention is paid to sustainable urban drainage systems (SuDS), which include porous pavements and rain gardens. Various numerical modeling software systems have been developed to simulate the hydrological performances of SuDS, e.g., GIFMOD and SWMM can be respectively applied to study the hydrological processes in small-scale SuDS and their effectiveness in large-scale drainage networks. However, it is sometimes desirable to combine the features of different software, such that the hydrological processes of various spatial-temporal scales can be simulated more accurately. Reusing the existing code to create new software, however, can be challenging, as various combinations of the software of very different structures might be interested. Therefore, this study develops a method and a toolbox in R programming language to couple and reuse existing software without modifying their source code. This toolbox automates the software application processes, including input file creation, simulation, and post-processing. A modeling scheme is adopted that the outflow time series from SuDS are first modeled using the software of choice, which are then treated as external inflows to the drainage networks modeling software. This toolbox also integrates evolutionary optimization algorithms and performance-assessment frameworks to form a flexible simulation-optimization framework for solving design optimization problems. For demonstration, SWMM, a data-driven model of SuDS, and a relative performance evaluation framework are coupled to solve a SuDS allocation problem in an urban catchment. This research demonstrates that file-based software coupling methods can be useful for reusing existing modeling software in developing integrated modeling systems.

Keywords: Urban hydrology · Numerical modeling · Software reuse

1 Introduction

Sustainable urban drainage systems (SuDS), such as porous pavements and rain gardens, are environmentally-friendly alternatives to the conventional drainage infrastructures. SuDS are decentralized semi-natural hydrological controls and connections that aim to restore the natural hydrologic regimes. The effectiveness of SuDS in terms

© Springer Nature Switzerland AG 2019
X. Peng et al. (Eds.): ICSR 2019, LNCS 11602, pp. 94–99, 2019.
https://doi.org/10.1007/978-3-030-22888-0_7

of stormwater management is often assessed using numerical modeling software. Various software systems have been developed in recent years for different applications. For example, GIFMod is an open-source software that can be applied to model the detailed hydrological process in small-scale SuDS of various designs; and SWMM is a popular open-source software that can be applied to model the integrated urban drainage system, which includes catchments, SuDS, conveyance systems (e.g., drainage conduits), and hydraulic controls (e.g., weirs). Researchers have coupled SWMM with a parameter estimation tool PEST++ [1], and the coupled system has been applied to optimize the parameters of SWMM [2].

However, it is sometimes desirable to combine the features of different software or to model different components of a catchment by using different software. For instance, SWMM uses simplified methods to model the hydrological processes in individual SuDS practices, which can be inadequate in certain applications; more sophisticated SuDS modeling methods used in other software might be more appropriate.

Developing new software by reusing the source code of existing ones may be more applicable than creating new software from the sketch. However, because the existing software systems are developed using different languages and can have very different structures, it might be difficult and impractical to develop ad-hoc software that reuses the existing code whenever a specific combination of software is of interest. In addition, the software of interest may not be open-source, preventing its source code from being reused directly by other researchers. To overcome these issues, researchers in the field of hydrology have proposed several software interface standards which aim to enable data exchange between different software at run-time. If the software systems are developed in compliance with these standards and are designed for modeling different hydrological processes, they may be reused and integrated easily to form an integrated modeling system; this may be considered as a practice of component-based software engineering. The commonly-used interface standards include Open Modeling Interface Standard (OpenMI) [3] and HydroCouple [4]. However, many existing software systems do not comply with these standards, and considerable effort may be required to make an existing piece of software compatible.

Alternatively, software integration and reuse might also be achieved through file-based information exchanges, i.e., the simulation results of a software can be used as input to drive the simulation of another software. Therefore, this study aims to develop a method and a programming toolbox to systematically implement file-based software integration, which allows the existing software to be reused without modifying their source code.

2 Methods and Materials

The file-based software integration is applicable because the hydrological processes in SuDS practices and their controlled areas are modeled relatively independently in the commonly used drainage networks modeling software (e.g., SWMM), such that the outflows from SuDS can be modeled using the software of choice and supplied to the drainage networks modeling software as externally-generated inflows. Apparently, the original input files to the drainage network modeling software should be updated to accommodate the effect that outflow from a part of the original catchment is modeled externally using other software. The proposed modeling scheme is depicted in Fig. 1a. A toolbox in R programming language is developed such that this modeling scheme can be implemented automatically once a SuDS modeling scenario is defined. Evolutionary optimization algorithms and performance evaluation frameworks are also coupled in the toolbox for deriving optimal SuDS designs (as shown in Fig. 1b). The evolutionary optimization algorithms can generate random SuDS designs and update these designs based on the evaluation results. As the performance of SuDS is often evaluated using multiple performance indicators and it is often necessary to account for the preferences of stakeholders, performance evaluation frameworks are thus often needed for generating an effectiveness score which reflects the overall effectiveness of each SuDS design.

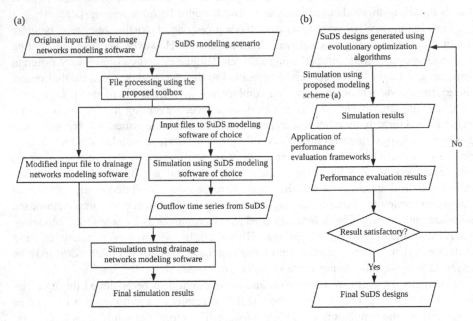

Fig. 1. (a) Workflow of the proposed modeling scheme; (b) illustration of the method to optimize SuDS designs with the aid of evolutionary optimization algorithms and performance evaluation frameworks.

As shown in Fig. 1a, the information exchange between different software is achieved by processing their input and output files. As the format of these files may be specific to each software, functions to read and write formatted files are developed and included in the proposed toolbox, where the string processing functions in R and regular expressions are employed.

In practice, modeling software may need to be executed for thousands of times to evaluate the effectiveness of different design alternatives. To speed up the evaluation process, the toolbox leverages the computing power of multi-core CPUs using the parallel processing functions provided by R, where parallel clusters (also known as "workers") communicating over sockets are created to independently perform the tasks of file processing, simulation, and post-processing. The simulation results are managed using data frame objects in R, where the creation, mutation, filtering, and merging of these objects are handled by functions provided by the tidyverse packages in R [5].

As a case study, the optimal layout design of SuDS was examined. A small urban catchment in the U.S. was considered, which was adapted from [6], where an urban catchment is subdivided into seven subcatchments (S1 through S7) with surface areas ranging between 0.80 and 2.75 hectares. The considered SuDS implementation options are: (1) installing green roofs on residential buildings in subcatchments S1 to S3 and (2) installing porous pavements and rain gardens in commercial lots in subcatchment S4 and S5. The goal is to find the optimal number of SuDS practices in each sub-catchment to maximize the hydrological performance of the drainage system while minimizing the cost.

The drainage networks and the green roofs were modeled using SWMM. The runoff generation process in the rain gardens and porous pavements were modeled using a data-driven model developed for a SuDS site in Geauga County, Ohio, U.S. (the site condition was described in [7]). The performance evaluation framework used in this study employed a relative performance evaluation method to collectively account for multiple performance targets [8]. Peak flow and runoff volume reductions under the 20 mm and the 40 mm design storms are of interest. In the performance evaluation framework, two parameters are used to reflect the management interests of the stakeholders: a is a parameter that reflects the relative degree of interests of stakeholders in SuDS' performances under 20 mm design storm; and b is a parameter that reflects the relative degree of interests of stakeholders in SuDS' performances in runoff volume reductions. $0 \leq a \leq 1$ and $0 \leq b \leq 1$, with 1 indicating of most interest and 0 indicating of no interest. A parameter c is used to specify how expensive per unit of porous pavement and rain garden is when compared to per unit of green roof. Forty-five unique optimization problems with varying a, b and c values were evaluated for assessing the effects of management interests and SuDS costs on the optimal solutions. The optimization algorithm was NSGA-II. Since SWMM, the SuDS modeling software, the performance evaluation framework, and the optimization solvers are developed using different languages, it is reasonable to integrate them through file-based information exchange.

3 Results and Discussions

The Pareto fronts of the 45 optimization problems are shown in Fig. 2, where the x-axis shows the cost of SuDS alternatives, which was calculated as the ratio between the cost of a SuDS alternative and the cost when all of the possible SuDS are implemented. The effectiveness score shown on the y-axis ranges between 0 and 1, with 1 indicating the best performance and 0 indicating the worst performance. As shown in Fig. 2, the effectiveness of SuDS increased non-linearly with their cost. It is apparent that the cost-effectiveness correlation was different when the management interests and the prices of SuDS practices varied (reflected by the values of a, b, and c).

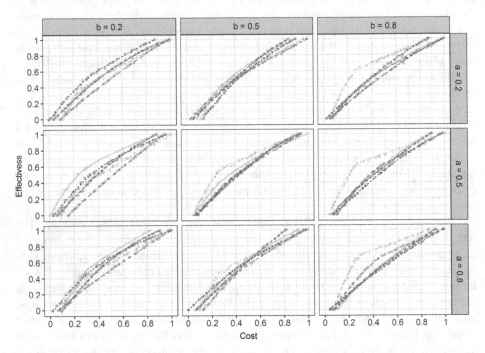

Fig. 2. Pareto fronts of the SuDS layout optimization problems when different values of parameters *a*, *b*, and *c* are used. The lines were fitted using locally weighted scatterplot smoothing.

The file processing functions developed in this study (e.g., the functions for processing SWMM input files) may be reused in future file-based software integration projects. To improve the reusability of software, developers are suggested to develop and provide such file processing functions together with the executable files to facilitate file-based software integration. Although the file-based software integration methods can be implemented relatively conveniently, it still has some limitations. First, domain knowledge is required for defining the modeling scheme and the subsequent software integration method, e.g., the scheme shown in Fig. 1a is proposed based on the understanding of the flow routing methods used in SWMM. It is the researchers' responsibility to identify the correct and efficient modeling scheme and integration method. Second, the involved repeated file reading and writing operations can be time-consuming. Run-time data exchange between software may be implemented to avoid these file operations, but it is also subject to higher software development costs. Although the hydrological modeling community is generally becoming more aware of the issue of software reusability and the importance of implementing common interface standards, it may not be realistic to expect all future software systems are compliant with the same interface standard. The proposed toolbox also includes functions to facilitate parallel simulations, which may be applied to enable the reuse of numerous existing single-thread hydrological modeling software in parallel computing.

4 Conclusions

The file-based software integration presented in this study allows the existing SuDS modeling software to be used together to achieve higher accuracy. The proposed method and toolbox significantly reduced the workload of creating new software, integrating with existing software, executing multiple simulations, and post-processing. The simulation-optimization framework developed in this study improves the current modeling and optimization practices in the following ways: (1) it allows different types of SuDS modeling software to be composed and reused directly without modifications; (2) it has a modular structure that the SuDS modeling software, evolutionary optimization algorithms, and performance assessment frameworks can all be easily updated or replaced.

This research demonstrates an application of file-based software composition methods in urban hydrological research, in which the existing modeling software and frameworks are reused without modifications to form an integrated simulation-optimization framework. As many hydrologists require integrated modeling systems for understanding the interactions among various hydrological processes, further studies on software integration and reuse in other branches of hydrology are recommended.

Acknowledgements. This study was supported by a grant from the Research Grants Council of the Hong Kong Special Administrative Region, China (Project No. HKU17255516). The authors would like to thank Robert A. Darner from the U.S. Geological Survey for providing data for this study.

References

1. Kamble, S., Jin, X., Niu, N., Simon, M.: A novel coupling pattern in computational science and engineering software. In: SE4Science@ICSE 2017, pp. 9–12 (2017)
2. Lin, X., Simon, M., Niu, N.: Hierarchical metamorphic relations for testing scientific software. In: SE4Science@ICSE 2018, pp. 1–8 (2018)
3. Gregersen, J.B., Gijsbers, P.J.A., Westen, S.J.P.: OpenMI: open modelling interface. J. Hydroinform. **9**(3), 175–191 (2007)
4. Buahin, C.A., Horsburgh, J.S.: Advancing the Open Modeling Interface (OpenMI) for integrated water resources modeling. Environ. Model Softw. **108**, 133–153 (2018)
5. Wickham, H.: tidyverse: Easily install and load the 'Tidyverse'. R package version 1.2.1 (2017). https://CRAN.R-project.org/package=tidyverse
6. Gironás, J., Roesner, L.A., Rossman, L.A., Davis, J.: A new applications manual for the Storm Water Management Model (SWMM). Environ. Model Softw. **25**, 813–814 (2010)
7. Darner, R.A., Shuster, W.D., Dumouchelle, D.H.: Hydrologic Characteristics of Low-Impact Stormwater Control Measures at Two Sites in Northeastern Ohio, 2008-2013. US Department of the Interior, US Geologic Survey, Reston (2015)
8. Yang, Y., Chui, T.F.M.: Integrated hydro-environmental impact assessment and alternative selection of low impact development practices in small urban catchments. J. Environ. Manag. **223**, 324–337 (2018)

Automatically Extracting Bug Reproducing Steps from Android Bug Reports

Yu Zhao[1(✉)], Kye Miller[1], Tingting Yu[1], Wei Zheng[2], and Minchao Pu[2]

[1] University of Kentucky, Lexington, USA
{yzh355,kemi232}@g.uky.edu, tyu@cs.uky.edu
[2] Northwestern Polytechnical University, Xi'an, China
pmcmc@mail.nwpu.edu.cn, wzheng@nwpu.deu.cn

Abstract. Many modern software projects use bug-tracking systems (e.g., Bugzilla, Google Code Issue Tracker) to track software issues and help developers reproduce these issues. There has been recent work on automatically translating the natural language text (i.e., steps to reproduce) of bug reports to reproducing scripts, targeted at Android apps, to facilitate app debugging process. The scripts describe the event sequences leading to the app issues and thus can be reused for testing newer versions of the apps. However, existing techniques require manually providing the text description of steps to reproduce for generating reproducing scripts, which is a non-trivial task because natural language text in bug reports can be complex and contain much information irrelevant for bug reproduction. In this paper, we propose an approach that can automatically extract the text description of steps to reproduce (S2R) from bug reports to advance automated software issue diagnosis and test script reuse. The approach is implemented as a tool, called S2RMiner, which combines HTML parsing, natural language processing, and machine learning techniques. We have evaluated S2RMiner on 1000 original Android bug reports. The results show that S2RMiner can extract S2R with high accuracy.

Keywords: Bug reports · Steps to reproduce · Android apps

1 Introduction

Mobile devices with advanced computing ability, such as smartphones and tablets, have become increasingly prevalent. Mobile applications (a.k.a apps) in different domains are developed and used on these devices. In 2017, there were over 3.5 million apps published in Google app store [4]. As mobile apps are becoming complex due to developers adding more features to make them competitive in the market, there is an urgent need to ensure the quality of the apps. A recent survey indicates that 88% users are likely to abandon the apps

© Springer Nature Switzerland AG 2019
X. Peng et al. (Eds.): ICSR 2019, LNCS 11602, pp. 100–111, 2019.
https://doi.org/10.1007/978-3-030-22888-0_8

if they repeated encounter the same issue [21]. Therefore, developers need to rapidly resolve app issues to avoid losing customers.

Many modern software projects use bug tracking systems (e.g., GitHub [2], Google Code [3], Bitbucket [1]) to help developers track and reproduce app issues and thus expedite the process of resolving the issues. These systems allow users or developers to submit *bug reports* describing the issues they encountered in the apps, typically involving bug symptoms, steps to reproduce (S2R), and expected behaviors. Once a developer receives a bug report, he or she will try to reproduce the bug according to the description of S2R. However, reproducing bugs from bug reports is a challenging task [20]. This is because bug reports are often written by natural language, which can be imprecise and often incomplete. In addition, even if a bug report is perfectly understood by developers, the event-driven nature of mobile apps can make actual process of bug reproduction complex as it may require developers to manually navigate through a number of actions before exposing the bug [26].

To help developers reproduce issues reported for mobile apps, there has been some work that can automatically translate the natural language text of a bug report into a test script that can directly execute on mobile apps [15,26]. The translated test scripts can reproduce bugs or be re-used to perform regression testing for future versions of apps. For example, YAKUSU [15] analyzes the natural language text of steps to reproduce (S2R) in an Android bug report and automatically translates it into actual test cases. ReCDroid [26] uses grammar patters to extract key information from S2R and then leverages dynamic GUI exploration to reproduce the app crash guided by the extracted information. The above work uses S2R as input and assumes it is readily available and manually provided by developers. This requires additional manual effort and prevents the bug reproduction tools from being used in fully automated environment (e.g., continuous integration). Therefore, *a tool that can automatically extract S2R from bug reports is needed to enhance the efficiency of bug reproduction and the generation of reusable test scripts.*

There has been little research on targeting at detecting S2R in bug report descriptions. Most existing techniques aim to detect other types of information, such as source code snippets [10,23] and stack traces [9,22]. While one approach has been proposed to detect S2R [13], it focuses on determining whether S2R exists in a bug report rather than extract the the actual text of S2R. In fact, extracting S2R is non-trivial because natural language bug descriptions are often unstructured. Although some bug tracking systems (e.g., Bugzilla) provide semi-structured templates for reporters to write bug symptoms, S2R, and expected behaviors, they cannot guarantee that reporters will provide such information.

In this paper, we propose a new technique, S2RMiner, targeted at Android apps, that can automatically analyze bug reports to extract S2R. The extracted S2R can achieve several straightforward benefits, such as providing succinct information to help developers understand the reported bug and providing insights for improving the quality of bug reports (e.g., an absent S2R indicates a low-quality bug report). Moreover, S2RMiner facilitates *software reuse* in the context of regression testing [25]. For example, bug-triggering test cases are often reused to test newer versions of software. Therefore, the extracted S2R by S2RMiner, once translated into automated test scripts, can be reused in regression testing.

S2RMiner leverages HTML parsing, natural language processing (NLP), and machine learning techniques to analyze the bug reports (in HTML format) directly downloaded from the issue tracking systems for extracting S2R. Specifically, HTML parsing extracts text relevant to S2R from the HTML files of bug reports. NLP is used to obtain different types of text features of each sentence by employing part-of-speech (POS) tags, dependency parsing, and stemming. With text features, a Support Vector Machine(SVM)-based machine learning method [17] is used to predict and extract S2R.

To determine the effectiveness of our approach, we apply S2RMiner on 1000 bug reports randomly selected from GitHub and Google code. The results showed that S2RMiner is effective at extracting S2R. The average F-measures are 0.65 and 0.65 on GitHub and Google code, respectively. The accuracy scores on the two datasets are 0.87 and 0.93.

In summary, our paper makes the following contributions:

- The design and development of the first approach that can extract S2R sentences directly from the textual description of bug reports.
- An empirical study showing that S2RMiner is effective at extracting S2R with high precision.
- The implementation of our approach as a publicly available tool, S2RMiner, along with all experiment data [5].

In the next section, we introduce a motivating example. We then present the details of S2RMiner in Sect. 3. Our empirical study and results are presented Sects. 4 and 5. We present the related work in Sect. 6, and then give our conclusions in Sect. 7.

2   A Motivating Example

Figure 1 shows an example bug report. Given the whole text description, it is unclear which sentence belongs to S2R. Therefore, existing bug reproduction tools (e.g., YAKUSU and ReCDroid) cannot directly work on the raw description of the bug report.

S2RMiner is designed and implemented to accurately extract all S2R sentences from the bug report. Specifically, S2RMiner takes the HTML format of the issue page (Fig. 2) as input and outputs a sequence of S2R sentences (i.e., the text inside the rectangle indicates S2R). If a bug report does not have S2R (e.g., Fig. 3), S2RMiner will report S2R is missing.

3   S2RMiner Approach

S2RMiner consists two major phases. In the first phase, S2RMiner uses a HTML parser to extract the key text containing S2R from the HTML format of an issue

Crash on Nexus 4, ACV 1.4.1.4:

1. start the app
2. click menu
3. choose "open"
4. go to directories like /mnt
5. long-press a folder, like "secure"
6. crash

The reason is that, when you don't have permission, File.list() would return null. But this is not checked. The problem happens in src/net/robotmedia/acv/ui/SDBrowserActivity.java:111, where you called file.list() and later used the result. The return code may be null.

In this case, it's due to permission, so maybe it's not that interesting. However, it may also return null due to other reasons. Anyway, showing an error message is better than crashing.

Fig. 1. A bug report

```
<task-lists disabled="" sortable="">
<table class="d-block">
  <tbody class="d-block">
    <tr class="d-block">
      <td class="d-block comment-body markdown-body  js-comment-body">

          <p>Crash on Nexus 4, ACV 1.4.1.4:</p>
<ol>
<li>start the app</li>
<li>click menu</li>
<li>choose "open"</li>
<li>go to directories like /mnt</li>
<li>long-press a folder, like "secure"</li>
<li>crash</li>
</ol>
<p>The reason is that, when you don't have permission, File.list() would
 return null. But this is not checked. The problem happens in
src/net/robotmedia/acv/ui/SDBrowserActivity.java:111, where you called
file.list() and later used the result. The return code may be null.</p>
<p>In this case, it's due to permission, so maybe it's not that
interesting. However, it may also return null due to other reasons.
Anyway, showing an error message is better than crashing.</p>
      </td>
    </tr>
  </tbody>
</table>
</task-lists>
```

Fig. 2. HTML format of Fig. 1

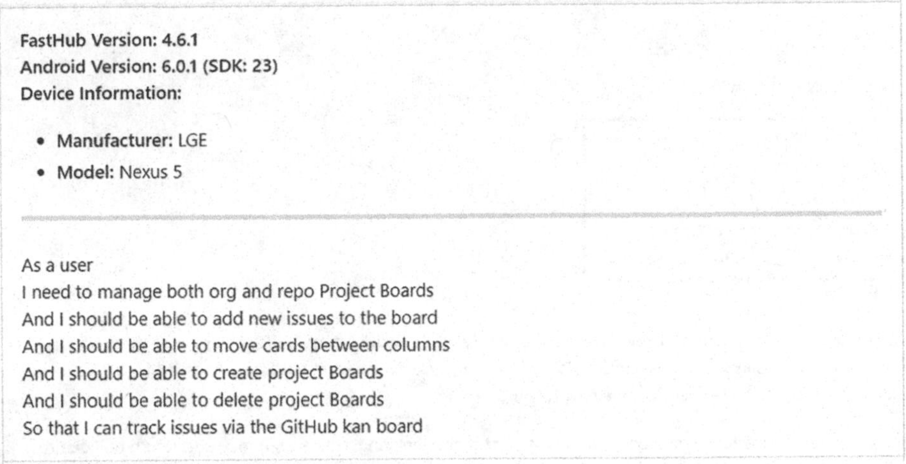

FastHub Version: 4.6.1
Android Version: 6.0.1 (SDK: 23)
Device Information:

- **Manufacturer:** LGE
- **Model:** Nexus 5

As a user
I need to manage both org and repo Project Boards
And I should be able to add new issues to the board
And I should be able to move cards between columns
And I should be able to create project Boards
And I should be able to delete project Boards
So that I can track issues via the GitHub kan board

Fig. 3. Missing S2R

page. As shown in Fig. 2, the HTML issue page contains HTML tags, such as </li>, </ol>, and <tbody class = "d-block">. S2RMiner filters out the HTML tags and obtains only text "start the app".

In the second phase, S2RMiner uses NLP techniques to extract text features from the sentences of the filtered text. It then uses machine learning to label whether a sentence belongs to S2R. Finally, the sentences labeled with S2R are saved into a output file. The output can either be manually analyzed by developers or provided as an input to the test script generation tool (e.g., YAKUSU) or the bug reproduction tool (ReCDroid).

3.1 Phase 1: HTML Parsing

Many bug tracking systems allow reporters to submit bug reports through web pages and developers can reply to the bug report by adding comments to the page. Therefore, bug report descriptions are often downloaded as HTML files. The original HTML file has a number of HTML tags. In addition, the raw HTML file contains many other types of information, such as bug symptoms, expected behaviors, developers' replies, CSS code, page information, and so on. These types of information are irrelevant to S2R. Even on a simple bug report shown in Fig. 1, the associated HTML file contains 1371 lines and is as large as 104 KB. S2RMiner needs to eliminate all such information to obtain the minimum amount of text containing S2R.

Specifically, S2RMiner removes all HTML tags and parses the first block of text in the HTML page. The intuition is that only the first comment involves S2R described by the reporter.

3.2   Phase 2: S2R Extraction

The problem of detecting S2R sentences can be formulated into the problem of text classification [12]. Given a sentence, a text classification tool can predict whether it is a S2R sentence or not. S2RMiner performs the classification in three steps. First, it splits the text into individual sentences by employing several heuristics. Second, for each sentence, S2RMiner extracts text features used for building a classifier. Third, leveraging the text features, S2RMiner builds a classifier that can predict whether a sentence is S2R. All S2R sentences are saved into an output file.

Splitting Text into Sentences. S2RMiner first needs to detect individual sentences for being labeled as S2R sentence or non-S2R sentence. We cannot simply view each text line as a sentence because a line may contain more than one sentence. In the example of Fig. 1, the first line in the second to last paragraph ("The reason is that ...") contains two sentences. While tools such as spaCy [7] have the capability of detecting sentences, they are not accurate because they are not intended to deal with bug report text.

To address this problem, S2RMiner designs several heuristics to identify sentences from each line of the text: (1) one text line contains at least one sentence; (2) a text segment ending with a full stop "." is a sentence; (3) if a full stop is preceded by a number (e.g., "1.") or a part of ellipsis, it is not considered to be the end of a sentence.

Extracting Text Features. S2RMiner employs a well-known NLP tool spaCy [7] to extract text features from each sentence. We consider three types of features. The first type of feature is *stemming*, which transforms each word in the sentence to its stem. Stemming is the process of removing the ending of a derived word to get its root form. For example, "clicking", "clicks", and "clicked" become "click". Without stemming, multiple words with the same meaning would be used as different features, resulting in too many features and thus a low quality machine learning model.

The second type of feature is *part-of-speech (POS)* tags, which labels each word with a POS tag. The features used by S2RMiner are words labeled as "noun", "verb", and "adjective".

The third type of features is *dependency parsing*, which analyzes the grammar structure of the sentence. Specifically, words labeled as root, predicate, and object are considered as features.

Building a Text Classifier. We use n-grams and CountVectorizer [19] to transform text features into numerical features, which is easy to process by a machine learning tool. A n-gram a contiguous sequence of n items from a given sequence of text. For example, 1-gram (or unigram) indicates single word tokens and 2-gram (or bigrams) indicates two consecutive word tokens.

The current implementation of S2RMiner uses Support Vector Machines [18] (SVM) to do binary classification given the extracted text features. SVM outputs a "1" if a sentence is a S2R and a "0" otherwise. S2RMiner saves the sentence labeled with "1" into the result file for each bug report.

4   Evaluation

To evaluate S2RMiner, we consider two research questions:

RQ1: What is the performance of S2RMiner in extracting S2R from bug reports?

RQ2: Which types of text features have the best performance in extracting S2R from bug reports?

RQ1 lets us evaluate the effectiveness of S2RMiner in extracting S2R. RQ2 lets us investigate how different types of text features influence of the performance of S2RMiner.

4.1   Datasets

We evaluated S2RMiner on bug reports from GitHub [2] and Google Code [3]. To prepare the training set, we randomly crawled 500 bug reports from GitHub and 500 reports from Google Code. We hired two undergraduate students to label the sentences of each bug report as S2R and non-S2R. During the labeling process, the inspector read the reports with sufficient details in the bug descriptions to identify S2R sentences. To ensure the correctness of our results, the manual inspections were performed independently by the two undergraduate students. Any time there was dissension, the authors and the inspectors discussed to reach a consensus.

We randomly divided the 500 bug reports from both datasets into two sets— 400 for training 100 for testing. Each bug report contains one or more sentences, which are the instances for building machine learning models.

4.2   Experiment Design

The experiment was conducted on a physical x86 machine running with Ubuntu 14.04 installed. The NLP techniques of S2RMiner was implemented by the spaCy dependency parser [7]. The classifier was implemented by Scikit-Learn [6].

Performance Metrics. We chose performance metrics allowing us to answer each of our two research questions. Specifically, we employ accuracy, precision, recall, and F1-measure. A sentence can be classified as: S2R when it is truly a S2R sentence (true positive, TP); it can be classified as a S2R sentence when it is actually not (false positive, FP); it can be classified as a non-S2R sentence when it is actually a S2R sentence (false negative, FN); or it can be correctly classified as a non-S2R sentence (true negative, TN).

- **Accuracy:** the number of instances correctly classified over the total number of instances.

$$Accuracy = \frac{TP + TN}{TP + FP + FN + TN}$$

- **Precision:** the number of instances correctly classified as S2R over the number of all instances classified as S2R.

$$P = \frac{TP}{TP + FP}$$

- **Recall:** the number of instances correctly classified as S2R over the total number of S2R instances.

$$R = \frac{TP}{TP + FN}$$

- **F-measure:** a composite measure of precision and recall for buggy instances.

$$F(b) = \frac{2 * P * R}{P + R}$$

Combinations of Different Text Features. RQ2 aims to evaluate how S2RMiner performs when using the combinations of different types of text features. Table 1 shows the features used for evaluation.

Table 1. Types of text features

No NLP techniques	Only use original words as features
Stem(1 gram)	Only stem of the word as features
Stem(3 gram)	Only stem of the word but consider 3 g relationship
Stem(3 gram)+pos	Combine stem and part of speech as features
Stem(3 gram)+dep	Combine stem and dependency as features
Stem(3 gram)+pos+dep	Combine three of them as features
(Stem+pos+dep)(3 gram)	Add 3 gram relationship to all of features

4.3 Threats to Validity

The primary threat to external validity for this study involves the representativeness of our subjects and bug reports. Other subjects may exhibit different behaviors. Data recorded in bug tracking systems can have a systematic bias relative to the full population of bug reports [11] and can be incomplete or incorrect [8]. However, we do reduce this threat to some extent by using two well studied open source projects and bug sources for our study. We cannot claim that our results can be generalized to all systems of all domains though.

The primary threat to internal validity involves the use of manual inspection to identify the S2R sentences To minimize the risk of incorrect results given by manual inspection, the sentences are labeled independently by two people.

The primary threat to construct validity involves the dataset and metrics used in the study. To mitigate this threat, we used bug reports from two bug tracking systems, which are publicly available and generally well understood. We also used the well known, accepted, and validated measures of accuracy, recall, precision, and F-measure.

5   Results and Analysis

Tables 2 and 3 summarizes the results of the two datasets.

RQ1: Performance of S2RMiner. Tables 2 and 3 show that S2RMiner is able to extract S2R from bug reports in GitHub and Google Code. The accuracy is above 0.85 for GitHub and above 0.92 for Google code. Regarding the precision and recall, the best F-score is above 0.6 for both Github and Google code. We consider F-measures over 0.6 to be good [14].

Table 2. GitHub result

GitHub result	TP	TN	FP	FN	Accuracy	Precision	Recall	F-score
No NLP techniques	79	612	33	84	0.85	0.69	0.47	0.56
Stem(1 gram)	99	596	49	69	0.86	0.66	0.62	0.64
Stem(3 gram)	88	612	33	71	0.87	0.72	0.55	0.63
Stem(3 gram)+pos	94	605	40	65	0.86	0.70	0.59	0.64
Stem(3 gram)+dep	94	609	36	65	0.87	0.72	0.59	0.65
Stem(3 gram)+pos+dep	90	607	38	69	0.86	0.70	0.57	0.63
(Stem+pos+dep)(3 gram)	87	605	40	72	0.86	0.69	0.55	0.61

In both bug tracking systems, the precision scores are better than the scores of recall. We analyzed the results and found that the low recall could be due to (1) the small training set; (2) incorrect labels. As part of the future, we intend to expand the training set and perform more robust labeling work.

In summary, the above results imply that *S2RMiner is effective at extracting S2R*.

RQ2: Comparison of Different Types of Text Features. As we can see from the two tables, comparing the text feature without using NLP technique (F_n) with the other feature combinations in the GitHub dataset, F_n performed the worst. However, this is not true in the Google Code dataset. When comparing different feature combinations with NLP applied, the dependency parsing feature type slightly improved the performance in terms of F-measures.

Overall, these results imply that the *the stemming and dependency parsing feature types can potentially improve the performance of S2RMiner.*

6   Related Work

Yukusu [15] translate S2R descriptions into executable test scripts. ReCDroid [26] use S2R descriptions to guide Android crash reproduction. Both tools assume that S2R is readily available and can be provided by users. In contrast, S2RMiner aims to automatically extract S2R sentences from raw bug reports.

Table 3. Google code result

Google Result	TP	TN	FP	FN	Accuracy	Precision	Recall	F-score
No NLP techniques	40	516	13	32	0.92	0.75	0.56	0.64
Stem(1 gram)	44	507	22	28	0.92	0.67	0.61	0.64
Stem(3 gram)	38	519	10	34	0.93	0.79	0.53	0.63
Stem(3 gram)+pos	36	518	11	36	0.92	0.77	0.5	0.61
Stem(3 gram)+dep	39	520	9	33	0.93	0.81	0.54	0.65
Stem(3 gram)+pos+dep	40	517	12	32	0.93	0.77	0.56	0.65
(Stem+pos+dep)(3 gram)	36	518	11	36	0.92	0.76	0.5	0.61

Chaparro et al. [13] proposed an approach, called DeMIBuD, to detect whether S2R is missing in a bug report. Their approach is probably most related to S2RMiner. However, DeMIBuD focuses on detecting whether a bug report contains S2R or not, whereas S2RMiner aims to extract all S2R in a bug report. In addition, S2RMiner analyzes original issue page of a bug report (e.g.,in the HTML format), whereas DeMIBuD can only handle the regular text.

There has been some research on mining bug repositories to classify and predict specific fault types. For example, Gegick et al. [16] classify bug reports as either security- or non-security-related. However, these techniques neither classify configuration bug reports nor identify concrete bug sources. Xia et al. [24] use text mining to categorize configuration bug reports related to system settings and compatibilities. In contrast, S2RMiner analyzes bug reports at the sentence to extract S2R.

7   Conclusion

We have presented S2RMiner, an automated approach to extract step to reproduce (S2R) sentences from bug reports. S2RMiner leverages HTML parsing, natural language processing, and machine learning techniques to analyze bug reports in the HTML formats and extract the needed contents from it. We have evaluated S2RMiner on two datasets from two popular bug tracking systems—GitHub and Google Code. The results showed that S2RMiner can extract S2R with a high accuracy and that the stem and grammar dependency text features play important roles in improving the performance of S2RMiner.

Acknowledgements. This research is supported in part by the NSF grant CCF-1652149.

References

1. Bitbucket. https://bitbucket.org
2. Github. https://github.com
3. Google code archive. https://code.google.com/archive/
4. Google play data. https://en.wikipedia.org/wiki/Google_Play
5. S2rminer publick link. https://github.com/AndroidTestBugReport/S2RMiner
6. Scikit-learn. https://scikit-learn.org/stable/
7. spaCy. https://spacy.io/
8. Aranda, J., Venolia, G.: The secret life of bugs: going past the errors and omissions in software repositories, pp. 298–308 (2009)
9. Bacchelli, A., Cleve, A., Lanza, M., Mocci, A.: Extracting structured data from natural language documents with island parsing. In: 2011 26th IEEE/ACM International Conference on Automated Software Engineering (ASE 2011), pp. 476–479. IEEE (2011)
10. Bettenburg, N., Premraj, R., Zimmermann, T., Kim, S.: Extracting structural information from bug reports. In: Proceedings of the 2008 International Working Conference on Mining Software Repositories, pp. 27–30. ACM (2008)
11. Bird, C., et al.: Fair and balanced?: bias in bug-fix datasets, pp. 121–130 (2009)
12. Burstein, J., Marcu, D., Andreyev, S., Chodorow, M.: Towards automatic classification of discourse elements in essays. In: Proceedings of the 39th Annual Meeting on Association for Computational Linguistics, pp. 98–105. Association for Computational Linguistics (2001)
13. Chaparro, O., et al.: Detecting missing information in bug descriptions. In: Proceedings of the 2017 11th Joint Meeting on Foundations of Software Engineering, pp. 396–407 (2017)
14. Dougherty, G.: Pattern Recognition and Classification: An Introduction. Springer, New York (2012). https://doi.org/10.1007/978-1-4614-5323-9
15. Fazzini, M., Prammer, M., d'Amorim, M., Orso, A.: Automatically translating bug reports into test cases for mobile apps. In: Proceedings of the 27th ACM SIGSOFT International Symposium on Software Testing and Analysis, pp. 141–152. ACM (2018)
16. Gegick, M., Rotella, P., Xie, T.: Identifying security bug reports via text mining: an industrial case study. In: International Working Conference on Mining Software Repositories, pp. 11–20 (2010)
17. Joachims, T.: Making large-scale SVM learning practical. Technical report, SFB 475: Komplexitätsreduktion in Multivariaten ... (1998)
18. Joachims, T.: Text categorization with support vector machines: learning with many relevant features. In: Nédellec, C., Rouveirol, C. (eds.) ECML 1998. LNCS, vol. 1398, pp. 137–142. Springer, Heidelberg (1998). https://doi.org/10.1007/BFb0026683

19. Kulkarni, A., Shivananda, A.: Converting text to features. In: Kulkarni, A., Shivananda, A. (eds.) Natural Language Processing Recipes, pp. 67–96. Springer, Heidelberg (2019). https://doi.org/10.1007/978-1-4842-4267-4_3
20. Moran, K., Linares-Vásquez, M., Bernal-Cárdenas, C., Poshyvanyk, D.: Autocompleting bug reports for android applications. In: Proceedings of the 2015 10th Joint Meeting on Foundations of Software Engineering, pp. 673–686. ACM (2015)
21. Packard, H.: Failing to meet mobile app user expectations: a mobile user survey. Technical report (2015)
22. Ponzanelli, L., Mocci, A., Lanza, M.: StORMeD: stack overflow ready made data. In: 2015 IEEE/ACM 12th Working Conference on Mining Software Repositories, pp. 474–477. IEEE (2015)
23. Rigby, P.C., Robillard, M.P.: Discovering essential code elements in informal documentation. In: 2013 35th International Conference on Software Engineering (ICSE), pp. 832–841. IEEE (2013)
24. Xia, X., Lo, D., Qiu, W., Wang, X., Zhou, B.: Automated configuration bug report prediction using text mining. In: Computer Software and Applications Conference, pp. 107–116 (2014)
25. Yoo, S., Harman, M.: Regression testing minimization, selection and prioritization: a survey. STVR **22**(2), 67–120 (2012)
26. Zhao, Y., Yu, T., Su, T., Liu, Y., Zheng, W., Zhang, J., Halfond, W.G.: Recdroid: automatically reproducing android application crashes from bug reports. In: Proceedings of the 2019 41st ACM/IEEE International Conference on Software Engineering (2019)

Intelligent Software Reuse

Searching Software Knowledge Graph with Question

Min Wang[1,2], Yanzhen Zou[1,2(✉)], Yingkui Cao[1,2], and Bing Xie[1,2]

[1] Key Laboratory of High Confidence Software Technologies, Peking University,
Ministry of Education, Beijing 100871, China
{wangmin1994,zouyz,caoyingkui,xiebing}@pku.edu.cn
[2] School of Electronics Engineering and Computer Science, Peking University,
Beijing 100871, China

Abstract. Researchers have constructed a variety of knowledge repositories/bases in different domains. These knowledge repositories generally use graph database (Neo4j) to manage heterogeneous and widely related domain data, which providing structured query (i.e., Cypher) interfaces. However, it is time-consuming and labor-intensive to construct a structured query especially when the query is very complex or the scale of the knowledge graph is large. This paper presents a natural language question interface for software knowledge graph. It extracts meta-model of software knowledge repository, constructs question related Inference Sub-Graph, then automatically transfers natural language question to structured Cypher query and returns the corresponding answer. We carry out our experiments on two famous open source software projects, build their knowledge graphs and verify our approach can accurately answer almost all the questions on the corresponding knowledge graph.

Keywords: Software reuse · Knowledge repository ·
Knowledge graph · Natural language search · Graph search

1 Introduction

Software reuse is a solution to avoid duplication of effort in software development, which can improve the efficiency and quality of software engineering [1,2]. In recent years, with the rapid development of open source software, a large number of reusable software projects have emerged on the Internet, such as Apache Lucene, Apache POI, jfreeChart, etc. Besides the source code, these software projects often contain different types of natural language text resources, such as user manuals, mailing-list, issue reports, user forum discussions, etc. To utilize and analyze these documents and source code, researchers propose and construct

Supported by the Foundation item: National Key Research and Development Program (2016YFB1000801), National Science Fund for Distinguished Young Scholars (61525201).

© Springer Nature Switzerland AG 2019
X. Peng et al. (Eds.): ICSR 2019, LNCS 11602, pp. 115–131, 2019.
https://doi.org/10.1007/978-3-030-22888-0_9

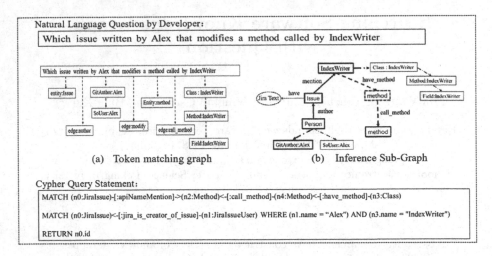

Fig. 1. A Search question and related Inference Sub-Graph (ISG)

various domain-specific software knowledge bases and knowledge graphs. Typically, Peking University proposed the specific-domain software projects knowledge graphs [3]; Fudan university proposed the software projects API knowledge graphs [27], etc.

These knowledge bases/knowledge graphs often utilize Neo4j and other graph database storage, which support formal query (i.e., Cypher). It requires the user be familiar with the Cypher grammar, and manually translate the user intention into a Cypher query statement. Meanwhile, the manual construction of Cypher query statement requires a clear understanding of the meta-model of the knowledge graph, i.e., the types of knowledge entities inside the knowledge graph. When the scale of meta-model becoming is very large, the cost of constructing Cypher query is very large too. Therefore, it is necessary to provide a knowledge base/knowledge graph query interface based on natural language, which can automatically transform users' natural language questions into formal query statements.

To address this problem, existing work in the process of natural language question parsing often rely on the large general domain knowledge base on the Internet (such as WordNet, DBpedia, Freebase, Yago, etc.), the calculation is very complex [6]. Typically, Percy Liang et al. utilized Lambda DCS (Dependency Based Composition Semantics) to get a logical representation of a natural language question and constructed a formal query for knowledge base or knowledge graph based on its logical representation. However, all these methods face the challenge of precise transformation of natural language descriptions. In our research, we found that the concepts in the software knowledge graph are quite different from those in the general open-domain knowledge base due to the characteristics of the specific-domain software. Therefore, it is not important that matching the specific predicate phrases. In contrast, we should pay more attention to the precise analysis of the overall semantics of the question. Figure 1 presents a natural language question from a developer and its corresponding construction process of structured Cypher query statement. When software developers reuse Apache Lucene's open source projects, they raise a query like this: *"Which issue written by Alex that modifies a method called by IndexWriter?"*, the key words included in this statement are *issue, Alex, modify, method, call, IndexWriter*, etc. Each key word has several concepts on the knowledge graph to correspond to it. *Alex*, for example, can be matched to a Person entity with a name attribute on the knowledge graph, but the knowledge graph has two similar conceptual entities, i.e., *GitAuthor: Alex developers* and *SoUser: Alex (stackOverflow users)*. Similarly, the *IndexWriter* can be matched to a software project source code knowledge of an entity on the knowledge graph, but it could match to *Class, Method,* and *Field*, three levels of entities. So what are the concepts that developers are trying to convey? Which concepts correspond to a knowledge graph entity? In order to address the problem of precise matching between natural language tokens and knowledge graph entities, we propose a method of reasoning and locating sub-graph in the knowledge graph corresponding to natural language questions, which is called Inference Sub-Graph. Inference Sub-Graph is an intermediate bridge from natural language questions to Cypher query statements: the generation of Inference Sub-Graph requires in-depth analysis and the use of knowledge graph information and knowledge graph meta-model to "match" the semantics in natural language questions.

Based on this insight, this paper proposes a natural language query approach on the software knowledge graph. It could transfer natural language question to structured Cypher query precisely through extracting software knowledge graph meta-model and constructing Inference Sub-Graph, then display the corresponding answer on the knowledge graph. Compared with the existing work, the main contributions of this work are:

- We propose a novel approach for transferring natural language question to formal Cypher query. Different from traditional semantic parsing, this algorithm generates an Inference Sub-Graph as a transformation bridge between natural language and formal query that can more accurately express the deep meaning of natural language. On the other hand, the ambiguity problem of natural language can be solved remarkably by measuring the Inference Sub-Graph;
- We implemented a natural language question interface and validated our approach on the software project knowledge graph of Apache Lucene and Apache Nutch's open source project. For each knowledge graph, we provided 66 real natural language questions in the process of software reuse, and we can achieve an accuracy of 93.9%.

2   Overview

We propose and implement a natural language question answering approach and system on software knowledge graph. In our approach, we firstly propose the concept of Inference Sub-Graph, and build a transformation bridge between natural

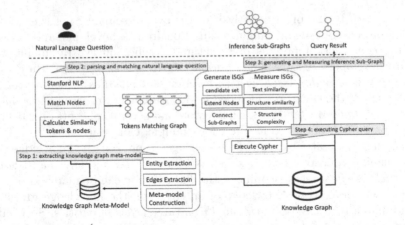

Fig. 2. The workflow of natural language Q&A solution

language questions and formal query statements by generating and measuring Inference Sub-Graph. On the one hand, compared with the traditional logical formal system of semantic parsing, the approach of sub-graph transformation [24, 25] is easier to express the semantic information of natural language. On the other hand, the generation and measurement of Inference Sub-Graphs can solve the ambiguity problem of natural language [25]. Figure 2 shows the workflow of our approach in this paper. Our approach is mainly composed of four parts: (1) extracting knowledge graph meta-model; (2) parsing and matching of natural language questions; (3) generating and measuring of Inference Sub-Graph; (4) constructing Cypher query statement.

2.1 Extracting Software Project Knowledge Graph Meta-Model

In order to adapt various Software Project Knowledge Graph, firstly, we define some concepts as follows:

(1) Entity-Type: each entity in the knowledge graph has a type. It defined as: {Entity-Type} = {Entity.type}.
(2) Relation-Type: each type of relationship in the knowledge graph is determined by the name of the relationship itself and the type of entity at both ends of the relationship. It defined as: {Relation-Type} = {(Relation.start.type, Relation.end.type, Relation.name)}.
(3) Attribute-Type: The type of each attribute in the knowledge graph is determined by its associated entity type and attribute name. It defined as: {Attribute-Type} = {(Attribute.entity.type, Attribute.name)}.
(4) meta-model: A schema graph with Entity-Type as the node, Relation-Type as the edge, and Attribute-Type as the property of the Entity-Type. It defined as: meta-model = {Entity-Type},{Relation-Type}.

Based on the above concepts, we traverse the software project knowledge graph, store all the entities in it and record all entity types as meta-model's entities;

then we traverse the software project knowledge graph, store all the relations in it and record all relation types as meta-model's relations.

2.2   Parsing and Matching Natural Language Question

In this subsection, we utilize Stanford NLP tools to parse natural language questions, including token segment, part-of-speech and filter stop-words, and then we match these tokens with elements from knowledge graph.

We propose a priority-based matching algorithm, i.e., hierarchically matching each tokens (i.e., parsing from natural language question) with elements from knowledge graph or knowledge graph meta-model. Each token may be matched to any elements about the knowledge graph, including: entity, entity type, attribute, attribute type, and relation, relation type, etc. We manually construct a synonym table based on software engineering specific-domain knowledge.

For example, the natural language question is *"when the class that call the method updatependingmerge is changed by Yonik Seeley ?"* Obviously, we can match *class* with one of entity type in the knowledge graph, i.e., Class, similarly, we can match *updatependingmerge* with one of entity in the knowledge graph, i.e., method named *updatependingmerge*. However, we can't directly match any elements with *call* and *changed*, so we utilize synonym table to match some synonym (e.g., *call* match with the relationship "call-method", *changed* match with the relationship "commit", etc.)

Obviously, it's possible that a token matches to more than one elements. To address this problem, firstly, we utilize Minimum Edit Distance algorithm to calculate the similarity between tokens and elements, so we can filter some irrelevant elements. However, we still retain some ambiguous matching pairs, we can eliminate this ambiguity in the latter approach. Finally, we obtain a {tokens,elements} matching graph, as shown in Fig. 1.

2.3   Generating and Measuring Inference Sub-Graph

Due to the ambiguity and complexity of natural language, tokens based on natural language processing may match to different knowledge graph elements, thus we obtain candidate sub-graphs with different semantics. In order to guarantee the quality of candidate sub-graphs, we propose an Inference Sub-Graph generation algorithm by extending hidden nodes and hidden edges, and calculate the feature values of each candidate Inference Sub-Graph. The measurement features include three aspects: textual similarity, structural similarity and Inference Sub-Graph structural complexity, and then we recommend the optimal Inference Sub-Graph to developers according to the measurement results. In this process, on the one hand, we construct the intermediate transformation bridge between natural language and formal query statement, on the other hand, we resolve the ambiguity problem of natural language by measuring the optimal sub-graph. Finally, we transform the optimal Inference Sub-Graph into a Cypher query statement and return the query result. In order to prevent possible semantic understanding deviation, we also support the visualization of the Inference Sub-Graph in the interactive process.

In the next section, we will introduce the details about the generation and measurement of Inference Sub-Graphs.

2.4 Constructing Cypher Query Statement

Here, we transform the Inference Sub-Graph into a Cypher query statement. The process of constructing a Cypher can be divided into three parts, corresponding to Match, Where and Return statement respectively.

- Match statement corresponds to the graph structure of Inference Sub-Graph. However, Inference Sub-Graph expresses a two-dimensional structure information, a Match statement only describes a one-dimensional structure information, namely a chain. So we adopt the heuristic method of dividing the path on the Inference Sub-Graph into a number of chain and set.
- Where statement corresponds to the all attribute values of nodes in the Inference Sub-Graph, each attribute value is the filter conditions of an entity, so attributes are added to the Where statement.
- Return statement is determined by the returned node properties. The returned node properties are determined by the interrogative in the question.

3 Generating and Measuring Inference Sub-Graph

In Sect. 2.2, after parsing natural language questions, their tokens may match to multiple knowledge graph elements. In order to ensure the correctness of the overall sentence meaning, we propose the concept of Inference Sub-Graph, and give the corresponding generation and measurement algorithm of Inference Sub-Graph.

Inference Sub-Graph: An Inference Sub-Graph is a sub graph in the knowledge graph, including: entities and edges, this sub-graph is inferred by the {tokens,elements} pairs from natural language question and knowledge graph, and so this sub-graph contains similar semantics with the natural language questions.

3.1 Generating Inference Sub-Graph

Inference Sub-Graph is a sub-graph on the knowledge graph meta-model. Due to the ambiguity of natural language, the semantics of natural language is often incomplete. As shown in Fig. 1, in the example of natural language question *"Which issue written by Alex that modifies a method called by IndexWriter"*, we need to extend a hidden method entity node (i.e., method) and a hidden association relation (i.e., have_method) between the entity class (i.e., IndexWriter) and the entity method called by IndexWriter. i.e., the complete semantics of the natural language question should be: a method is modified because of an issue proposed by Alex, and the method is called by a method member method in the class IndexWriter.

To address this problem, we propose a novel approach, which is called Inference Sub-Graph. Algorithm 1 illustrates the process of generating Inference Sub-Graph. The input is a set of disconnected sub-graphs, which extracting from knowledge graph according the {tokens,elements} matching graph (Sect. 2.2). The output is a set of connected Inference Sub-Graphs. Firstly, as shown in algorithm in line 2–6, by parsing natural language questions and matching elements in the knowledge graph, we obtain a matching graph. Due to the ambiguity of natural language, each natural language token may correspond to multiple knowledge graph related elements. We retain these ambiguities in the previous process. We utilize a Bean-Search algorithm to connect all possible {tokens,elements} matching graph, and so we can obtain a set of candidate disconnected sub-graph, i.e., $S_{disconnect} = G_{disconnect}$. Each set represents a possibility of the knowledge graph element set corresponding to the natural language question. Then, in line 7–11 in algorithm 1, we extend the hidden nodes of the disconnected sub-graphs by inferring the knowledge graph, and we get the graphs with hidden nodes and hidden edges, i.e., $S_{hidden} = G_{hidden}$. Finally, in line 12–17 in algorithm 1, we utilize a Minimum Spanning Tree algorithm to connect these disconnected sub-graphs, so we obtain a set of connected Inference Sub-Graphs, i.e., $S_{connect}$.

Algorithm 1. Inference Sub-Graph Generation
Input: A set of disconnected Sub-Graphs : $S_{disconnect}$
Output: A set of candidate connected Sub-Graphs : $S_{connect}$
1.   **Function** Connect($S_{disconnect}$)
2. $S_{hidden} := \{\}$
3.   **For each** ($G_{disconnect}$ in $S_{disconnect}$)
4. $S_{sub\text{-}hidden} := $getG-hidden($G_{disconnect}$)
5. $S_{hidden} := S_{hidden} \cup S_{sub\text{-}hidden}$
6.   **End for**
7. $S_{forest} := \{\}$
8.   **For each** (G_{hidden} in S_{hidden})
9. $S_{sub\text{-}forest} := $ getG-forest (G_{hidden})
10. $S_{forest} = S_{forest} \cup S_{sub\text{-}forest}$
11.   **End for**
12. $S_{connect} := \{\}$
13.   **For each** (G_{forest} in S_{forest})
14. $S_{sub\text{-}connect} := $ getG-connect (G_{forest})
15. $S_{connect} = S_{connect} \cup S_{sub\text{-}connect}$
16.   **End for**
17.   **Return** $S_{connect}$
18.   **End Function**

3.2   Measuring Inference Sub-Graphs

In the above steps, we generate a set of Inference Sub-Graphs, we have to select the optimal Inference Sub-Graph as a bridge with a Cypher query statement.

We propose a series of heuristic rules to calculate some measured features as follows:

(1) Textural Similarity between Inference Sub-Graph and NL-Question

In Sect. 2.2, as the Fig. 1 shows, we retain some candidate elements which match the tokens, i.e., each token has a candidate elements list, each element in this list has a similar rank with tokens, so, we can calculate the similarity between Inference Sub-Graph and Natural Language Question as follows:

$$Score_{T-similar} = \omega_{T-similar} \times \sum_{t \epsilon token} (1 - \frac{t.mapping.rank}{k}) \tag{1}$$

In the above formula, t denotes the tokens from the parsed natural language questions (Sect. 4.2), $t.mapping.rank$ denotes the element's rank in the candidate list, k denotes the number of all elements in the matching graph, and $\omega_{T-similar}$ denotes the weight of textural similarity in the feature set, we can manually assign a weight value.

(2) Structural Similarity between Inference Sub-Graph and NL-Question

Calculating the structural similarity between the Inference Sub-Graph and the natural language question, we consider the difference between the relative distance between the pair of nodes in the Inference Sub-Graph and the relative distance of the corresponding words in the natural language question as the metric factor. We can calculate the structural similarity as follows:

$$Score_{S-similar} = \omega_{S-similar} \times (\sum_{i \epsilon V(G)} \sum_{j \epsilon outVertex(i)} (Position_i - Position_j)$$
$$+ \sum_{i \epsilon V(G)} \sum_{e \epsilon outEdge(i)} (Position_e - Position_i + token_e.direct)) \tag{2}$$

In the above formula, $Position$ denotes the position of the natural language token in the question corresponding to the node or edge in each sub-graph. $outVertex(i)$ denotes $node_i$'s adjacent node set. $outEdge(i)$ denotes $node_i$'s outgoing edge. $token_e.direct$ denotes tense of natural language token corresponding to the direction of edge e. $\omega_{S-similar}$ denotes the weight of structural similarity in the feature set.

(3) Structural Complexity of the Inference Sub-Graph

In the process of generating the Inference Sub-Graph, we extend the hidden nodes of the matching graph, which leads to the change of the structure of the Inference Sub-Graph. Considering the complexity of this structural change and the connection between natural language questions, we calculate the structural complexity of the Inference Sub-Graph as one of the measured features:

$$Score_{complex} = \omega_{complex} \times (|E(G)| + |v(G)| - |V(G_{hidden})| - |E(G_{hidden})|) \tag{3}$$

In the above formula, $E(G)$ and $V(G)$ respectively denotes original number of the nodes and edges in the Inference Sub-Graph. $V(G_{hidden})$ and $E(G_{hidden})$ respectively denotes the number of hidden nodes and edges that we extend. $\omega_{complex}$ denotes the weight of structural complexity in the feature set.

Finally, we calculate these feature values to measure a Inference Sub-Graph, and so we can obtain a optimal Inference Sub-Graph. On the one hand, it resolves the gap between natural language and formal query, and on the other hand, it resolves the ambiguity when natural language matches knowledge graph elements.

4   Experiment and Evaluation

Based on the above solution, we designed and implemented a natural language question answering system for software project knowledge graph, which is called SnowSearch (**S**oftware **K**nowledge **Search**).

Our experiments are used to answer the following research questions:

RQ1: Does SnowSearch effectively answer natural language questions?

We are concerned about whether our approach could effectively return the correct query results when the developers input a natural language question.

RQ2: Does our Inference Sub-Graph solve the transformation between natural language and Cypher query?

We propose a approach of Inference Sub-Graph on the knowledge graph to serve as a bridge between natural language and formal query statements. We are concerned about whether the Inference Sub-Graph could express natural language more effectively and accurately.

RQ3: Are the three metric features of the Inference Sub-Graph reasonable?

We propose three metrics of textural similarity, structural similarity and Inference Sub-Graph complexity to measure the Inference Sub-Graph, so as to obtain the optimal Sub-Graph. We are concerned about whether the three metric features proposed in this paper are reasonable.

4.1   Software Project Knowledge Graph

Our work is based on software project knowledge graph proposed by Lin et al. [3,26]. Software knowledge graph is defined as a graph for representing relevant knowledge in software domains, projects, and systems. In a software knowledge graph, nodes represent software knowledge entities (e.g., classes, issue reports and business concepts), and directed edges represent various relationships between these entities (e.g., method invocation and traceability link). Based on their tools, we can automatically construct a software project knowledge graph.

To evaluate our approach, we constructed knowledge graph of two famous open source software projects, Apache Lucene and Apache Nutch. The open source project Lucene is a Java-implemented information retrieval program library; the open source project Nutch is a Java-implemented Open source search engine. We collected a large number of multi-source heterogeneous data on Lucene and Nutch on the Internet, including software source code, mailing-lists, issue reports, and StackOverflow posts. The statistics of related resources

Table 1. Software resources statistics in Apache Lucene and Nutch

Project	Source Code		Documents			Knowledge Graph		Time min
	version	Code File	Issue Report	Mailing-list	StackOverflow Post	Entities	Edges	
lucene	6.3.0	1941	7439	15769	9376	39,419	176,3694	28
nutch	1.5.1	553	1254	2759	947	13,861	8,4908	7

Table 2. Meta-Model of Software Project Knowledge Graph

Data Type	Knowledge Entity	Relation Type
Source code	Class, Interface, Field, Method	extends, implements, dependency, call, include, type, method parameters, return, throw
Issue Report	Issue report, patches, comments, jira user	Issue-patches, Issue-Comments
Mailing-list	mail content, mail user	mail-send, mail-reply
StackOverflow Posts	questions, answers, comments, SoUser	Question-proposed, answer-question, answer-received

are shown in Table 1. For example, the open source project Lucene is a well-known information retrieval library implemented by the Java language. We collected more than 8 GB of Lucene project data on the Internet, including 67 Versions, more than 800,000 lines of source code, 244,000 e-mails, more than 7,500 issue reports, and a large number of related StackOverflow posts. Finally, we constructed Apache Lucene's knowledge graph, and statistics of the graph are shown in Table 2.

4.2 Question Example

We invited four developers who are familiar with Apache Lucene and Nutch to ask some natural language questions related to these two projects. These questions mainly cover factual questions such as *Who, What, When,* and the *List.* Finally, the four developers proposed 66 questions about the Lucene project and 66 questions about the Nutch project. As shown in Table 3, we randomly select 22 sample questions that developers ask for Lucene open source projects. Among them, the number of entities in the Inference Sub-Graph corresponding to *What/Which* type, *Who* type and *When* type questions is about 4 on average, and the number of edges in Inference Sub-Graph is about 3 on average. The number of entities in Inference Sub-Graph corresponding to the questions of *List* type is about 97 on average, and the number of edges in Inference Sub-Graph is

Table 3. 22 questions used to search on Lucene knowledge graph

Type	Natural Language Questions	Entity Num	Edge Num
What/Which	what's the superclass of the Class that is extended by the Class call updatependingmerge	5	3
	which class have updatependingmerge	2	1
	which class call updatependingmerge	2	1
	Which commit is about "custom MergeScheduler implementation"	4	3
Who	Who change IndexWriter	3	2
	who change IndexWriter and change IndexReader	5	4
	who mention a method called by IndexWriter	4	3
	Who write a commit about "custom MergeScheduler implementation"	4	3
	who write a jiraissue about "custom MergeScheduler implementation"	4	3
	who write a answer about IndexWriter	3	2
When	When a commit about "custom MergeScheduler implementation" is written	4	3
	When Dave Kor send a mail about IndexWriter	3	2
	When is IndexWriter changed	3	2
	When IndexWriter is change by a commit written by Yonik Seeley	4	3
List	list method belong to IndexWriter	53	52
	list field belong to IndexWriter	9	8
	list Class mentioned by Yonik Seeley	20	19
	list method of Class IndexWriter	53	52
	Issue about IndexWriter changed by Alexb	8	7
	list all mail sent by Dave Kor	75	74
	list all JiraIssue that mention IndexWriter	478	477
	id of Issue written by Alexb that mention a method called by Class IndexWriter	76	75

Table 4. The precise results of 132 Q&A about Lucene and Nutch

Project	What/Which		Who		When		List		Amount	
	P@1	P@2	P@1	P@2	P@1	P@2	P@1	P@2	P@1	P@2
lucene	12/12	12/12	17/18	18/18	12/12	12/12	21/24	22/24	62/66	64/66
nutch	14/14	14/14	16/16	16/16	11/12	12/12	21/24	22/24	62/66	64/66

about 96 on average. The data analysis results of 22 examples of natural language questions show that the natural language questions raised by developers in the process of software reuse exist objectively, and have certain reasoning complexity and Q&A difficulty for the knowledge base query.

4.3   RQ1: Q&A Effectiveness Evaluation

We think that only the accuracy of top-1 and top-2 Cypher need to be considered. i.e., the generated correct Cypher query is ranked in the top k position in all possible Cypher candidate sets, thus the question answering result is correct. The experimental results are shown in Table 4. It can be seen that 62 of the 66 questions for the knowledge graph of Lucene project return correct Cypher query in top-1, while 64 questions return correct Cypher query in top-2. The same experimental results were obtained in 66 questions for Nutch project knowledge graph, which indicate that most natural language questions of different software projects can be correctly answered.

The experiment result shows that our approach of natural language question answering on the software project knowledge graph can achieve more than 93.3% accuracy. Considering the natural language grammar of *List* type questions are more complicated, and the corresponding entities in the Inference Sub-Graph are more complicated, natural language question parsing and matching may produce a certain error. For example: In natural language question *"list all JiraIssue that mention IndexWriter"*, because the JiraIssue and IndexWriter get involved with large number of entities, lead to natural language questions answering get failed. For the other questions such as *what/which, When, who*, our approach has good effect of Q&A.

4.4   RQ2: Inference Sub-Graph Effectiveness Evaluation

Inference Sub-Graph is a bridge between natural language and formal query statement. To better express the full semantics of a natural language question, during the generation of Inference Sub-Graph, we have to extend hidden nodes and hidden edges. For example, in the natural language question example *"Which issue written by Alex that modifies a method called by IndexWriter"* shown in Fig. 1, it is necessary to add three hidden nodes, i.e., *method, GitAuthor* and *Commit*, as well as two hidden edges, i.e., *have_method* and *code_mention*. In order to verify the role of the Inference Sub-Graph in the transformation from natural language to formal query, we statistically analyze the number of hidden node elements added to the Inference Sub-Graph. As shown in Fig. 3, 64% questions in Apache Lucene need to add hidden nodes in Inference Sub-Graphs, and as shown in Fig. 4, 55% questions in Apache Lucene need to add hidden edges in Inference Sub-Graphs. The same statistics are presented in Apache Nutch project. This shows that in the process of converting natural language questions into formal query statements, more than half of the natural language questions need to be extended. If we don't use the Inference Sub-Graph to extend the hidden nodes and edges, but simply combine natural language tokens and construct formal queries, then more than half of the natural language questions cannot be correctly answered. Therefore, Inference Sub-Graph proposed in our approach can effectively solve the transformation between natural language and Cypher query.

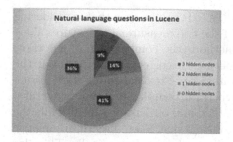

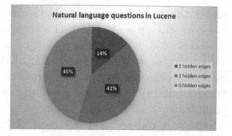

Fig. 3. The Distribution of Hidden nodes and edges in Inference Sub-Graph of Lucene Search Questions

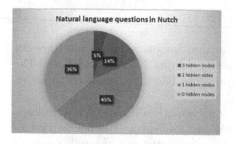

Fig. 4. The Distribution of Hidden nodes and edges in Inference Sub-Graph of Nutch Search Questions

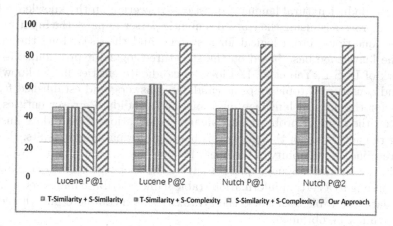

Fig. 5. The precise results of 3 kinds Measurement methods comparison analyse

4.5 RQ3: Measurement Strategy Comparison Evaluation

We designed a series of comparison experiments in order to compare the measurement effects of the three metrics: "textural similarity + structural similarity", "textural similarity + structural complexity", "structural similarity + structure complexity", so we can verify the role of each metric in the metrics. Figure 5 shows the experiment results: As shown in Fig. 5, It can be seen that, considering the correct Cypher in top-1, the accuracy of the two measurement features alone is about 50%, while the accuracy of our method (the combination of the three measurement features) is up to 94%. Considering the correct Cypher in top-2, the accuracy achieved by the measurement strategies of "textual similarity + structural similarity", "textual similarity + structural complexity" and "structural complexity + structural similarity" is 55%, 63% and 59% respectively, while the accuracy of our method can reach 97%. It means that if we discard any metric feature, the accuracy of the question answering will drop dramatically. This also proves that the three metrics we propose are reasonable.

5 Related Work

A lot of work have tried to construct a natural language query interface for graph database/knowledge [12], which mostly adopts NoSQL database. The existing researches mainly include: (1) approaches based on syntactic analysis; (2) approaches based on machine learning.

The basic process of the approach based on syntactic analysis [7] is as follows: firstly, the natural language query is parsed and its syntactic dependency tree is constructed, then the query transformation is carried out through methods such as node matching and rule extension, and finally formal query statement is obtained. Typically, Berant et al. [16] proposed to train a semantic parser, which is used to conduct natural language questions answering on the knowledge base. The basic process is: using the trained semantic parser to parse the input natural language questions into a logical form system, and then searching the answer from the knowledge base based on the structured logical expression; Based on the work of DCS-L, Yao et al. [17] located candidate entities in the knowledge base and constructed topic maps as candidate answers, and established feature vectors for the natural language questions and candidate answer entities, and converted the original problem into binary classification of candidate answers. Among the advantage of this method is based on formal query results, the user can determine the reliability of the query results. But in these research work, the words in the natural language query input by the user still need to be explicitly corresponding to a certain information (table name, attribute name, record, etc.) in the database table, otherwise the syntax tree is incomplete and the correct answer cannot be obtained.

In terms of the research based on machine learning method for the natural language query of knowledge base, the early work is mainly to record the feedback information when the user makes the query and use it to assist the next query according to the historical query information. Freitas et al. [11] utilize interactive algorithms to optimize query results, design user feedback methods to improve accuracy. The basic idea is to record feedback information when users input query, and then historical queries is used to assist the next query input. This method can optimize most methods, but it needs to be used more frequently to accumulate the user's usage history. Tunstall-Pedoe et al. [9] utilize human factors in the process of generating templates. Zheng et al. [10] extract the correct natural language question template from the existing questions from Yahoo and other communities. Other recent representative work mainly rely on machine learning including sequence model, neural network model, attention mechanism, etc. [18,19]. Especially, the deep learning approach has become one of the main technologies of the knowledge base natural language question answering [21, 22]. Wen-tauYih et al. [23] defined a query sub-graph method, and the query sub-graph can be directly converted from the knowledge base to Logical formal system, the task of defining semantic parsing is to generate query sub-graph, use the knowledge base to perform pre-physical chain index, and use Deep CNN to calculate the matching degree of question and logical predicate, and obtain significant effect.

6 Conclusion

This paper proposes and implements a natural language question interface for software project knowledge graph. It extracts meta-model of software knowledge repository, constructs question related Inference Sub-Graph, then automatically transfers natural language question to structured Cypher query and returns the corresponding answer. We evaluated our approach with the open source software project Lucene and the open source software project Nutch's knowledge graph. The results show that our approach is effective in answering natural language questions from developers for software reuse. In the future, we will try to solve the more complex natural language question answering problems by increasing the human-computer interaction.

References

1. Fuqing, Y., Hong, M., Keqin, L.: Software reuse and software component technology. Acta Electronica Sinica **27**(2), 68–75 (1999)
2. Fuqing, Y.: Software reuse and its correlated techniques. Comput. Sci. **26**(5), 1–4 (1999)
3. Lin, Z.Q., Xie, B., Zou, Y.Z., et al.: Intelligent development environment and software knowledge graph. J. Comput. Sci. Technology **32**(2), 242–249 (2017)
4. McFetridge, P., Groeneboer, C.: Novel terms and cooperation in a natural language interface. In: Ramani, S., Chandrasekar, R., Anjaneyulu, K.S.R. (eds.) KBCS 1989. LNCS, vol. 444, pp. 331–340. Springer, Heidelberg (1990). https://doi.org/10.1007/BFb0018391
5. Lin, J., Liu, Y., Guo, J., et al.: TiQi: a natural language interface for querying software project data. In: Proceedings of the 32nd IEEE/ACM International Conference on Automated Software Engineering, pp. 973–977. IEEE Press (2017)
6. Mike, L., Mark, S.: A* CCG parsing with a supertag-factored model. In: Proceedings of the 2014 Conference on Empirical Methods in Natural Language Processing (EMNLP), pp. 990–1000, 25–29 October 2014
7. Li, F., Jagadish, H.V.: Understanding natural language queries over relational databases. ACM SIGMOD Rec. **45**(1), 6–13 (2016)

8. Tunstall-Pedoe, W.: True knowledge: open-domain question answering using structured knowledge and inference. AI Mag. **31**(3), 80–92 (2010)
9. Unger, C., Bühmann, L., Lehmann, J., et al.: Template-based question answering over RDF data. In: Proceedings of the 21st International Conference on World Wide Web, pp. 639–648. ACM (2012)
10. Zheng, W., Zou, L., Lian, X., et al.: How to build templates for RDF question/answering: an uncertain graph similarity join approach. In: Proceedings of the 2015 ACM SIGMOD International Conference on Management of Data, pp. 1809–1824. ACM (2015)
11. Freitas, A., de Faria F.F., O'Riain, S., et al.: Answering natural language queries over linked data graphs: a distributional semantics approach. In: Proceedings of the 36th International ACM SIGIR Conference on Research and Development in Information Retrieval, pp. 1107–1108. ACM (2013)
12. Krishna, S.: Introduction to Database and Knowledge-Base Systems, p. 18. World Scientific, Singapore (1992)
13. Siva, R., Mirella, L., Mark, S.: Large-scale semantic parsing without question answer pairs. Trans. Assoc. Comput. Linguist. **2**, 377–392 (2014)
14. Siva, R., Oscar, T., Michael, C., et al.: Transforming dependency structures to logical forms for semantic parsing. Trans. Assoc. Comput. Linguist. **4**, 127–140 (2016)
15. Zettlemoyer, L.S., Collins, M.: Online learning of relaxed CCG grammars for parsing to logical form. In: Empirical Methods in Natural Language Processing and Computational Natural Language Learning (EMNLP/CoNLL), pp. 678–687 (2007)
16. Berant, J., Chou, A., Frostig, R., et al.: Semantic parsing on freebase from question-answer pairs. In: Proceedings of the Conference on Empirical Methods in Natural Language Processing, pp. 1533–1544 (2013)
17. Yao, X., Van Durme, B.: Information extraction over structured data: question answering with freebase. In: Proceedings of the 52nd Annual Meeting of the Association for Computational Linguistics (Volume 1: Long Papers), vol. 1, pp. 956–966 (2014)
18. Zhang, Y., Liu, K., He, S., et al.: Question Answering over Knowledge Base with Neural Attention Combining Global Knowledge Information. arXiv preprint arXiv:1606.00979 (2016)
19. Chen, J., Siva, R., Vijay, S., et al.: Learning structured natural language representations for semantic parsing. In: Proceedings of the 55th Annual Meeting of the Association for Computational Linguistics, 30 July–4 August, Vancouver, Canada, pp. 44–55 (2017)
20. Shen, Y., He, X., Gao, J., Deng, L., Mesnil, G.: Learning semantic representations using convolutional neural networks for web search. In: Proceedings of the Companion Publication of the 23rd International Conference on World Wide Web Companion, pp. 373–374 (2014)
21. Xiao, C., Marc D., Claire, G.: Symbolic priors for RNN-based semantic parsing. In: Proceedings of the Twenty-Sixth International Joint Conference on Artificial Intelligence (IJCAI 2017) (2017)
22. Yih, W.-T., Chang, M.-W., He, X., Gao, J.: Semantic parsing via staged query graph generation: question answering with knowledge base. In: Proceedings of the Joint Conference of the 53rd Annual Meeting of the ACL and the 7th International Joint Conference on Natural Language Processing of the AFNLP, vol. 1 (2015)
23. Chang, Z., Zou, L., Li, F.: Privacy preserving subgraph matching on large graphs in cloud. In: SIGMOD 2016, 26 June–01 July, San Francisco, CA, USA (2016)

24. Sun, Z., Wang, H., Wang, H., et al.: Efficient subgraph matching on billion node graphs. Proc. VLDB Endowment **5**(9), 788–799 (2012)
25. Zou, L., Huang, R., Wang, H., et al.: Answering, natural language question, over RDF a graph data driven approach. In: SIGMOD 2014, 22–27 June 2014, Snowbird, UT, USA (2014)
26. Li, W., Wang, J., Lin, Z., et al.: Software knowledge graph building method for open source project. J. Front. Comput. Sci. Technol. **11**(6), 851–862 (2017)
27. Li, H., et al.: Improving API caveats accessibility by mining API caveats knowledge graph. In: 2018 IEEE International Conference on Software Maintenance and Evolution ICSME (2018)

SemiTagRec: A Semi-supervised Learning Based Tag Recommendation Approach for Docker Repositories

Jiahong Zhou[1,2], Wei Chen[1,2,3(✉)], Guoquan Wu[1,2,3],
and Jun Wei[1,2,3]

[1] Institute of Software, Chinese Academy of Sciences, Beijing, China
{zhoujiahong17,wchen,gqwu,wj}@otcaix.iscas.ac.cn
[2] University of Chinese Academy of Sciences, Beijing, China
[3] State Key Laboratory of Computer Sciences, Beijing, China

Abstract. Docker has been the mainstream technology for providing reusable software artifacts by packaging applications, dependencies, and execution environments into images. Developers can easily build and deploy their applications using Docker. Currently, a large number of reusable Docker repositories are in the online open source communities, especially Docker Hub and Docker Store. Effectively reusing these artifacts requires a well understanding of them, and semantic tags provide this way. However, the communities do not support tags well, and little training data is available. This paper addresses the problem and proposes a semi-supervised learning based tag recommendation approach, SemiTagRec, for Docker repositories. SemiTagRec contains four components. (1) Predictor calculates the probabilities of assigning tags to Docker repositories. (2) Extender introduces in new tags as the candidates based on tag correlation analysis. (3) Evaluator measures the candidate tags. (4) Integrator combines the results of predictor and evaluator, and then takes the tags with high scores as the final result. SemiTagRec uses the newly tagged repositories together with the original ones as training data for the next round of training. In this iterative manner, SemiTagRec trains the predictor with the cumulative labeled data set and the extended tag vocabulary to achieve high accuracy of tag recommendation. Finally, we conducted some experiments and evaluated SemiTagRec by comparing it with other related works. Experimental results show that Semi-TagRec outperforms the other approaches in terms of Recall@5 and Recall@10.

Keywords: Tag recommendation · Docker repositories · Dockerfile · L-LDA · Semi-supervised learning

1 Introduction

Docker is a well-known open source container engine with flourishing communities. So far, Docker Store has stored more than 2.16 million repositories (accessed in April 2019), and the number is still growing fast. Developers can reuse these artifacts by pulling down the off-the-shelf images or building images using the Dockerfiles. According to the statistics, Docker Hub serves 12+ billion image pulls per week [1].

© Springer Nature Switzerland AG 2019
X. Peng et al. (Eds.): ICSR 2019, LNCS 11602, pp. 132–148, 2019.
https://doi.org/10.1007/978-3-030-22888-0_10

Given such a huge number of Docker repositories, effective reuse of them requires a good understanding of them, and semantic tags provide this way. Semantic tags facilitate artifact classification and efficient search [2]. For example, users can obtain the Docker artifacts by using the relevant tags as search keywords. Moreover, semantic tags add bookmarks to the repositories, which makes them easy to understand, without reading their description documents and code.

However, Docker Hub and Docker Store do not support tags well, and manual tagging is exhausting and time-consuming. Some approaches have been proposed to automatically tag the conventional software objects [3]. For instance, EnTagRec [4] takes description documents as input and recommends tags based on a supervised learning method. The existing approaches cannot be directly applied, because little training data is available and the tag vocabulary is limited, which affects the recommendation results.

This paper addresses the problem and proposes a semi-supervised learning based tag recommendation approach, **SemiTagRec**, for Docker repositories. SemiTagRec works in an iterative manner. It trains the predictor with the cumulative labeled data and the extended tag vocabulary, to achieve high tag recommendation accuracy. In summary, the main contributions of this work are as follows.

- **Approach.** We propose a self-optimized approach to tag a large number of Docker repositories. It incrementally generates the training data and extends the tag vocabulary, and with which it is capable of improving the tagging accuracy.
- **Evaluation.** We conduct several experiments to evaluate SemiTagRec. (1) We compare it with some other related works. The experimental results show that SemiTagRec outperforms these works in terms of Recall@5 and Recall@10. (2) We analyze the effect of iterative training on the performance of SemiTagRec. (3) We evaluate whether the recommended tags are reasonable based on a small scale survey.

The rest of this paper is organized as follows. Section 2 introduces the background and analyzes the problem. Section 3 elaborates the details of SemiTagRec. Section 4 presents the experimental setup, and Sect. 5 discusses the experimental results. Section 6 surveys the related work, and finally, Sect. 7 gives a conclusion.

2   Background and Problem Analysis

2.1   Background

In general, a Docker repository stores Docker images and Dokcerfiles for reuse. Specifically, a Docker repository contains several important kinds of information, including repository name, Docker images, text descriptions (short and full), Dockerfiles, version information, and pull command for downloading the image. It is worth noting that the repository already contains so-called tags, but they are version information and not the semantic tags we refer to in this paper.

In particular, a Dockerfile, following the notion of Infrastructure-as-Code (IaC) [7], is a configuration file containing several kinds of instructions, such as 'FROM', 'RUN',

'ENV' and 'CMD'. 'FROM' specifies the base image. 'RUN' executes shell scripts to build the image. 'ENV' sets environment variables. 'CMD' starts services packaged in the image. Therefore, Dockerfiles contain a lot of semantic information, and we use them as an important input in our approach.

2.2 Problem Analysis

Content-based tag recommendations have been widely used for reusing software objects, including Q&A (Question and Answer) entries, Apps and open source softwares. Most approaches take textual information as input (particularly online profiles, comments and readme files) and use machine learning algorithms (particularly supervised learning) to perform tag recommendations. In general, state-of-the-art approaches like EnTagRec [4] and TagMulRec [8] use the rich labeled data for training and use pre-defined tag vocabularies for recommendations.

However, tagging Docker repositories is very different, making these existing approaches inapplicable. The reasons are as follows.

First of all, little training data is available in the online Docker communities. The popular online communities, Docker Hub and Docker Store, do not provide semantic tags for stored repositories. We crawled 88,226 repositories from Docker Hub and found that they have no tags.

Secondly, unlike other software communities such as Stack Overflow, Docker communities do not have predefined tag vocabulary. We surveyed the 5,532 Docker repositories (among the crawled 88,226 ones) whose code bases contain GitHub topics and found that there are only over 700 high-quality GitHub topics associated with them. As a result, the tag vocabulary is too small to provide sufficient semantic information.

To solve the above problems, we are motivated to propose a semi-supervised learning based approach to automatically tagging a large number of Docker repositories.

3 Approach Details

As shown in Fig. 1, SemiTagRec contains four components, namely *predictor*, *extender*, *evaluator* and *integrator*. Basically, SemiTagRec works in two phases, i.e., training and prediction.

Algorithm 1 lists the training process using pseudo-code. At the beginning, Semi-TagRec makes the initialization. Specifically, it trains a topic correlation model with GitHub Repository Library (*GRL*) and an LR model with manually labeled training data (Evaluator Training Data, *ETD*), for the evaluator and the extender respectively (line 1–2). SemiTagRec then iteratively trains the predictor in multiple rounds to improve the prediction accuracy and to extend the tag vocabulary of the predictor (*PredTagSpace*, a set of unique tags) (line 3–17). In each round, SemiTagRec trains an L-LDA model with Tagged Docker repositories Set (*TDS*) for the predictor (line 4), and the predictor takes as input the Untagged Docker repositories Set (*UDS*) and recommends the top n tags

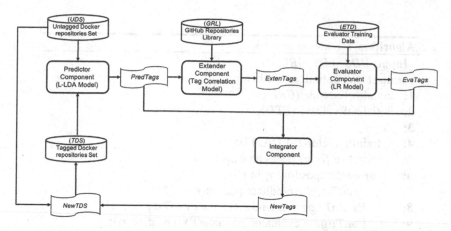

Fig. 1. SemiTagRec's working process overview

(*PredTags*, *PredTags* = $\{(tag_1, proba_1), \ldots, (tag_n, proba_n)\}$, where *proba$_i$* is the probability score of *tag$_i$* from predictor) for each repository in *UDS* (line 6–7). Next, the extender analyzes the correlations between the tags in *PredTags* and the topics in GitHub Topic Library (*GTL*) and takes the closely related topics together with *PredTags* as the extended tag set (*ExtenTags*) (line 8), where *GTL* is a set of top popular tags generated from *GRL* (see Sect. 4.1). Then the evaluator calculates the probability scores for the tags in *ExtenTags* of taking them as the candidates and outputs the evaluation results (*EvaTags*) (line 9). After that, for each tag in *PredTags* and *EvaTags*, the integrator calculates a linear combination score and takes the tags with high scores as the final result (*NewTags*) (line 10). For the repository, if its *NewTags* is not empty (*NewTags* is empty means the repository has no high score tags), it will be added into the Newly Tagged Docker repositories Set (*NewTDS*) (line 11–13). Finally, SemiTagRec updates *UDS* and *TDS* by removing *NewTDS* from the former and adding *NewTDS* into the latter, for the next round training (line 15–16).

This way, the amounts of *TDS* and *PredTagSpace* incrementally increase, and the performance of the predictor will improve and tend to be stable after multiple iterations. Finally, we will obtain an optimized L-LDA model as the final predictor.

The prediction is similar to the training. Given an untagged Docker repository, the four components execute in sequence, and finally, SemiTagRec outputs the top *q* tags as the final recommendation.

3.1 Predictor

The predictor calculates the probability score of recommending a tag to an untagged Docker repository. It is based on L-LDA [5], a state-of-the-art Bayesian inference algorithm working in the supervised learning based way. L-LDA model has been proved effective in solving the multi-label learning problems [9].

Algorithm 1 Training process
Input: UDS, TDS, GRL, ETD
Output: the optimized predictor
1: initializeExtender(GRL);
2: initializeEvaluator(ETD);
3: **do**
4:      trainPredictor(L-LDA, TDS);
5:      initialize $NewTDS$ as an empty list
6:      **for each** repository r_i in UDS
7:          $PredTags$ = predictor.predict(r_i);
8:          $ExtenTags$ = extender.extend($PredTags$);
9:          $EvaTags$ = evaluator.evaluate($ExtenTags, r_i$);
10:         $NewTags$ = integrator.combine($EvaTags, PredTags$);
11:         **if** $NewTags$ is not empty
12:             $NewTDS$.append(($r_i, NewTags$));
13:         **end if**
14:     **end for**
15:     $UDS = UDS - NewTDS$;
16:     $TDS = NewTDS \cup TDS$;
17: **until** predictor's performance converges

SemiTagRec models a labeled Docker repository as a document d and a tag set ts. Each document d is represented as a tuple consisting of a list of word indices $w^{(d)} = (w_1, w_2, \ldots, w_{N_d})$, and the tag set ts is represented by a list of binary tag presence/absence indicators $\Lambda^{(d)} = (t_1, t_2, \ldots, t_K)$, where each $w_i \in \{1, 2, \ldots, V\}$ $(1 \leq i \leq N_d)$ and each $t_j \in \{0, 1\}$ $(1 \leq j \leq K)$. Here N_d is the document length, V is the vocabulary (word vocabulary) size and K is the total number of the tags in *PredTagSpace*.

When performing training, the predictor computes the probability distribution of all the words in vocabulary for each tag in *PredTagSpace*. The predictor constructs a $K \times V$ matrix Φ, where $\varphi_{k,v} \in [0, 1]$ $(1 \leq k \leq K, 1 \leq v \leq V)$ and $\sum_{v=1}^{V} \varphi_{k,v} = 1$. $\varphi_{k,v}$ is the probability of a certain word w_v being generated from tag t_k.

When performing prediction, the predictor computes the probability distributions of all the tags in *PredTagSpace* for each untagged Docker repository. The predictor constructs an $M \times K$ matrix Θ, where $\vartheta_{m,k} \in [0, 1]$ $(1 \leq m \leq M, 1 \leq k \leq K)$ and $\sum_{k=1}^{K} \vartheta_{m,k} = 1$, $\vartheta_{m,k}$ is the likelihood of assigning tag t_k to the Docker repository $docker_m$. M is the number of untagged Docker repositories. For a certain untagged Docker repository $docker_m$, whose probability score vector of taking the tags in *PredTagSpace* is $\vartheta_{docker_m} = (\vartheta_{m,1}, \vartheta_{m,2}, \ldots, \vartheta_{m,K})$. Finally, all the tags are ranked according to their probability scores, and the top n tags are recommended as *PredTags*.

3.2   Extender

Initially, there are a few available tags since only a small number of Docker repositories whose code bases contain GitHub topics. The small number of tags are not enough to tag the large number of unlabeled repositories.

The extender addresses this problem. It adds into *PredTags* the GitHub topics closely correlating to the tags already in *PredTags*, according to their co-occurrences in GitHub repositories. The rationale is that most of the Docker repositories have source code repositories in GitHub, and thus the two repositories (Docker and source code) of a certain software system would have the same (or similar at least) semantics information. According to the statistics from STAR [6], it crawls 118,427 Docker repositories from Docker Hub and among which there are 105,606 (almost 90%) ones have GitHub code repositories. Therefore, it is reasonable to use those most popular GitHub topics for tagging Docker repositories. In practice, we crawl the GitHub topics and select the most popular ones as *GTL*, which is represented as $GTL = \{tag_1, tag_2, \ldots, tag_N\}$. The popularity of a topic is measured as its total occurrences in GitHub repositories.

The extender computes the tag correlation score for each pair of tags in *GTL*. As Eqs. 1 and 2 show, extender creates an $N \times N$ Tag Correlation Matrix (*TCM*). In the matrix, $TCM_{i,j}$ is the conditional probability $P(tag_j|tag_i)$, which denotes the probability of taking tag_j as a candidate when tag_i is selected.

$$TCM = \begin{pmatrix} TCM_{1,1} & TCM_{1,2} & \ldots & TCM_{1,N} \\ TCM_{2,1} & TCM_{2,2} & \ldots & TCM_{2,N} \\ \ldots & \ldots & \ldots & \ldots \\ TCM_{N,1} & TCM_{N,2} & \ldots & TCM_{N,N} \end{pmatrix} \tag{1}$$

$$TCM[i,j] = P(tag_j|tag_i) = \frac{Count(tag_i, tag_j)}{Count(tag_i)} \tag{2}$$

In Eq. 2, $Count(tag_i)$ is the number of GitHub repositories containing tag_i, and $Count(tag_i, tag_j)$ is the number of repositories containing both tag_i and tag_j.

Given a Docker repository $docker_m$ that contains tag_i, the extender can predict the probability of tag_j being a tag of $docker_m$ with Eq. 2. In this way, extender takes the closely related topics together with *PredTags* as *ExtenTags*.

3.3   Evaluator

The evaluator, based on LR (Logistic Regression) model [10], is responsible for computing a probability score for each candidate in the set *ExtenTags*. For a tag and a specific Docker repository, the evaluator calculates the probability of the tag belonging to the Docker repository.

In particular, the evaluator propose a feature vector to model a tag. Table 1 lists the feature details. It is worth noting that some features are based on Docker domain knowledge. For instance, 'in_df_comments', 'in_df_from' and 'in_df_env' are three features extracted from Dockerfile. 'FROM' specifies the base images and

'ENV' sets the environment variables, and thus we use 'in_df_from' and 'in_df_env' features to model whether a tag is in 'FROM' and 'ENV' instructions, respectively. Besides, comments in a Dockerfile is another kind of important information that might reflect the developer intentions and the functionalities. As such, we use 'in_df_comments' feature to model whether the tag is in the comments of a Dockerfile. 'gh_weight' is extracted from *GTL*, which indicates the popularity of tag in GitHub repositories. 'in_full_title' and 'occur_count' are extracted from descriptions of Docker repository, the former indicates whether the tag in the title of full description (full description is a markdown document) and the later indicates the times of tag occurrence in all descriptions. The rest features come from STAR [6].

We model the tags in *ExtenTags* for a Docker repository by analyzing its descriptions (short description and full description) and Dockerfile. For example, the candidate tag 'nginx' in the exemplary repository nytimes/nginx-vod-module[1] (see Sect. 2.1) will be modelled as $(1, 5, 0, 0, 1, 1, 1, 0, 3, 0, 0, 1)$.

Table 1. The details of all features.

Feature	Encoding	Description
word_nums	Integer	number of words in the tag
length	Integer	number of characters in the tag
is_username	Boolean	is user name or not
contain_num	Boolean	contains numeric characters or not
in_full_desc	Boolean	is in the full description or not
in_short_desc	Boolean	is in the short description or not
gh_weight	Integer	the weight of tag in the GitHub Tag Library
in_full_title	Boolean	is in the title of full description or not
occur_count	Integer	times of tag occurrence in all descriptions
in_df_comments	Boolean	is in the comments of Dockerfile or not
in_df_from	Boolean	is in the FROM command or not
in_df_env	Boolean	is in the ENV command or not

We manually label 1000 samples (500 positive samples and 500 negative samples) as *ETD* and train the LR model. After training, the evaluator can predict the probability of a candidate tag belonging to a Docker repository.

3.4 Integrator

If a tag represents a latent topic and does not occur in the description and the Dockerfile, the evaluator cannot determine whether to assign the tag to the Docker repository due to the limitation of the LR model. Therefore, some tags output by the predictor would not be considered as the right ones despite their high probability scores of the predictor.

---

[1] https://hub.docker.com/r/nytimes/nginx-vod-module.

To handle such situations, the integrator combines the results of predictor and evaluator. In detail, given a Docker repository $docker_m$ and a tag tag_i, the integrator computes a final ranking score $Score_{m,i}$ based on Eq. 3. In Eq. 3, $Predictor_{m,i}$ and $Evaluator_{m,i}$ are the probability scores of tag_i belonging to $docker_m$, which are computed by the predictor and the evaluator, and $\alpha, \beta \in [0, 1]$ are the weights.

$$Score_{m,i} = \alpha \times Predictor_{m,i} + \beta \times Evaluator_{m,i} \qquad (3)$$

Finally, SemiTagRec ranks the tags with their final scores in descending order. In training phase, we select the tags with high scores and add them into *NewTags*, and in prediction, we recommend the top q ones as the final result (TAG_i^{top-q}).

4 Experimental Setup

4.1 Dataset

GitHub Repository Library (GRL). We crawled 1,193,875 GitHub repositories as *GRL* and investigated their topics. We found that the topics are of very different qualities, depending on the developers' preferences and domain knowledge. Some topics of high qualities are very common and occur frequently among the repositories, and in contrast, the low-quality ones only occur a few times. We made statistics of the tag occurrences, although there are thousands of unique topics in *GRL*, only a very small part of them are of high-quality ones. In detail, the statistical results are as follows.

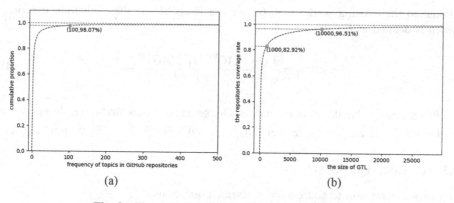

(a)   (b)

Fig. 2. The statistics of the topic occurrences in *GRL*

We obtained 5,438,644 topics and among which there are 344,881 unique ones.

1. There are 98.07% topics occurring in less than 0.00837% (100/1,193,875) repositories. Figure 2(a) shows the cumulative distribution of the GitHub topics frequency. (This figure does not show the very few topics whose occurrences exceed 500.)

2. We further made the statistics of the top 1,000 and the 10,000 most popular topics (occurring most frequently). Figure 2(b) shows the change of repositories coverage rate along with the size of the *GTL*, which indicates that the 1,000 topics occur in 82.92% repositories and the 10,000 topics occur in 96.51% repositories.

As a result, we made a trade-off between improving tagging result and reducing time cost and selected the 1,000 most popular topics as the *GTL* for the extender. It is worth noting that, if necessary, the *GTL* can be extended to contain much more popular topics.

Table 2. The three-round filtering of the crawled Docker repositories.

Round	Description	# of Remaining
1st	Filter out the repositories without GitHub code bases	81,233
2nd	Filter out the untagged repositories	7,276
3rd	Filter out the repositories whose tags are not in *GTL*	5,532

UDS and TDS. We crawled 88,226 Docker repositories from Docker Hub (accessed in March 2018), which contain rich description information. Similar to the existing work [6], we made a three-round filtering, and the details are in Table 2. We took the remaining 5,532 repositories after the 3rd filtering as the initial *TDS* and took the rest 82,694 ones of crawled Docker repositories as *UDS*.

4.2   Evaluation Metrics

Similar to the existing work [3, 4, 6], we use *Recall@q* as the evaluation criterion, which is defined as Eq. 4.

$$Recall@q = \frac{1}{n} \sum_{i=1}^{n} \frac{\left| TAG_i^{top-q} \bigcap TAG_i^{original} \right|}{\left| TAG_i^{original} \right|} \tag{4}$$

It is supposed that there are n untagged Docker repositories, and for each repository $docker_i$, we generate a top q tag set TAG_i^{top-q}, and $TAG_i^{original}$ are its original tag set.

4.3   Research Questions

Our experiments aim to address some research questions.

RQ1. Is the iterative training effective in optimizing the predictor of SemiTagRec? This question includes two sub ones. (1) Is the iterative training effective in extending *PredTagSpace*? (2) Can the iterative training improve the accuracy of predictor?

To answer this question, we conducted the experiment with the 5,532 repositories and their GitHub topics. We first randomly selected one-tenth of the repositories as test data and the remaining ones as the initial training data. We then trained the predictor and SemiTagRec in the different iterations and evaluated the effects on the tag recommendation accuracy in terms of Recall@5 and Recall@10.

RQ2. Is SemiTagRec effective in tagging a large number of Docker repositories? To answer this question, we also conducted the experiment with the 5,532 repositories and their GitHub topics and compared SemiTagRec with the other existing approaches in terms of Recall@5 and Recall@10.

RQ3. How about the tag recommendation result of SemiTagRec? This question includes two sub ones. (1) Are the recommended tags reasonable? (2) Is SemiTagRec helpful in bookmarking Docker repositories?

To answer this question, we randomly selected 100+ untagged Docker repositories and used SemiTagRec to generate tags for them. We then made a small scale survey on some interviewees (of software engineering field) about the reasonability of the tags. In addition, we performed some case studies on how SemiTagRec helps to semantically describe the repositories with tags.

4.4 Parameter Settings

SemiTagRec contains two parameters α and β and they should be set appropriately. We employed the grid search [20] to determine the parameter values, setting them with 0.91 and 0.09 respectively for final SemiTagRec recommender.

5 Evaluation

All of the experiments were conducted on a server with 8-core 3.50 GHz, 32 GB memory and Ubuntu 18.04.01 LTS (Linux version 4.15.0-34-generic).

5.1 RQ1

We used 4,979 repositories of the 5,532 ones as the initial *TDS* and iteratively trained the predictor in multiple rounds. We then used the rest ones (553 tagged repositories) as the test data to evaluate the predictor. We conducted the experiment by increasing the number of iterative trainings from 0 to 70, and Fig. 3 shows the experimental results.

Table 3. The statistics of *PredTagSpace* and the *TDS*

Iteration	0	10	20	30	40	50	60	70
|PredTagSpace|	740	785	802	817	824	834	844	846
|TDS|		4,979	9,078	13,327	17,619	21,901	26,194	30,563	34,836

Overall, the accuracy of the predictor (in terms of Recall@5 and Recall@10, represented as the red dash line and the green dash line) firstly increases as the number of iterations increases and tends to be stable when the iteration number exceeds 50. In particular, the accuracy of the predictor increase from 0. 514 to 0.590 (Recall@5) and from 0.589 to 0.652 (Recall@10), accounting for 14.79% and 10.70% increase respectively. When the number of iterations increases from 50 to 70, the accuracy changes slightly, only increases from 0.590 to 0.598 (Recall@5) and from 0.652 to

0.655 (Recall@10). We further investigated the experimental results from 40 iterations to 70 iterations and found that the predictor after 53 iterative trainings is optimal, whose accuracy is 0.600 and 0.661 respectively. As such, in the following experiments, we integrate the predictor after 53 iterations into SemiTagRec.

We also made the statistics of *PredTagSpace* and *TDS* during the iterative training. Table 3 lists the results, we notice that the size of *PredTagSpace* increase from 740 to 846, which proves that our approach is capable of extending the tag vocabulary.

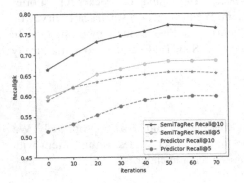 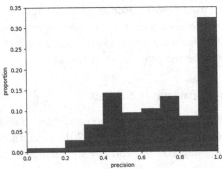

Fig. 3. The result of iterations for Semi-TagRec and Predictor (Color figure online)

Fig. 4. The precision distribution of repositories on survey

5.2   RQ2

We first evaluated the overall performance of SemiTagRec, and the results are also in Fig. 3. SemiTagRec's accuracy (also in terms of Recall@5 and Recall@10, represented as the orange solid line and the blue solid line) is higher than that of the individual predictor, which means that the other three components are also helpful in improving the tag recommendation performance. In particular, after the 53 iterative trainings, there are 838 tags in *PredTagSpace* and 27,191 tagged repositories, and the accuracy of SemiTagRec is 0.688 (Recall@5) and 0.781 (Recall@10) respectively, which is 14.67% and 18.15% higher than that of the individual predictor.

We then compared SemiTagRec with some other approaches, including EnTagRec [4] and STAR [6]. In addition, we also implemented some approaches which employed the components of SemiTagRec. LR is the approach only uses the evaluator and PEE is the approach combines the predictor, the extender and the evaluator. Note that we use the same training data and test data for all the approaches.

Table 4. The experimental results of the different approaches.

Accuracy	SemiTagRec	STAR	EnTagRec		LR	PEE
			0 Iter.	53 Iter.		
Recall@5	**0.688**	0.613	0.569	0.646	0.497	0.557
Recall@10	**0.781**	0.678	0.667	0.743	0.591	0.651

Table 4 lists the experimental results. SemiTagRec outperforms all of the other approaches, and EnTagRec (with 53 iterations) and STAR take the second and the third place respectively. LR is with the lowest accuracy, which means that LR is inefficient in tagging the large number of Docker repositories. We compared the results of SemiTagRec and PEE and found that SemiTagRec outperforms PEE, which also denotes that the integrator component is effective in improving the overall accuracy since it considers the latent tags generated from the predictor. EnTagRec contains two prediction components, Bayesian Inference Component (BIC) and Frequentist Inference Component (FIC), and BIC is also based on L-LDA model. As such, we used two different L-LDA models as BIC and FIC remained the same, and the two experimental results are different. The different results also imply that the iteratively trained L-LDA model is more effective than that only trained with the limited tagged repositories. As to STAR, it first uses an LR model to generate a large number of training data and then trains an L-LDA model with the large amount of data. There are two shortcomings, on the one hand, STAR cannot ensure all of the generated training data is of high quality, and on the other hand, STAR requires the much larger amount data as its input. Even though with more training data, STAR's accuracy is still lower than that of SemiTagRec.

5.3   RQ3

We made a survey on the reasonabilities of the recommended tags. We invited 11 masters majoring in software engineering to take part in our survey. Considering the cost of time and human efforts is expensive, we only randomly selected 105 tagged Docker repositories (with 645 tags in total) and sent each participant 10 repositories and their tags. The participants evaluated whether the tags are reasonable according to the repository description documents and their domain knowledge. As a result, each tag might be thought of unreasonable (0), reasonable (1) or neutral (2).

Table 5. The survey result

Score	Evaluation	# of tags	Pct.
0	Unreasonable	152	23.56%
1	Reasonable	402	62.33%
2	Neutral	91	14.11%

Table 5 shows the survey result. Among all the 645 tags, 402 ones are thought of reasonable, 152 ones are unreasonable and the rest are neutral. Therefore, the overall precision is 62.33% (take the neutral ones and unreasonable ones as negative) or 72.56% (ignore the neutral ones and take the unreasonable ones as negative).

In addition, we made the statistics of the repository distributions according to their precision. As Fig. 4 shows, a large part of the 105 tagged repositories whose tags are of high precision. Statistically, 88.57%, 72.38%, 56.19% and 50.48% of the repositories whose reasonable tags exceed 50%, 60%, 70% and 80%, respectively.

We further investigated the evaluation result and performed some case studies on how SemiTagRec helps to describe and bookmark the Docker repositories.

Case 1: Docker repository `vhtec/jupyter-docker`[2] provides a Jupyter notebook with tensorflow-stack, PHP kernel, JavaScript kernel, C++ kernel and Bash kernel. For this repository, SemiTagRec predicts 7 tags, 'jupyter-notebook', 'php', 'tensorflow', 'javascript', 'ssl', 'python' and 'ipython'. All of these tags are thought of reasonable by the participants.

Case 2: Docker repository `mtinx/tensorflow`[3] provides a image of customized tensorflow based on Python 3 but not Python 2.7. For this repository, SemiTagRec predicts 7 tags, and 5 ones are reasonable. The reasonable tags are 'tensorflow', 'artificial-intelligence', 'ubuntu', 'jupyter', 'cuda' and 'python3', among which 'artificial-intelligence' is a latent tag that never occurs in the description. Besides, it is worth mentioning that the full description of this repository includes both phrase "Python 2.7" and phrase "Python 3", SemiTagRec can smart recommend 'python3' but not 'python2' as the final tag.

Case 3: Docker repository `mitsutaka/mediaproxy-relay`[4] provides a mediaproxy-relay image. For this repository, SemiTagRec predicts 5 tags, 'emoji', 'postgres', 'kibana', 'dotnetcore' and 'relay', and only 'relay' is thought of reasonable by the participants. We inspected the repository and found that its description is very short. As such, SemiTagRec is limited to recommend high-quality tag for it, and the participants cannot make the evaluation.

5.4   Threats to Validity

Several threats that may potentially affect the validity of our work are discussed as follows.

Threats to internal validity come from several aspects. The first threat is about using GitHub topics as tags. We investigate a large number (88,226) of Docker repositories and find that the majority of them (81,233) have the corresponding GitHub based code repositories. Furthermore, we manually examined the GitHub topics, and find that they can be used to describe the corresponding Docker repositories. In consequence, it is reasonable to use GitHub topics. The second threat comes from the quality of the GitHub topics. We mitigate the threat by only using the most popular GitHub topics as tags. We make the statistics of the crawled GitHub topics and find that only a very small proportion of the topics occur frequently. As such, we use the top 1,000 most popular topics to form the tag vocabulary, which can ensure the quality of the tags. The third threat is the implementation of the different approaches compared for answering RQ3. To ensure the fairness of the comparison, if a specific model is used by different approaches, we use the same implementation of the model in all of these approaches. For example, L-LDA model is also employed in EnTagRec, and the code which implements of the L-LDA in EnTagRec is exactly the same with that in SemiTagRec,

---

[2] https://hub.docker.com/r/vhtec/jupyter-docker.

[3] https://hub.docker.com/r/mtinx/tensorflow.

[4] https://hub.docker.com/r/mitsutaka/mediaproxy-relay.

which would reduce the bias introduced by different implementation in the experimental results.

External validity concern the generality of our work. We crawl a large number of Docker repositories (88,226) from Docker Hub, the most popular community specialized for Docker, which ensures that the data we used is popular and representative. Furthermore, the tags derive from a large number of GitHub code repositories and the tag vocabulary of the predictor can be extended during the iterative training, which can handle the diversity of Docker repositories.

Construct validity refers to the suitability of our evaluation measures. Similar to the existing related studies, we use Recall@5 and Recall@10 as our evaluation metrics. In addition, we conduct a survey with 11 participants, who have rich expertise in software engineering, to evaluate the quality of recommended tags. The knowledge background of the participants also ensures the validity of the survey result.

6   Related Work

6.1   Researches Focusing on Docker

Docker has become attractive, and there are studies solving the related problems.

RUDSEA [11] extracted software code changes between two versions and analyzed their impacts on the software environment. According to the analysis, it recommended Dockerfile item updates. A study [12] addressed the problems of how outdated container packages are and how this relates to the presence of bugs and severity vulnerabilities, by empirical analyzing technical lag, security vulnerabilities and bugs for Docker images. Zhang et al. [13] conducted an empirical study to analyze the impact of Dockerfile evolutionary trajectory on the quality and latency of Docker-based containerization. They found six Dockerfile evolution trajectories and made a number of suggestions for practitioners. A NIER (New Ideas and Emerging Results) work [1] introduced the idea of mining container image repositories and showcased the opportunities that can benefit from it. Cito et al. [14] conducted an empirical study to characterize the Docker container ecosystem. They discovered the prevalent quality issues and studied the evolution of Docker images. In addition, to lay the groundwork for research on Docker, they collected structured information about the state and the evolution of Dockerfiles on GitHub and released it as a PostgreSQL database archive [15].

Overall, the goal of our work is totally different to the existing ones. Rather than focusing on software maintenance and evolution, SemiTagRec aims to support Docker repository reuse by providing semantic tags for them.

6.2   Tag Recommendation

Tag recommendation has been widely studied. Currently, content-based tag recommendation is popular. Most of the approaches take text information and code as input, and use machine learning algorithms.

FastTagRec [16] is an automated scalable tag recommendation method using neural network-based classification. It accurately infers new tags for postings in Q&A sites, by learning existing postings and their tags from existing information. TagMulRec [17] is an approach that recommends tags for software objects. It creates index for software object descriptions and recommends tags based on similarity computation and multi-classification of software objects. GRETA [18] is a graph-based approach to assigning tags for repositories on GitHub. Sally [19] is a tagging approach for Maven-based software repositories. It is able to produce tags by extracting identifiers from bytecode and harnessing the dependency relations between repositories. EnTagRec [4] makes some improvements on TagCombine [3]. It combines Bayesian inference based method and frequentist inference based method together. However, most of the existing studies base on a large volume of training data and use supervised learning based method.

The most related work is STAR [6], which also recommends tags for Docker repositories based on supervised learning. STAR directly generates a large amount of training data based on the LR algorithm, which uses manually labeled data for training. With the generated training data, STAR then recommends tags for the untagged Docker repositories based on the L-LDA model. Compared with SemiTagRec, the limitations of STAR are as follows: (1) The quality of generated training data is not guaranteed, which will further affect the overall recommendation performance; (2) There are too many configuration parameters in STAR, and tuning the parameters is cumbersome and time-consuming, which makes STAR hard to use in practice.

7 Conclusion

This paper proposes a semi-supervised learning based tag recommendation approach, SemiTagRec, for Docker repositories. SemiTagRec incrementally generates the training data and extends the tag vocabulary of the predictor. By self-adapting the model iteratively, SemiTagRec is capable of improving tagging accuracy. We compare it with other related works, such as STAR [6] and EnTagRec [4]. The experimental results show that SemiTagRec outperforms these works in terms of Recall@5 and Recall@10.

In future work, we plan to explore improving the search and reuse of Docker repositories with semantic tags. Furthermore, we also plan to empirically investigate the quality issues of Docker artifacts and explore the ways to solve them, helping developers effectively and correctly creating Docker artifacts.

Acknowledgement. The authors would like to thank the contributions of the participants in our work and the comments of the reviewers. This work was partially supported by the National Key R&D Program of China under Grant No. 2016YFB1000803 and the National Natural Science Foundation of China under Grant No. 61732019.

References

1. Xu, T., Marinov, D.: Mining container image repositories for software configuration and beyond. In: Proceedings of the 40th International Conference on Software Engineering: New Ideas and Emerging Results, pp. 1–13. ACM (2018)
2. Chen, W., Xu, P., Dou, W., Wu, G., Gao, C., Wei, J.: A hierarchical categorization approach for configuration management modules. In: 2017 IEEE 41st Annual Computer Software and Applications Conference (COMPSAC), vol. 1, pp. 160–169. IEEE (2017)
3. Xia, X., Lo, D., Wang, X., Zhou, B.: Tag recommendation in software information sites. In: Proceedings of 10th IEEE Working Conference on Mining Software Repositories (MSR), pp. 287–296. IEEE (2013)
4. Wang, S., Lo, D., Vasilescu, B., Serebrenik, A.: Entagrec: an enhanced tag recommendation system for software information sites. In: Proceedings of 2014 IEEE International Conference on Software Maintenance and Evolution (ICSME), pp. 291–300. IEEE (2014)
5. Ramage, D., Hall, D., Nallapati, R., Manning, C.: Labeled LDA: a supervised topic model for credit attribution in multi-labeled corpora. In: Proceedings of the 2009 Conference on Empirical Methods in Natural Language, vol. 1, pp. 248–256 (2009)
6. Yin, K., Chen, W., Zhou, J., Wu, G., Wei, J.: STAR: a specialized tagging approach for docker repositories. In: 25th Asia-Pacific Software Engineering Conference (2018)
7. Hummer, W., Rosenberg, F., Oliveira, F., Eilam, T.: Testing idempotence for infrastructure as code. In: Eyers, D., Schwan, K. (eds.) Middleware 2013. LNCS, vol. 8275, pp. 368–388. Springer, Heidelberg (2013). https://doi.org/10.1007/978-3-642-45065-5_19
8. Zhou, P., Liu, J., Yang, Z., Zhou, G.: Scalable tag recommendation for software information sites. In: Proceedings of 24th-International-Conference-on Software-Analysis, -Evolution-and-Reengineering-(SANER), pp. 272–282. IEEE (2017)
9. Zhang, M., Zhou, Z.: A review on multi-label learning algorithms. IEEE Trans. Knowl. Data Eng. **26**(8), 1819–1837 (2014)
10. Hosmer, D., Lemeshow, J., Sturdivant, R.: Applied Logistic Regression, vol. 398. Wiley, Hoboken (2013)
11. Hassan, F., Rodriguez, R., Wang, X.: RUDSEA: recommending updates of Dockerfiles via software environment analysis. In: Proceedings of the 33rd ACM/IEEE International Conference on Automated Software Engineering, pp. 796–801. ACM (2018)
12. Ahmed, Z., Tom, M., et al.: On the Relation Between Outdated Docker Containers, Severity Vulnerabilities and Bugs. arXiv preprint arXiv:1811.12874 (2018)
13. Zhang, Y., Yin, G., Wang, T., et al.: An insight into the impact of dockerfile evolutionary trajectories on quality and latency. In: Proceedings of 2018 IEEE 42nd Annual Computer Software and Applications Conference (COMPSAC), pp. 138–143. IEEE (2018)
14. Cito, J., Schermann, G., Wittern, J., Leitner, P., Zumberi, S., Gall, H.: An empirical analysis of the docker container ecosystem on github. In: Proceedings of the 14th International Conference on Mining Software Repositories, pp. 323–333. IEEE (2017)
15. Schermann, G., Zumberi, S., Cito, J.: Structured information on state and evolution of dockerfiles on github. In: Proceedings of the 15th International Conference on Mining Software Repositories (2018)
16. Liu, J., Zhou, P., Yang, Z., Liu, X., Grundy, J.: FastTagRec: fast tag recommendation for software information sites. Autom. Softw. Eng. **25**(4), 675–701 (2018)
17. Zhou, P., Liu, J., Yang, Z., Zhou, G.: Scalable tag recommendation for software information sites. In: Proceedings of IEEE 24th International Conference on Software Analysis, Evolution and Reengineering (SANER), pp. 272–282. IEEE (2017)

18. Cai, X., Zhu, J., et al.: Greta: graph-based tag assignment for github repositories. In: 2016 IEEE 40th Annual Computer Software and Applications Conference (COMPSAC), vol. 1, pp. 63–72. IEEE (2016)
19. Vargas-Baldrich, S., Linares-V'asquez, M., Poshyvanyk, D.: Automated tagging of software projects using bytecode and dependencies. In: 2015 30th IEEE/ACM International Conference on Automated Software Engineering (ASE), pp. 289–294. IEEE (2015)
20. Bergstra, J., Bengio, Y.: Random search for hyper-parameter optimization. J. Mach. Learn. Res. **13**, 281–305 (2012)

Slicing Based Code Recommendation
for Type Based Instance Retrieval

Rui Sun, Hui Liu$^{(\boxtimes)}$, and Leping Li

Beijing Institute of Technology, Beijing, China
{sr1993,liuhui08,lileping}@bit.edu.cn

Abstract. It is common for developers to retrieve an instance of a certain type from another instance of other types. However, it is quite often that developers do not exactly know how to retrieve the instance although they know exactly what they need (the instance to re retrieved, also known as the *target instance*) and where it could be retrieved (i.e., the *source instance*). Such kind of instance retrieval is popular and thus their implementations, in different forms, are often publicly available on the Internet. Consequently, a number of approaches have been proposed to retrieve such implementations (code snippets) and release developers from reinventing such snippets. However, the performance of such approaches deserves further improvement. To this end, in this paper, we propose a slicing based approach to recommending code snippets that could retrieve the target instance from the source instance. The approach works as follows. First, from a large code base, it retrieves methods that contain the source instance and the target instance. Second, for each of these methods, it locates the target instances, and extracts related code snippets that generate the target instances by backward code slicing. Third, from the extracted code snippets, it removes those that do not contain the source instance. Fourth, it merges code snippets whose corresponding target instances are at parallel execution paths. Fifth, it removes duplicate code snippets. Finally, it ranks the resulting code snippets, and presents the top ones. We implement the approach as an Eclipse plugin called *TIRSnippet*. We also evaluate it with real type based instance retrieval queries. Evaluation results suggest that compared to the state-of-the-art approaches, the proposed approach improves the precision and recall by 8.8%, and 25%, respectively.

Keywords: Reuse · Slicing · Code search

1 Introduction

It is common for developers to retrieve an instance of a certain type from another instance they have [12]. For convenience, we call the retrieve Type Based Instance Retrieval (TIR). For example, they may want to retrieve the *IDocument* instance associated with an *IFile* instance. The following is a typical code snippet that accomplishes the task:

© Springer Nature Switzerland AG 2019
X. Peng et al. (Eds.): ICSR 2019, LNCS 11602, pp. 149–167, 2019.
https://doi.org/10.1007/978-3-030-22888-0_11

```
IFile file = ...
IPath path= file.getFullPath();
ITextFileBufferManager bufferManager = FileBuffers.getTextFileBufferManager();
bufferManager.connect(path, LocationKind.IFILE, null);
ITextFileBuffer textFileBuffer = bufferManager.getTextFileBuffer(path, LocationKind.
    IFILE);
IDocument document = textFileBuffer.getDocument();
```

For convenience, code snippets (like the example) that accomplish a TIR are noted as TIR code snippets. The instance (*document* in the example) that a TIR code snippet returns is called *target instance*, and the input (*file* in the example) is called *source instance*.

Automatic or semi-automatic recommendation of TIR code snippets is desirable. TIR code snippets could be quite complicated. Consequently, it is challenging for programmers who are not familiar with relevant framework or library to create such a code snippet from scratch. However, it is likely that the programming task has been implemented by others and such implementation (TIR code snippet) is available on the Internet. Retrieving such reference implementation for reuse (or at least as learning material) can significantly facilitate the programming task at hand [9]. To this end, a number of approaches have been proposed [12, 17, 20] to retrieve TIR code snippets according to their target instances and source instances. Mandelin et al. [12] proposed *PROSPECTOR*. It accepts a query in the form of (Tin, $Tout$), where Tin, $Tout$ represent two different types. *PROSPECTOR* utilizes API method signatures and a corpus of examples to synthesize API client code automatically which achieves the transformation from Tin to $Tout$. Shavechaphan and Claypool [17] use a graph-based module to mine for paths for the instantiation of a certain type. These paths form suggested code snippets which are extracted from a sample repository. Thummalapenta and Xie [20] use a code search engine to collect relevant code samples, and extract method-invocation sequences that retrieve the target instance by static code analysis. Such approaches [12, 17, 20] have greatly facilitated the reuse of type based instance retrieval code snippets. However, the performance (e.g., precision and recall) of such approaches deserve significant improvements.

To this end, in this paper, we propose a slicing based approach to recommending TIR code snippets. For a given TIR query in the form of <*source type*, *target type*>, the proposed approach retrieves code snippets that accomplish the given TIR query. The approach works as follows. First, from a code repository, it retrieves methods that contain both source instance and target instance. Second, for each such method, it employs code slicing to extract code snippets that generate target instances. Third, it merges extracted code snippets whose corresponding target instances are at parallel execution paths. Fourth, it removes duplicate code snippets, and ranks the resulting code snippets to recommend the top ones. We also implement the proposed approach as an Eclipse plugin, called *TIRSnippet*.

The paper makes the following contributions:

- A slicing based approach to recommending code snippets for TIR queries.
- Implementation of the proposed approach as an Eclipse plugin.
- Evaluation of the proposed approach with real TIR queries. Evaluation results suggest that the proposed approach improves the state-of-the-art.

The rest of the paper is structured as follows. Section 2 presents a motivating example. Section 3 presents details of the proposed approach. Section 4 presents an evaluation of the proposed approach. Section 5 provides a review of related research. Section 6 makes conclusions.

2 Motivating Example

Suppose that we are assigned the following programming task: For a given method invocation, retrieve the type of the instance on which the method is invocated. For example, given the method invocation '*assign.getOperator()*', we should retrieve the type of *assign*. If we decide to accomplish this task with JDT framework [2] (a widely used Java development toolkit), we should retrieve an *ITypeBinding* instance (initializing the data type of an instance) from a given *MethodInvocation* instance. An example code snippet (we call it *ExampleSnippet*) that can accomplish this task is presented as follows:

```
1    Expression expression = invocation.getExpression();
2    if(expression == null){
3      typeBinding = invocation.resolveMethodBinding().getDeclaringClass();
4    }
5    else {
6      typeBinding = expression.resolveTypeBinding();
7    }
```

where *invocation* on Line 1 is a *MethodInvocation* instance and *typeBinding* on Line 3 and Line 6 is an *ITypeBinding* instance.

We expect existing TIR approaches to retrieve the *ExampleSnippet* for the given task. However, these approaches, e.g., *PARSEWeb* [20], fail. *PARSEWeb* creates a graph for the *ExampleSnippet* where nodes represent statements (method invocation, constructor or typecast statement) and edges represent control information between statements. Based on the graph, *PARSEWeb* searches for paths that connect the source instance (*invocation* in the example) and the target instance (*typeBinding* in the example). For each of the resulting paths, statements on the path that are relevant to the target instance make up a TIR code snippet. Consequently, code snippet 1# and code snippet 2# (as presented in Fig. 1) are retrieved. However, both of the retrieved code snippets are incomplete and may result in buggy implementation. For example, code snippet 1# may result in *Null Pointer Exception* during execution if a *MethodInvocation* instance has no expression (e.g., for method invocation '*getFullName()*').

Code Snippet 1#
Expression expression = invocation.getExpression();
typeBinding = expression.resolveTypeBinding();

Code Snippet 2#
typeBinding = invocation.resolveMethodBinding().getDeclaringClass();

Fig. 1. Code snippets retrieved by existing approaches

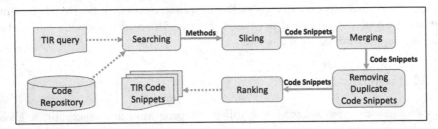

Fig. 2. Overview of the proposed approach

In contrast, the proposed approach retrieves the complete *ExampleSnippet* successfully. It first locates target instances (*typeBinding* on Line 3 and Line 6 in the example). After that, for each target instance, it employs code slicing to extract all statements (including complex control statements) that are relevant to the generation of the target instance. In the example, two code snippets are extracted. They are noted as TIRC (*typeBinding*, Line 3) = {1, 2, 3, 4} and TIRC (*typeBinding*, Line 6) = {1, 2, 4, 5, 6, 7} where the integer set represents line numbers, and statements on these lines make up the extracted TIR code snippets. Unlike code snippet 1# and code snippet 2# retrieved by existing approaches, such code snippets retrieved by the proposed approach contain control statements as well. The proposed approach notices that the two target instances on Line 3 and Line 6 are at parallel execution paths, and thus it merges their corresponding TIR code snippets: TIRC (*typeBinding*)={1, 2, 3, 4, 5, 6, 7}. As a result, the whole code snippet (*ExampleSnippet*) is retrieved by the proposed approach.

3   Approach

3.1   Overview

An overview of the proposed approach is presented in Fig. 2. The input of the proposed approach is a TIR query in the form of *<source type, target type>*. The output is the resulting TIR code snippets that could retrieve the target instance associated with the given source instance. For a TIR query, the proposed approach works as follows:

- First, from a code repository, it retrieves all methods which contain both source instance and target instance.

- Second, for each of these methods, it locates the target instances, and extracts related code snippets that generate the target instances by backward code slicing. From extracted code snippets, it removes those that do not contain the source instance.
- Third, it merges extracted code snippets whose corresponding target instances are at parallel execution paths of the involved programs.
- Fourth, from the resulting code snippets, it removes the duplicate ones.
- Finally, it ranks the resulting code snippets, and present the top ones.

3.2 Searching

The first step of the proposed approach is to search for all methods (noted as RMS) that contain both source instance and target instance from a code repository. Algorithm 1 shows the details of how to search for these methods. For each source code file in a code repository, we retrieve all methods contained in this file (Lines 2–3). For each retrieved method (noted as rm), we check whether this method contains both source instance and target instance. If yes, the method rm is added to RMS. The checking process is explained as follows. First, we retrieve all instances (noted as $INSES$) contained in the method rm (Line 5). Second, for each instance in $INSES$, we check whether it is a source instance or target instance (Lines 8–14). Finally, the method rm is added to RMS if it contains both source instance and target instance (Lines 15–16).

3.3 Slicing

From retrieved methods RMS which contain both source instance and target instance, backward code slicing is employed to extract the smallest code snippets that could generate the target instances. The slicing works as follows. First, for each method in RMS, we locate all target instances. Second, based on each of the target instances, we extract code snippet that could generate the target instance by backward code slicing. Third, from extracted code snippets, we remove those that do not contain the source instance. We take code snippet $ExampleSnippet$ (as presented in Sect. 2) as an example to illustrate the detailed process. $ExampleSnippet$ is a solution for the TIR query $<MethodInvocation,$ $ITypeBinding>$. From this code snippet, the proposed approach first locates two target instances. These two target instances (noted as $t3$ and $t6$) are on Line 3 and Line 6, respectively. Based on target instances $t3$ and $t6$, backward code slicing is employed to extract two code snippets that could generate $t3$ and $t6$, respectively. Code snippet 3# (as presented in Fig. 3) is extracted based on target instance $t3$ and code snippet 4# (as presented in Fig. 3) is extracted based on target instance $t6$. These two code snippets both contain the source instance $invocation$, and thus we do not remove any of them.

In some special cases, slicing could not retrieve some TIR code snippets. These code snippets have the following two features: (1) Their source instances or target instances are not explicitly denoted (e.g., the source

Algorithm 1. Searching for Methods that Contain Source Instance and Target Instance

Input: *sourceFiles* //source code files in a code repository
   source type //source type in a query
   target type //target type in a query
Output: *RMS* //methods that contain source instance and target instance

1: $RMS \leftarrow \emptyset$
2: **for each** *source* in *sourceFiles* **do**
3: *allMethods* $\leftarrow$ *source*.getMethods() //retrieve methods of a source code file
4: **for each** *method* in *allMethods* **do**
5:    *INSES* $\leftarrow$ *method*.getInsideInstances() //retrieve all instances
6:    *containSource* $\leftarrow$ False
7:    *containTarget* $\leftarrow$ False
8:    **for each** *instance* in *INSES* **do**
9:      **if** *instance*.getType().equals(*sourceType*) **then**
10:       *containSource* $\leftarrow$ True
11:      **end if**
12:      **if** *instance*.getType().equals(*targetType*) **then**
13:       *containTarget* $\leftarrow$ True
14:      **end if**
15:      **if** *containSource* $==$ True && *containTarget* $==$ True **then**
16:       *RMS*.add(*method*)
17:       break
18:      **end if**
19:    **end for**
20: **end for**
21: **end for**
22: **return** *RMS*

instance is the instance returned by a method invocation). (2) They consist of method invocation sequences only. We take the following example to explain how to retrieve these code snippets. Suppose that we have a code snippet *PlatformUI*.*getWorkbench*().*getActiveWorkbenchWindow*().*getActivePage*() (noted as *MI*), and we want to retrieve an *IWorkbenchWindow* instance from an *IWorkbench* instance. To achieve that, we first list all instances contained in *MI* from left to right. These instances are *PlatformUI*, *IWorkbench*, *IWorkbenchWindow*, and *IWorkbenchPage* instance. The last three instances are listed because they are the instances returned by method invocation *getWorkbench*(), *getActiveWorkbenchWindow*() and *getActivePage*(), respectively. After that, we check whether the source instance appears ahead of the target instance. If yes, a correct TIR code snippet is found. In this example, the source instance (the *IWorkbench* instance) appears ahead of the target instance (the *IWorkbenchWindow* instance). Consequently, a correct TIR code snippet

```
Code Snippet 3#
Expression expression = invocation.getExpression();
If(expression == null){
    typeBinding = invocation.resolveMethodBinding().getDeclaringClass();
}


Code Snippet 4#
Expression expression = invocation.getExpression();
If(expression == null){

}
else {
    typeBinding = expression.resolveTypeBinding();
}
```

Fig. 3. Extracted code snippets based on different target instances

$PlatformUI.getWorkbench().getActiveWorkbenchWindow()$ is retrieved. In this TIR code snippet, the source instance is the instance returned by the method invocation $PlatformUI.getWorkbench()$ and the target instance is the instance returned by the method invocation $getActiveWorkbenchWindow()$.

3.4 Merging

Extracted TIR code snippets that satisfy the following conditions are merged: (1) First, they are from the same method of a source code file; (2) Second, their corresponding target instances are at parallel execution paths of the involved program. Each of such snippets presents a special condition where the target instance could be generated. To guarantee that a target instance could be successfully generated under different conditions (i.e., handling some exceptional cases), we merge code snippets whose corresponding target instances are at parallel execution paths (i.e., these target instances could not be generated with one execution path). For example, the target instances generated by code snippet 3# and code snippet 4# (as presented in Fig. 3) are at parallel execution paths, and they are generated under different conditions. When a *MethodInvocation* instance has no expression (e.g., '*getFullName()*'), code snippet 3# is used to generate the target instance. When a *MethodInovcation* instance contains an expression (e.g., '*var.getFullName()*'), code snippet 4# is used to generate the target instance. We merge code snippet 3# and code snippet 4# into a complete code snippet (*ExampleSnippet* as presented in Sect. 2) to guarantee that a target instance could be generated no matter whether a *MethodInvocation* instance contains an expression or not. After merging, we get a set of TIR code snippet candidates (noted as *snippetCandidates*).

3.5 Removing Duplicate Code Snippets

From TIR code snippet candidates *snippetCandidates*, we remove the duplicate or nearly duplicate ones. When users look through the top k recommended TIR code snippets, the duplicate ones are meaningless and redundant. To remove these duplicates, we first make some pretreatments for each TIR code snippet in *snippetCandidates*. These pretreatments include: (1) Replacing all the variable names with a special character '#'. (2) Removing blank characters from all statements. These pretreatments are conducted in order. After that, we compare any pair of TIR code snippets (noted as *snippetA* and *snippetB*) to check whether they are duplicate. To avoid comparing twice for a pair of code snippets, we guarantee that the index of *snippetA* is not larger than that of *snippetB* in the *snippetCandidates*. *SnippetA* and *snippetB* are considered as duplicate if they meet the following two conditions. The first condition is that they have the same number of statements. The second condition is that they share the same characters for all statements. If *snippetA* and *snippetB* are duplicate code snippets, we remove *snippetA* that has a smaller index.

3.6 Ranking

We rank TIR code snippet candidates *snippetCandidates*, and present the top ones. Existing investigation suggested that users usually look through only the first around ten recommendations of search or mining process [3]. Consequently, we rank *snippetCandidates* as the following process. First, we rank them by frequency. Frequency is selected for the following reasons. (1) Generally speaking, a specific function could be implemented by various approaches. (2) An approach has a higher frequency in programs, which suggests that the approach is generally acceptable and more standardized. Second, we rank *snippetCandidates* by Mccabe Cyclomatic Complexity (MCC) [13] in descending order if two TIR code snippets share the same frequency.

4 Evaluation

In this section, we present the evaluation of the proposed approach on 26 real type based instance retrieval requests post on *Stackoverflow*.

4.1 Research Questions

- **RQ1:** Are type based instance retrieval code snippets popular?
- **RQ2:** Can the proposed approach outperform the state-of-the-art approaches in retrieving TIR code snippets?
- **RQ3:** How does the code slicing influence the performance of the proposed approach?
- **RQ4:** How does the ranking influence the performance of the proposed approach?

The proposed approach is based on the assumption that type based instance retrieval code snippets are popular (i.e., it is common for developers to write type based instance retrieval code snippets). If not, the proposed approach will not be used frequently, and thus useless. Answering research question RQ1 helps to validate the assumption.

RQ2 concerns the performance of the proposed approach against the-state-of-art approaches. To answer RQ2, we compare the proposed approach against *PARSEWeb* [20] and *Google* (https://www.google.com). *PARSEWeb* is the state-of-the-art approach and *Google* is the state-of-the-practice general purpose search engine. We select PARSEWeb for the following reasons. First, it is designed to retrieve type based instance retrieval code snippets, just as the proposed approach is. Second, we fail to get the implementation of other approaches for type based instance retrieval. *PARSEWeb* is the only one of such approaches whose implementation is publicly available. Third, *PARSEWeb* has proved to have a better performance than other type based instance retrieval approaches (e.g., *PROSPECTOR* and *XSnippet*) [20]. *Google* is selected because of the following reasons. First, programmers tend to use the general purpose search engine to search for code to reuse [8,18,19]. Second, *Google* is the most frequently used search engine for code search [16,18]. It should be noted that the evaluation results do not suggest that the proposed approach is better in general than *Google*. The proposed approach is only confined to type based instance retrieval, while *Google* is more generic. Consequently, it is unfair to compare them in general. The purpose of our evaluation is to validate that better performance could be achieved by focusing on a special and common case, type based instance retrieval.

As specified in Sect. 3.3, the proposed approach is based on code slicing. Answering research question RQ3 helps to reveal the influence of code slicing in retrieving type based instance retrieval code snippets.

RQ4 concerns the influence of ranking. As specified in Sect. 3.6, we rank code snippets to present the top ones. Answering research question RQ4 helps to reveal whether the performance is influenced by the ranking.

4.2   Type Based Instance Retrieval Requests and Code Repository

To evaluate the proposed approach, we need some real TIR requests for evaluation. A request is called TIR request if it could be translated into a TIR query <*source type, target type*>. In the evaluation, we select TIR requests related to JDT framework [2]. This framework is chosen for the following reasons. First, the data types in a TIR request are various. They could be from any framework or library. Second, JDT framework is popular for developers to reuse. To get these requests, we search *Stackoverflow* (https://stackoverflow.com, one of the most popular online community for developers to ask and answer questions) with keywords like 'jdt get from', 'jdt convert from', 'jdt change to', etc. We manually check the top 50 returned requests to identify whether any request could be translated into a TIR query according to its description. For example, the following request is post on *Stackoverflow*:

"This plugin processes each Java file as a ICompilationUnit. However, in my approach I can only get an instance of IFile. How can I create a ICompilationUnit from this IFile object?"

According to the description, this request could be translated into a TIR query $<IFile, ICompilationUnit>$. Consequently, this request is a TIR request. Finally, 26 TIR requests (noted as *selectedRequests*) are selected for evaluation.

To search for solutions (TIR code snippets) for *selectedRequests*, we need a relevant code repository. In this evaluation, the code repository (noted as CR) is composed of 5 closed-source applications developed previously in Beijing Institute of Technology and 33 open-source applications (https://github.com/sr1993/TIRSnippet) downloaded from *Github*. All these applications are related to JDT framework. To get these open-source applications, we searched *Github* with keywords like 'jdt -language-:java', 'eclipse -language-:java', etc. We sorted returned applications by their stars in descending order, and selected applications. The selected applications meet the following criteria: (1) They are written in Java. (2) They are related to JDT framework. (3) They could be imported into Eclipse IDE successfully. The third criteria makes sure that we could create Abstract Syntax Tree successfully for the source code files, and thus retrieve the binding information of program elements. The size (LOC) of applications in the code repository CR varies from 136 to 545638.

4.3   RQ1: Type Based Instance Retrieval Code Snippets in Programs

To answer research question RQ1, we first acquire TIR code snippets from code repository CR which is used in the evaluation. After that, we classify those TIR code snippets into different categories. Two TIR code snippets are classified into the same category if they share the same source type and target type. Finally, we calculate the following metrics: the number of TIR code snippets, involved files, involved methods, TIR code snippet categories and the average number of TIR code snippets per application, per involved file, per involved method. Evaluation results are presented in Table 1.

Table 1. TIR code snippets in the code repository

Number of TIR code snippets	102,420
Number of involved files	5,225
Number of involved methods	56,905
Number of TIR code snippet categories	12,590
Average number of TIR code snippets per application	2,695
Average number of TIR code snippets per involved file	20
Average number of TIR code snippets per involved method	2

From Table 1, we make the following observations:

- First, the number of TIR code snippets is quite large. The results suggest that 102,420 TIR code snippets exist in 5,225 involved source code files and 56,905 involved methods. The average numbers of TIR code snippets per application, per involved file and per involved method are 2,695, 20 and 2, respectively.
- Second, the number of TIR code snippet categories is large. The result suggests that required TIR code snippets could be classified into 12,590 categories.

From the analysis in the preceding paragraphs, we conclude that type based instance retrieval code snippets are popular.

4.4 RQ2: Comparison Against Existing Approaches

To address RQ2, we compare the proposed approach against *PARSEWeb* and *Google* on 26 TIR requests in *selectedRequests*. The process is as follows:

- First, for each TIR request in *selectedRequests*, we translate it into a TIR query in the form of *<source type, target type>*.
- Second, for each TIR query, we apply each approach to search for TIR code snippets. It is noted that Google Code Search (www.google.com/codesearch) used in *PARSEWeb* is not available anymore. We replace it with Search Code (https://searchcode.com, a free source code search engine).
- Finally, for each query, we manually check the correctness of the top k code snippets recommended by various approaches. A code snippet is considered as correct if it could solve the query functionally and answer the corresponding request. The manual checking is conducted by three postgraduate students in Beijing Institute of Technology. They all have rich experience in Java development. They first check the recommended code snippets independently. After that, they discuss together to remove inconsistence.

Metrics. To evaluate the performance of various approaches, we employ metrics $p@k$ to measure precision and $r@k$ to measure recall. $p@k$ is calculated as follows: $p@k = \frac{tp@k}{retrievedN_k}$ where $tp@k$ represents the number of retrieved correct code snippets and $retrievedN_k$ represents the total number of retrieved code snippets, when the top k results are inspected. $r@k$ is calculated as follows: $r@k = \frac{solved@k}{N_{query}}$ where N_{query} represents the number of queries and $solved@k$ represents the number of solved queries, when the top k results are inspected.

We also assess the performance of various approaches with the Mean Reciprocal Rank (MRR). It is a statistical metric to evaluate a process that produces a list of possible responses to a specific query [4]. It is calculated as follows: $MRR = \frac{1}{|Q|} \sum_{i=1}^{|Q|} \frac{1}{rank_i}$ where $rank_i$ represents the rank of the first correct code snippet for query i and Q represents all queries. The approach with a higher MRR has a better performance.

Table 2. Comparison against existing approaches

	Proposed approach	PARSEWeb	Google
$p@1$	87%	80%	23.1%
$p@5$	68%	66.3%	30.8%
$p@10$	65%	58.5%	25.8%
$r@1$	76.9%	61.5%	19.2%
$r@5$	84.6%	76.9%	69.2%
$r@10$	84.6%	76.9%	80.8%
MRR	0.825	0.609	0.395

Results. Evaluation results are presented in Table 2. From Table 2, we make the following observations:

- First, the proposed approach is accurate. The precision is 87% when the top 1 results are inspected. Compared to *PARSEWeb* and *Google*, the proposed approach improves the precision by $8.8\% = (87\% - 80\%)/80\%$ and $276.6\% = (87\% - 23.1\%)/23.1\%$, respectively.
- Second, the proposed approach improves recall significantly. Its recall is always greater than that of *PARSEWeb* and *Google*. When the top 1 results are inspected, it improves recall by $25\% = (76.9\% - 61.5\%)/61.5\%$ and $300.5\% = (76.9\% - 19.2\%)/19.2\%$, compared to *PARSEWeb* and *Google* respectively.
- Third, the proposed approach is significantly more effective in ranking resulting code snippets than *PARSEWeb* and *Google*. It improves the MRR by $35.5\% = (0.825 - 0.609)/0.609$ and $108.9\% = (0.825 - 0.395)/0.395$, respectively.

Analysis. To investigate the reasons why the proposed approach has a better performance than the state-of-the-art approach *PARSEWeb*, we look through and compare code snippets retrieved by these two approaches, and we attribute the advantage of the proposed approach to the following two points:

First, the exact type information of Java elements in source code files could be acquired in the proposed approach. Consequently, some correct code snippets whose source instance or target instance is not explicitly denoted could be retrieved, e.g., the assignment (code snippet) *IType type = baseType.getJavaProject().findType(refTypeName, (IProgressMonitor)null);* where an *IType* instance *type* is at the left hand of this assignment and an *IJavaProject* instance *baseType.getJavaProject()* (the return type of this method invocation is *IJavaProject*) is at the right hand of this assignment. Consequently, this code snippet is a solution for the query *<IJavaProject, IType>*. The proposed approach gets the type information through Abstract Syntax Tree, and thus it could acquire exact type information of any Java elements. Consequently, it could retrieve this kind of code snippet. However, *PARSEWeb* gets the type information heuristically and has no idea about the return type of the method invocation *baseType.getJavaProject*(), and thus this code snippet could not be retrieved.

Second, the proposed approach could retrieve complete code snippets. We check the code snippets retrieved by the proposed approach, and observe that all retrieved code snippets are complete. Additionally, due to code slicing and merging are employed in the proposed approach, control statements (e.g., *if*, *for* statements) could be included in the retrieved code snippets. Because of these control statements, the biggest advantage of corresponding code snippets is that they are more ready-to-use. The following code snippet is an example:

```
Iterator iter = selection.iterator();
while(iter.hasNext()){
    Object element = iter.next();
    if(element instanceof IJavaProject){
        project = (IJavaProject) element;
    }else if(element instanceof IPackageFragment){
        IPackageFragmentRoot pf = (IPackageFragmentRoot) element;
        project = pf.getJavaProject();
    }else if(element instanceof ICompilationUnit){
        ICompilationUnit cu = (ICompilationUnit) element;
        project = cu.getJavaProject();
    }else if(element instanceof IProject){
        IProject p = (IProject) element;
        if(p.isOpen() && p.hasNature(JavaCore.NATURE_ID)){
            project = JavaCore.create(p);
        }
    }
}
```

where *selection* is an *IStructuredSelection* instance and *project* is an *IJavaProject* instance.

This code snippet is one of the code snippets retrieved by the proposed approach for the query <*IStructuredSelection, IJavaProject*>. From the code snippet, we observe it has two features. First, it is complete and could be safely reused. It contains several *if/else* statements. These statements guarantee that a target instance (*project* in the example) could be generated under different conditions. Second, it is easy to reuse. Only the name of *selection* or *project* is needed to modify if necessary. Consequently, code snippets containing control statements are more ready-to-use. We also observe that this kind of code snippets account for 30.4%, 37.1%, 32.8% of the top k ($k = 1, 5, 10$) code snippets recommended by the proposed approach, respectively. Whereas, *PARSEWeb* could retrieve method invocation sequences only, and they may be difficult to reuse without needed modification.

4.5   RQ3: Influence of Code Slicing

To reveal the influence of code slicing, we first look through the code snippets (noted as *SlicedSnippets*) retrieved by the proposed approach in Sect. 4.4. After that, for each code snippet in *SlicedSnippets*, we compare it with its corresponding non-sliced snippet which is retrieved by collecting all statements between the source instance and the target instance (inclusive) from source code file. The following code snippet (we call it *SourceSnippet*) is taken as an example to illustrate what we did.

```
1  ASTParser astParser = ASTParser.newParser(AST.JLS8);
2  astParser.setSource(compilationUnit);
3  astPasrser.setKind(ASTParser.K_COMPILATION_UNIT);
4  astPasrser.ResolveBindings(true);
5  Visitor vistor = new Vistor();
6  int relativeNumberOfMethodPairs = 0;
7  int totalNumberOfMethods = mapOfMethodAndAtrributeBinding.size();
8  CompilationUnit unit = (CompilationUnit) (astParser.createAST(null));
```

The code snippet *SourceSnippet* is from a source code file, and *compilationUnit* on Line 2 is an *ICompilationUnit* instance. For a TIR query <*ICompilationUnit, CompilationUnit*>, the source instance *compilationUnit* is on Line 2 and the target instance *unit* is on Line 8. From *SourceSnippet*, code slicing is used in the proposed approach to retrieve code snippet 5# (as presented in Fig. 4). If code slicing is not applied, collecting statements between the source instance *compilationUnit* one Line 2 and the target instance *unit* one Line 8 (inclusive) will result in the code snippet 6# (as presented in Fig. 4).

```
Code Snippet 5#
1 ASTParser astParser = ASTParser.newParser(AST.JLS8);
2 astParser.setSource(compilationUnit);
3 astPasrser.setKind(ASTParser.K_COMPILATION_UNIT);
4 astPasrser.ResolveBindings(true);
8 CompilationUnit unit = (CompilationUnit) (astParser.createAST(null));
   Code Snippet 6#
2 astParser.setSource(compilationUnit);
3 astPasrser.setKind(ASTParser.K_COMPILATION_UNIT);
4 astPasrser.ResolveBindings(true);
5 Visitor vistor = new Vistor();
6 int relativeNumberOfMethodPairs = 0;
7 int totalNumberOfMethods = mapOfMethodAndAtrributeBinding.size();
8 CompilationUnit unit = (CompilationUnit) (astParser.createAST(null));
```

Fig. 4. Sliced and non-sliced code snippets

From code snippet 5# and code snippet 6#, we make the following observations:

Table 3. Influence of ranking

	Default	Disabling *Ranking*	Disabling $C1$	Disabling $C2$
$p@1$	87%	60.9%	60.9%	82.6%
$p@5$	68%	58.8%	60.8%	68%
$p@10$	65%	54.4%	58.3%	59.4%
$r@1$	76.9%	53.8%	53.8%	73.1%
$r@5$	84.6%	76.9%	76.9%	80.7%
$r@10$	84.6%	80.7%	84.6%	84.6%
MRR	0.825	0.629	0.694	0.765

- First, code slicing could remove statements that are useless for the generation of the target instance. The statements on Line 5, 6, 7 in *SourceSnippet* are removed by code slicing (as presented in code snippet 5#). These statements are redundant for the generation of the target instance *unit*.
- Second, code slicing could retrieve additional statements that are related to the generation of other instances besides the target instance. Compared to code snippet 6#, the statement on Line 1 in *SourceSnippet* is retrieved by code slicing (as presented in code snippet 5#). This statement is about the initialization of the *ASTParser* instance *astParser* which is involved in the process of retrieving the target instance *unit* from the source instance *compilationUnit*. This additional statement is necessary. Without this statement, code snippet 5# may not be successfully reused because developers might not know how to retrieve the *ASTParser* instance *astParser*.

We analyze all code snippets in *SlicedSnippets* as the aforementioned process. The results suggest that redundant statements removed by code slicing accounts for 49.6% of all statements in non-sliced *SlicedSnippets*, and additional necessary statements retrieved by code slicing accounts for 55.1% of all statements in *SlicedSnippets*.

4.6   RQ4: Influence of Ranking

As introduced in Sect. 3.6, the proposed approach ranks resulting code snippets (noted as *Ranking*) to present the top ones. The ranking contains two criteria. The first criterion is frequency (noted as $C1$) and the second criterion is Mccabe Cyclomatic Complexity (noted as $C2$). To answer RQ4, we repeat the evaluation for three times. On the first time, we disable the whole *Ranking*. On the last two times, we disable two criteria (i.e., $C1$, $C2$), respectively. Evaluation results are presented in Table 3. From Table 3, we make the following observations:

- First, disabling *Ranking* leads to significant reduction in precision and recall. When the top 1 results are inspected, the reduction is as much as $30\% = (87\% - 60.9\%)/87\%$ for precision and $30\% = (76.9\% - 53.8\%)/76.9\%$ for recall. The evaluation results suggest that *Ranking* is critical for the proposed approach to achieve better performance.

- Second, disabling $C1$ has more influence on the performance of the proposed approach compared to disabling $C2$. It leads to significant reduction in precision and recall. By contrast, disabling $C2$ has little influence on the performance of the proposed approach.

4.7   Threats to Validity

A threat to the external validity is that only one framework JDT is involved in the evaluation and it may be unrepresentative. In order to support other type based instance retrievals, we prepare to involve more applications that are related to other frameworks or libraries. Another threat to the external validity is that the proposed approach is only evaluated on Java applications. Conclusions on Java applications may not hold for applications written in other languages.

A threat to internal validity is that we replace Google Code Search used in the state-of-the-art approach *PARSEWeb* with Search Code because Google Code Search is not available anymore. *PARSEWeb* may achieve better performance by using Google Code Search. Another threat to internal validity is that the manual checking of correctness for recommended code snippets could be inaccurate. Three participants are not familiar with all the recommended code snippets in the evaluation. Consequently, they may make incorrect judgements. To reduce the threat, we select three participants who all have experience in reusing JDT framework (the involved framework in the evaluation).

A threat to construct validity is the uncertainty of the existence of the solution for the requests which are selected for evaluation. We search *Stackoverflow* by keywords and manually identify requests that could be translated into type based instance retrieval queries. However, we have no idea if there really exists a code snippet that could retrieve the target instance from the source instance for a query. Maybe it is impossible to achieve that.

5   Related Work

To the best of our knowledge, *PROSPECTOR* [12] is the first approach for type based instance retrieval. The input of *PROSPECTOR* is a query in the form of $(Tin, Tout)$, where Tin and $Tout$ specify the types of the source instance and target instance, respectively. The output of *PROSPECTOR* is a synthesized code snippet that instantiates a $Tout$ instance via a Tin instance. To synthesize the code snippet, *PROSPECTOR* creates a Jungloid graph according to API method signatures and adds downcast information to the graph according to a corpus of code examples. By traversing the graph from Tin to $Tout$, the approach may find out some paths that connect Tin to $Tout$. Based on such paths, it generates corresponding code snippets that retrieve the expected instance. *XSnippet* proposed by Sahavechaphan and Claypool [17] is the second approach for type based instance retrieval. The input of *XSnippet* is an object instantiation query and the output is all possible code snippets that accomplish the instantiation. To retrieve such code snippets, *XSnippet* creates a source code model for each source code file in a code example repository. After that, it employs a graph based snippet mining algorithm to mine paths that end at the instantiation specified by the given query, and statements on the paths make up code snippets. *PARSEWeb* [20] is the third and latest approach for type based instance retrieval. The input of *PARSEWeb* is a query in the form of '*Source object type -> Destination object type*'. The output of *PARSEWeb* is a set of method invocation sequences that retrieve the destination object type instance from the source object type instance. First, *PARSEWeb* searches for source code files that contain the source object type instances and destination object type instances using Google Code Search Engine. Second, it conducts a static analysis on the files to extract method invocation sequences that could retrieve the destination object from source object. All such approaches have significantly facilitated type based instance retrieval. The proposed approach differs from such approaches for the following two points. First, the proposed approach employs code slicing to include control statements into the retrieved code snippets while existing approaches fail. Second, the merging process in the proposed approach makes the resulting code snippets more complete which could handle various cases for the generation of the target instance.

Code search is applied to search for existing code snippets to reuse [6, 7, 21]. There exists a number of researches about code search. *Sourcerer* [1] is a search engine for open source code. It uses structural information from open source code to make fine-grained code search. *Portfolio* [14] is a code search system that retrieves and visualizes relevant functions and their usages. *CodeHow* [11] finds potential APIs related to the query by looking through descriptions and online documents of APIs to expand the query. *PRIME* [15] takes partial programs as input and outputs semantic relevant code snippets based on type state. *DeepAPI* [5] uses a neural language model called RNN Encoder-Decoder to generate API usage sequences for a given natural language query. *FACOY* [10] is a code-to-code search engine to statically find code fragments which may be semantically similar to user input code with a query alternation strategy. All such approaches significantly facilitate code search. However, they can not retrieve type based instance retrieval code snippets directly.

6   Conclusion

In this paper, we validate that type based instance retrieval code snippets are popular. We also propose an accurate and effective approach to retrieve these code snippets. The proposed approach employs code slicing to extract relevant statements (including complex control statements) that are related to the generation of the target instance. To retrieve complete code snippets, we also merge extracted code snippets whose corresponding target instances are at parallel execution paths. The proposed approach has been evaluated on twenty-six real type based instance retrieval queries. Evaluation results suggest that compared to the state-of-the-art approaches, the proposed approach improves both precision and recall.

Acknowledgments. The work is supported by the National Key Research and Development Program of China (2016YFB1000801), and the National Natural Science Foundation of China (61690205, 61772071).

References

1. Bajracharya, S., et al.: Sourcerer: a search engine for open source code supporting structure-based search. In: Companion to the 21st ACM SIGPLAN Symposium on Object-Oriented Programming Systems, Languages, and Applications, pp. 681–682. ACM (2006)
2. D'Anjou, J., Fairbrother, S., Kehn, D., Kellerman, J., McCarthy, P.: The Java Developer's Guide to Eclipse. Addison-Wesley Professional, Boston (2005)
3. Drori, O.: Algorithm for documents ranking: idea and simulation results. In: Proceedings of the 14th International Conference on Software Engineering and Knowledge Engineering, pp. 99–102. ACM (2002)
4. Grechanik, M., Fu, C., Xie, Q., McMillan, C., Poshyvanyk, D., Cumby, C.: A search engine for finding highly relevant applications. In: Proceedings of the 32nd ACM/IEEE International Conference on Software Engineering, pp. 475–484. ACM (2010)
5. Gu, X., Zhang, H., Zhang, D., Kim, S.: Deep API learning. In: Proceedings of the 2016 24th ACM SIGSOFT International Symposium on Foundations of Software Engineering, pp. 631–642. ACM (2016)
6. Henninger, S.: Retrieving software objects in an example-based programming environment. In: Proceedings of the 14th Annual International ACM SIGIR Conference on Research and Development in Information Retrieval, pp. 251–260. ACM (1991)
7. Holmes, R., Murphy, G.C.: Using structural context to recommend source code examples. In: Proceedings of the 27th International Conference on Software Engineering, pp. 117–125. IEEE (2005)
8. Hucka, M., Graham, M.J.: Software search is not a science, even among scientists. arXiv preprint arXiv:1605.02265 (2016)
9. Jaskowski, W., Krawiec, K., Wieloch, B.: Multi-task code reuse in genetic programming. In: Proceedings of the 10th Annual Conference Companion on Genetic and Evolutionary Computation, pp. 2159–2164. ACM (2008)
10. Kim, K., et al.: FaCoY: a code-to-code search engine. In: Proceedings of the 40th International Conference on Software Engineering, pp. 946–957. ACM (2018)
11. Lv, F., Zhang, H., Lou, J.G., Wang, S., Zhang, D., Zhao, J.: CodeHow: effective code search based on API understanding and extended boolean model (e). In: Proceedings of the 30th IEEE/ACM International Conference on Automated Software Engineering, pp. 260–270. IEEE (2015)
12. Mandelin, D., Xu, L., Bodík, R., Kimelman, D.: Jungloid mining: helping to navigate the API jungle. In: ACM SIGPLAN Notices, vol. 40, pp. 48–61. ACM (2005)
13. Mccabe, T.J.: A Complexity Measure. IEEE Press, Piscataway (1976)
14. McMillan, C., Grechanik, M., Poshyvanyk, D., Xie, Q., Fu, C.: Portfolio: finding relevant functions and their usage. In: Proceedings of the 33rd International Conference on Software Engineering, pp. 111–120. ACM (2011)
15. Mishne, A., Shoham, S., Yahav, E.: Typestate-based semantic code search over partial programs. In: ACM SIGPLAN Notices, vol. 47, pp. 997–1016. ACM (2012)
16. Rahman, M.M., et al.: Evaluating how developers use general-purpose web-search for code retrieval. In: Proceedings of the 15th International Conference on Mining Software Repositories, pp. 465–475. ACM (2018)

17. Sahavechaphan, N., Claypool, K.: XSnippet: mining for sample code. In: ACM SIGPLAN Notices, vol. 41, pp. 413–430. ACM (2006)
18. Sim, S.E., Umarji, M., Ratanotayanon, S., Lopes, C.V.: How well do search engines support code retrieval on the web? ACM Trans. Softw. Eng. Methodol. (TOSEM) **21**(1), 4 (2011)
19. Stolee, K.T., Elbaum, S., Dobos, D.: Solving the search for source code. ACM Trans. Softw. Eng. Methodol. (TOSEM) **23**(3), 26 (2014)
20. Thummalapenta, S., Xie, T.: Parseweb: a programmer assistant for reusing open source code on the web. In: Proceedings of the 22nd IEEE/ACM International Conference on Automated Software Engineering, pp. 204–213. ACM (2007)
21. Ye, Y., Fischer, G.: Supporting reuse by delivering task-relevant and personalized information. In: Proceedings of the 24th International Conference on Software Engineering, pp. 513–523. ACM (2002)

NLI2Code: Reusing Libraries
with Natural Language Interface

Qi Shen[1,2], Bing Xie[1,2]([✉]), Yanzhen Zou[1,2], Zixiao Zhu[1,2], and Shijun Wu[1,2]

[1] Key Laboratory of High Confidence Software Technologies, Ministry of Education,
Beijing 100871, China
[2] School of Electronics Engineering and Computer Science, Peking University,
Beijing 100871, China
{shenqi16,xiebing,zouyz,zhuzixiao,wushijun}@pku.edu.cn

Abstract. Modern software development typically involves composing functionality by reusing existing libraries. This task is difficult due to the gap of abstraction levels between user tasks and APIs. In this paper we propose a new concept *LibNLI* (Library Natural Language Interface) to bridge the gap. LibNLI is a domain-specific language encapsulating APIs into library functions, which is more high-level and instructive than library APIs. In LibNLI, user can reuse libraries with the description of the current programming task. We design an abstract framework *NLI2Code* to illustrate how to build and use LibNLI.

The framework combines three components: functional feature summarizes functionality of a library, code pattern maps each functional feature to its implementation, synthesizer creates local variables to complete code patterns into well-typed snippets. The main goal of NLI2Code is to show feasibility of reusing libraries with natural language interface and lay out the design space to motivate further related research.

We have performed a preliminary evaluation by instantiating this framework in a tool *NLI4j* to reuse Java libraries. The results affirm its capability to summarize accurate functional features and synthesize correct implementation. LibNLI for the evaluated libraries is published.

Keywords: Library reuse · Code pattern · Program synthesis

1 Introduction

Developers often reuse existing libraries to implement certain functionality. Useful libraries typically evolve into complex application programming interfaces (APIs). When faced with a programming task, developers need to learn related APIs and invoke them in certain usage pattern. However, a popular library could contain hundreds or even thousands of APIs, learning them can be difficult [27]. A field study [28] found that a huge obstacle for API users is to discover the subset of the APIs for certain functionality.

We address the main challenge for library reusing problem is the gap of abstraction levels between user tasks and APIs. The gap comes in two ways. On

© Springer Nature Switzerland AG 2019
X. Peng et al. (Eds.): ICSR 2019, LNCS 11602, pp. 168–184, 2019.
https://doi.org/10.1007/978-3-030-22888-0_12

one hand, APIs contain many implementation details while user tasks are usually high-level. A real-world task usually requires cooperation of multiple APIs. On the other hand, API functionalities might not be implemented as user supposed to be [28]. When lack of enough background knowledge, users need extra time and effort to learn the related APIs. Even for a simple task like *set color for an Excel cell*, the implementation requires invoking five API calls in sequence:

$$Workbook.createCellStyle();$$
$$CellStyle.setFillBackgroundColor(short);$$
$$CellStyle.setFillForegroundColor(short);$$
$$CellStyle.setFillPattern(FillPatternType);$$
$$Cell.setCellStyle(CellStyle);$$

To bridge the gap, libraries usually provide documentation to help user understand APIs. However, many libraries are not well documented [32]. In a survey conducted by Microsoft, 67.6% respondents mentioned that there are obstacles caused by inadequate or absent resources for learning APIs [27]. Besides, many official documents, such as user tutorials, are prepared for learning the library in detail, rather than seeking information with specific goals.

There are two main ideas to help developers reuse libraries. The first one works by organizing library functions with high-level specifications, which help developers rapidly understand the library. Treude et al. [30] defines *tasks* as verbs associated with a direct object and/or a prepositional phrase, such as *get iterator, get iterator for collection*. Tasks directly reflect the developers' reuse requirements, indexing a library at the task level would narrow the gap in library reuse and provide API guide in a more understandable and fast-to-learning manner. However, most of existing tools [5,29,31] for task generation are designed to give developers an overview of library functionality like a tutorial or FAQ, which did not build traceability between tasks and concrete code. Users can quickly locate related functionality with the tasks but they still need to manually implement the code. The second solution is automatic programming technique like program synthesis [12]. Such techniques [8,19,25,26] diverse in input and output form, we focus on those transforming natural language queries to code invoking large-scale library APIs. Existing synthesis tools can recommend related APIs and their usage patterns for a given natural language query. However, natural language is vague and improper for validation compared to other forms of input (e.g. input/output pairs, partial programs). A universal problem for existing synthesis tools based on natural language is the validation for the generated programs, they can only recommend the most likely program for a given query.

In this paper, we present an abstract framework *NLI2Code* for library reusing problem. As Fig. 1 shows, the framework builds a natural language interface (LibNLI) for user to describe their programming tasks and synthesizes well-typed code implementation. NLI2Code combines three components: *Functional feature* concludes common functions of a library. A functional feature is a brief description of library function, which is in the form of verb phrase. e.g. *set color*

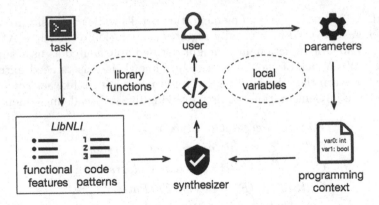

Fig. 1. NLI2Code framework

for an Excel cell. In LibNLI, user can literally compose an identified functional feature to describe a programming task. *Code pattern* builds traceability between functional features with the corresponding code implementation. The traceability plays the role of an interpreter for LibNLI, which interprets functional features to concrete code. *Synthesizer* is supposed to complete code patterns with local variables. Consider the functional feature *set color for an Excel cell*, it did not specify the color or the cell to operate. These missing variables could come from current programming context or provided by user as parameters. Finally, NLI2Code generates well-typed code snippets for user to reuse library functions.

The main contributions of this paper are:

- the concept of *LibNLI* to bridge the gap between user tasks and APIs.
- an abstract framework *NLI2Code* build and use LibNLI, which consists of three sub-components: functional feature, code pattern and synthesizer.
- an implementation for the abstract framework for reusing Java libraries, with evaluation on two libraries to prove feasibility of NLI2Code.

2   Framework

2.1   Overview

We first give an overview of NLI2Code from the perspective of a user. The framework is designed to build a domain-specific language LibNLI for a given library. Based on the programming language of the library, LibNLI extends its grammar with functional features. Each functional feature is a brief description of certain library function. Figure 2 displays the example of using LibNLI for Apache POI, a java library processing Microsoft documents. To set color for an Excel cell, user only need to compose the functional feature *set cell color*. The feature is then mapped to the corresponding code pattern, which requires nine local variables. Our synthesizer captures six of them from the current context

```
public class Main {
    public static void main(string[] args) {
        Workbook workbook = new HSSFWorkbook();
        Cell cell = workbook.createSheet().createRow(0).createCell(0);
        set cell
    }                set cell alignment   (Statement in jetbrains.mps.baseLanguage)
}                    set cell borders     (Statement in jetbrains.mps.baseLanguage)
                     set cell color       (Statement in jetbrains.mps.baseLanguage)
                     set cell font        (Statement in jetbrains.mps.baseLanguage)
```

(a) User can type the functional feature *set cell color* in LibNLI

```
public class Main {
    public static void main(string[] args) {
        Workbook workbook = new HSSFWorkbook();
        Cell cell = workbook.createSheet().createRow(0).createCell(0);
        set color for cell cell {
            background color: <IndexedColors.RED.getIndex()>
            foreground color: <IndexedColors.RED.getIndex()>
            pattern: <FillPatternType.BIG_SPOTS>
        }
    }
}
```

(b) The code pattern exposes three parameters for user to specify

```
public class Main {
    public static void main(String[] args) {
        Workbook wb = new HSSFWorkbook();
        Cell cell = wb.createSheet().createRow( i 0).createCell( i 0);
        CellStyle style = wb.createCellStyle();
        style.setFillBackgroundColor(IndexedColors.RED.getIndex());
        style.setFillForegroundColor(IndexedColors.RED.getIndex());
        style.setFillPattern(FillPatternType.BIG_SPOTS);
        cell.setCellStyle(style);
    }
}
```

(c) The synthesized code snippet for the functional feature

Fig. 2. Example usage of LibNLI for Apache POI

and exposes the rest three ones to user with hint in grey characters. After user fills the parameters, a well-typed snippet will be generated.

In NLI2Code, functional features provide natural language aliases for library functions, code patterns map them to concrete implementation and synthesizer completes the patterns by filling local variables. In the rest of this section, we discuss three key issues in NLI2Code.

2.2   Functional Feature Extraction

Extracting functional features in a library is the first step to build LibNLI. Functional feature is the description of a library function in verb phrase form. Open-source libraries typically have multiple types of software documents, such as mailing lists, issue tracker system and online forums like Stack Overflow. These documents are the natural corpus to extract functional features because they contain rich information of how library functions are used. Figure 3 is a Stack

Overflow post, it mentioned the functional feature *set an Excel cell background color* in Apache POI. All verb phrases from library documents are considered as candidate functional features, which need to be refined due to noises and ambiguity in natural language. We issue two challenges to get usable functional features: (1) Noises. Phrases like *want to* and *try many things* in Fig. 3 are unrelated to library functionality and have little semantic information, which should be pruned off. (2) Ambiguity. There are many ways to express the same library function. Such verb phrases of the same meaning should be clustered and normalized, e.g. *set an Excel cell color* and *set the color of an Excel cell*.

The extracted functional features are supposed to satisfy two properties:

- Accurate: Each feature should clearly corresponds to certain library function and describes the usage of one or more APIs.
- Complete: The complete set of functional features should cover library functions as much as possible.

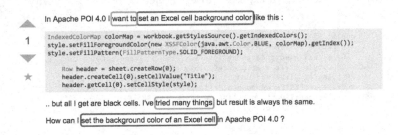

Fig. 3. Verb phrases in a Stack Overflow post

2.3   Code Pattern Mining

After extracting functional features of a library, the role of code pattern mining is to match each feature with the corresponding implementation. A code pattern describes that in a certain usage scenario, some API methods are frequently called together and their usages follow some sequential rules [33]. The technique of code pattern mining is widely used in many automatic programming tools [20,25], which follows a common procedure: (1) construct a code corpus, (2) abstract code into certain data structure (e.g. call sequence [25], abstract syntax tree [4], data flow graph [21]), (3) apply corresponding frequent pattern mining algorithm on the corpus and finally transform the frequent items back to code.

For corpus construction phase in NLI2Code, user can feed extracted functional features to any code search tools [16] to find related code. We want to mention that functional features are extracted from library documents, which tend to have nature traceability to their implementation. For example, suppose functional features are extracted from Stack Overflow posts, then code snippets in the accepted answers will be helpful in corpus construction. For the latter two phases, NLI2Code does not enforce any concrete data structure for code abstraction. User could choose the data structure that fits best to their problem and apply the corresponding frequent pattern mining algorithm (e.g. PrefixSpan or BIDE for sequence structure, gSpan for graph structure).

The mined code patterns are only supposed to be frequently-used, which do not guarantee to implement the functional feature. We address validation for the code patterns because:

- NLI2Code is not designed to recommend possible solutions. The generated code should solve user tasks for sure.
- Each code pattern in NLI2Code corresponds to a functional feature. The amount of functional features in a library is limited, which is feasible for high-cost validation.

2.4 Synthesizer

Code patterns are incomplete because they usually miss local variables. Some of them can be synthesized from the current context while others need to be specified by user. Existing Integrated Development Environments (IDEs) provide simple code completion functionality. Two popular Java IDEs, Eclipse [1] and IntelliJ [2] recommend methods applicable to an object, and allow the developer to fill in additional method arguments. Such completion typically considers one step of computation but it is common to create an object with a sequence of method calls and each method call may require new variables as parameters. For example, suppose there is an object with type *Workbook*, you can invoke the following methods to get a *Cell* object: *Workbook.createSheet().createRow(x).createCell(y)*. In the process of creating the object for *Cell*, another two variables x and y are needed to specify the index of row and column. These efforts suggest a general direction for code completion in NLI2Code: introduce the ability to synthesize entire type-correct code fragments for a given type T and a type environment Γ (a map from identifiers to their types). Formally, find e such that $\Gamma \vdash e : T$.

There are two main ideas behind related research. The first one [14,23] is based on type-directed search. A direct solution for expression synthesis is to enumerate all possible expressions that return the desired type, which could start from ASTs with depth 1 and gradually extend the depth. Two key issues in type-directed search are: (1) a heuristic function to guide the search and rank the output expressions, (2) the search algorithm. Search strategies like beamer search and stochastic search are also proper choices besides enumerative search. The second idea [11,17,24] recommends expressions according to statistical analysis of the large code corpus, represented by probabilistic models like neural networks. Suppose we need a variable of type T, 50% files in the corpus create the object by the constructor function of T, other 40% files invoke certain method with return type of T. Then presenting the two expressions to user would be helpful.

Sometimes, the users themselves do not imagine the full scope of their intent until they begin an interaction with a programmer or a program synthesis system

[12]. Thus, real-world program synthesis is much a human-computer interaction (HCI) problem as an algorithmic one. NLI2Code recommends some HCI-related technique like [10] to cooperate with two ideas above.

3   Implementation

To understand the potential and feasibility of this framework, we instantiate NLI2Code as a tool *NLI4j* for reusing Java libraries. Following the framework, NLI4j consists of three sub-tools:

- a functional feature extractor to extract library functions from Stack Overflow posts tagged with the library name
- a code pattern miner to mine code patterns for each functional feature
- a synthesizer to complete code patterns with local variables

At last, we combined output of the three tools and manually composed LibNLI using Jetbrains MPS [3].

3.1   Functional Feature Extractor

Figure 4 demonstrates our approach to extract functional features. First, we use natural language processing techniques to parse Stack Overflow posts and extract verb phrases from the syntax tree. A filtering pipeline is used for filtering noises in candidate verb phrases. We normalize the phrases and convert them into graphs. The recognized gSpan [34] algorithm is applied to mine frequent subgraphs. Finally, we rebuild phrases from subgraphs as functional features. We will not discuss all the steps in detail considering this is only one possible solution under our framework. Instead, we illustrate how our implementation solves the two challenges mentioned in Sect. 2.2.

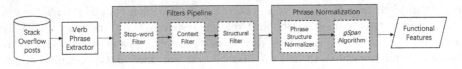

Fig. 4. The process of extracting functional features

Filtering Pipeline. The filtering pipeline consists of three rule-based phrase filters. If a phrase matches the rule of a filter, one piece of evidence will be added to the phrase. A piece of evidence might be counted as one vote up or one vote down or veto to accept the phrase. Then we collect all the evidence added to a phrase and count the vote. Intuitively, we remove a phrase when the up votes are less than the down votes.

The first filter is based on a handcrafting stop-word list. We downvote three types of verb phrases because they are not likely to appear in a meaningful functional feature: (1) special grammatical ingredients: auxiliary verbs (including be, do, have), modal verbs (can, may, must, should,...) and pronouns (it, this, that, them, me) usually do not have actual meanings. (2) Q&A special words. The sentences from Stack Overflow often contain trivial words for describing the questioners' requirements. e.g. ask, try, want. (3) Programming special terms. Some programming terms, keywords in programs, or development special words are usually not part of valid functional feature, such as extend, return and stack trace.

The second filter judge the phrases based on information from the context. Though the phrases containing Q&A special expressions are considered invalid, the phrases following some special Q&A expressions could be a good candidate. We upvote verb phrases behind such preceding expressions because they are very likely to refer to the functional features.

The third filter is based on structure of the phrase in the syntax tree. We use syntactic structure characteristics to filter out some invalid verb phrases. There are usually some complex sub-clauses in the noun phrase or prepositional phrases of the parse tree. We hope to keep our generated features as concise as possible, therefore we remove the most sub-clauses except for those modifying the phrase with some pre/post-conditions. Another important purpose of filtering parse tree structures is to get the candidate phrases ready for graph-based clustering. We later transform the phrases into the normal form. The structural filter ensures the phrase candidates are compatible with the normal form.

Phrase Normalization. In order to cluster verb phrases with similar meaning, we: (1) define the normal form of feature phrases (formalization definition in Table 1), (2) transform phrases from the original parse trees to graphs of normalized form, (3) employ gSpan algorithm to mine frequent subgraphs.

Table 1. The normal form of feature phrases

Feature	::= Action Object Condition
Action	::= verb [particle]
Object	::= dt adj noun noun
Condition	::= prep [verb] Object

The normal form is necessary for the accuracy of graph mining. Figure 5 explains the reason. Figure 5(a) is the parse tree of the verb phrase *set the print area*. Figure 5(b) depicts another candidate phrase *set up the print areas for the excel file*. The original parse trees contain many detailed grammatical ingredients, which prevent us from mining valuable common subgraphs. As shown in the graphs, the two largest common subgraphs between graph (a) and graph (b) are (VP (VB set) (NP)) (in red color and bold font) and (NP (DT the)

(NN print)) (in blue color and underscored), which are meaningless. In contrast, the normalized trees (c) and (d), which omit unnecessary details like POS tags, and unify the structures of the top layers, show us a reasonable result.

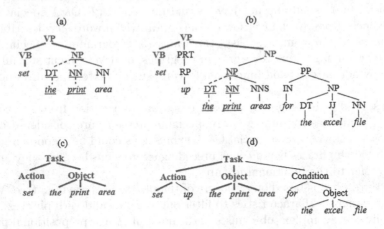

Fig. 5. Comparison between parse tree and normalized tree in mining frequent subtrees (Color figure online)

3.2 Code Pattern Miner

We download all client code repositories of the reused library from Github by searching the library name. e.g. Apache POI. For each functional feature, we build a corpus for mining code patterns. The corpus construction takes two phases. In the first phase, the functional feature is mapped to an API. Many tools can help locate related APIs for a given natural language statement [15]. In our implementation, all library API names are splitted according to the CamelCase rule. We count the number of common words between the splitting result of each API and the functional feature. We only keep the APIs with the maximum number of common words. If multiple APIs have the same number, we break the tie with the co-occurrence times of the API and the feature in Stack Overflow posts. Recall that our functional features are extracted from Stack Overflow posts, it is easy to recover the posts they come from. After the first phase, we get an API which is frequently used and lexically similar to the functional feature. Given an API of interest, the second phase scans and parses all the methods in the client code repositories. If a method invokes the API we concerned, it will be added to the corpus for the functional feature.

After constructing the corpus for a functional feature, we extract the sequence of API calls for each method in the corpus. At last, we apply the PrefixSpan [22] algorithm to mine the most frequent closed sub-sequences as the code pattern. A pattern is closed if there is no super-pattern with the same frequency.

3.3 Synthesizer

We implemented a search-based synthesis tool to complete code patterns in NLI4j. A graph model is built to define search space, which organizes APIs of the reused library. Tables 2 and 3 display schema of the graph.

Table 2. Node types of CAG

Node type	Description	Properties
Class	A Java class	name, comment
Interface	A Java interface	name, super interface name, comment
Method	A Member method	name, parameter list, static or not

Table 3. Edge types of CAG

Edge type	From	To	Description
haveMethod	Class/interface	Method	A class/interface to its member methods
return	Method	Class/interface	A method to its return type
implement	Class/interface	Interface	A class/interface to interfaces it implements
extend	Class/interface	Class/interface	Inheritance between classes/interfaces

The synthesis problem can be stated as: given a programming context, how to create a variable with certain type τ. There are three strategies:

- pick a variable of τ from context
- call the constructor function of τ
- start from a variable in context, invoke several methods in sequence, return type of the last one is τ.

The last strategy is a search process on our graph model. To be more specific, we explain one step of the search in detail. Suppose the current variable we visit has type ϕ and the desired type is τ. We pick the class node for ϕ in the graph and get all edges with type *haveMethod* from the node. Target nodes of theses edge form a set S, each element is a method. If any method from S returns type τ, which means an edge with type *return* starts from the member and ends with class node τ, the search ends and we successfully synthesize the variable with type τ. Otherwise, the search continues until it reaches the desired type or comes to the limit for search depth.

We define a cost model as the heuristic rule to guide the search process. The model evaluates goodness of different ways for variable creation by mapping them to integers. Using existing variables in context is encouraged, with zero cost. If there are multiple variables with the same type, we choose the one created most recently due to software localness. If a variable is the return value of certain method, it costs 2 when the method is a constructor and 1 for else. Empirically, avoiding frequent constructor functions can synthesize snippets with higher quality. The process for variable synthesis could be recursive, which means in the process of synthesizing the current variable, the invocations require parameters not in the context. Our cost model adds the costs for synthesizing these parameters as well.

Finally, we sum up cost for creating all variables in a code pattern as the total cost. The synthesized snippets are ranked by their total costs and the one with the smallest cost is returned to user.

4   Preliminary Evaluation

We have performed a preliminary evaluation of NLI4j on two open-source Java libraries. The implemented LibNLI for the two libraries is published[1]. We investigate the following two research questions:

- **RQ1: Are the generated functional features accurate and complete?**
- **RQ2: How many functional features can be mapped to their implementation?**

The first research question is concerned with the accuracy and completeness of the extracted functional features. The second research question reveals the quality of our mined code patterns and performance of the synthesizer.

4.1   Experiment Design

In our evaluation, we use two open-source Java libraries as the subjects: JFreeChart and Apache POI. JFreeChart is a Java chart library for data presenting. Apache POI manipulates the Microsoft documents.

We manually create a list of library functions and their implementation as benchmarks. The process of creating the benchmarks for library functions is as follows. The participants are provided with all the available documents, including JavaDoc, user tutorials, quick guide, FAQ, etc. Each library is annotated by two participants who are familiar with the library. They are requested to extract function-like phrases mentioned in the documents. They are told to classify the functions into higher-level categories if possible. The two annotators for a library create the function list separately. Afterwards they discuss with each other to reach an agreement on the benchmark. At last, we identified 59 functions for JfreeChart and 50 for Apache POI and we manually implemented each of them using the library APIs.

We use our NLI4j tool to generate the function features and corresponding implementation. We clarify the data for our experiment here. The source code are downloaded from official site and the Stack Overflow threads are parsed from

---

[1] https://github.com/Wusjn/MPS-Projects.

the official data dump. The corpus of code pattern mining is built from client code repositories from Github. We collect all repositories with at least 2 stars in the Github search result. The number of repositories is 42 for JfreeChart and 60 for Apache POI.

4.2   RQ1-Functional Feature Accuracy and Completeness

Metrics. Given a library, we ask the two annotators to rate our functional features. They are requested to give a score for each feature: two points for an actual library function, one point for a likely function that requires further information to make it clear, zero point for a meaningless phrase. We count all the ratings by annotators and calculate the average score for all the functional features.

Table 4. Accuracy of the generated functional features

Library	#Phrases	# Features	Score			Average score
			2	1	0	
JfreeChart	10126	67	41	22	4	1.55
Apache POI	24226	149	73	61	15	1.39
Total	**34352**	**216**	**114**	**83**	**19**	**1.44**

Table 5. Completeness of the generated functional features

Library	# Functions	Score			Average score
		2	1	0	
JfreeChart	59	25	13	21	1.07
Apache POI	50	21	16	13	1.16
Total	**109**	**46**	**29**	**34**	**1.11**

Results Analysis. Table 4 presents the rating scores of the generated functional features for each subject. The second column depicts the number of extracted verb phrases for each subject. The third column depicts the number of functional features generated by NLI4j. Columns 4–6 depict the number of features rated as two points, one point, and zero point, respectively. Column 7 depicts the average rating score of the functional features. From the total statistics, we observe that 52.8% the features are rated as actual functions of the library. About 8.8% of are rated as meaningless phrases. The other features are rated a middle score.

The average scores show that our functional features get an approximately 1.44 points out of two.

We asked the benchmark annotators to review their handcrafted benchmark function by function, and judge whether the function is included in our generated functional features. For each benchmark function, if it is included in our generated features, our result get two points on this benchmark item. If our result include a similar function but not precise, our result get one point. Otherwise, our result get zero point. Table 5 depicts the rating scores of our results on the benchmark. Our generated functional features earn a full mark on 42.2% of the functions in the benchmark. This performance is not as good as the accuracy aspect. We have found that the functions in the benchmarks are much longer and more detailed than the extracted features. The benchmark functions usually contain a sub-clause that modifies or restricts the function itself. But our generated features are based on the frequent subgraphs, which tend to be more concise.

Table 6. Accuracy of code patterns

Library	# Features	# Features mapped to code	Average Jaccard distance
JfreeChart	38	35	0.11
Apache POI	37	31	0.17
Total	**75**	**66**	**0.14**

Table 7. Analysis of variable synthesis

Library	# Average API	# Average variables	# Average synthesized variables
JfreeChart	2.6	5.8	4.0
Apache POI	3.4	5.1	3.2
Total	**3.0**	**5.5**	**3.6**

4.3 RQ2-Code Implementation Accuracy

For each manual function included in our generated features (functions with two or one point in Table 5), we pick one related functional feature. Totally, there are 38 functions included for JfreeChart and 37 for Apache POI, the number is the sum of column 3 and 4 in Table 5. For each selected functional feature, we manually check the code pattern NLI4j mines for it. The validated code patterns are fed to our synthesizer to complete the missing variables from an empty context.

Table 6 presents the number of functional features mapped to correct code patterns. As column 2 and 3 show, for JfreeChart, NLI4j mines correct code patterns for 35 functional features out of total 38 ones. The number is 31 out of 37 for Apache POI. We manually check the correctness of a code pattern to see whether it can implement the corresponding functional feature. Besides, Column 4 gives a feel about the equivalence between manual code implementation and the mined code patterns. As there is no universal metric to measure program equivalence, we approximate the equivalence by calculating the average *Jaccard distance* between the sets of API calls made by the manual implementation and the mined code patterns. The average Jaccard distance between manual implementation and mined code patterns is 0.14, which proves the mined code patterns are close to our manual implementation.

Table 7 shows performance of our synthesizer on the two evaluated libraries. In our experiment, each code pattern contains 3 APIs on average, which proves that our functional features are more high-level than APIs. Each API call requires several local variables for its caller and parameters. We ask NLI4j to synthesize an expression for each local variable. On average, there are 5.5 variables to synthesize in each code pattern. We manually judge the synthesized result to check whether the variables are created correctly. A variable is considered to be correctly created if the synthesized expression is meaningful and we can find such usage in real-world client code. On average, our synthesizer can correctly create 3.6 variables for a code pattern out of total 5.5 ones. There are mainly two reasons for failed variable synthesis. The first one is that the local variable should be specified by user, e.g. a specific file name. The second reason is that the correct expression requires APIs from JDK, which is out of knowledge for our synthesizer. For the rest variable synthesis, the recommended synthesis results are quite usable, which proves the capability of our heuristic function.

5   Related Work

Several studies [7,31] try to organize library functions with high-level specifications. The concept of *task* defined by Treude et al. [30] offers a new perspective for user to read documents. Indexing documentation with such high-level specifications can help users quickly locate what they need when they have a specific goal. The tool NLP2Code [7] can map tasks to code snippets from Stack Overflow answers. However, its hard to meet the diversity of user requirement with simple copy of existing snippets. Different from such work, NLI2Code emphasizes the process to build the traceability between high-level specifications and concrete code implementation.

Several studies [32,33] apply statistical methods to mine code patterns because code has been shown to be highly repetitive [9]. Such work abstracts source code to certain data structure and then apply frequent pattern mining algorithm. Mining code patterns for functional features is an important part in

NLI2Code. Compared with existing tools, which are designed to solve a particular problem, NLI2Code is designed as an abstract framework, which does not specify the approach to mine code patterns. Existing tools may rely on properties of their problem and cannot be easily generalized to others.

Several studies [18, 20, 25] focus on synthesizing API usages from natural language. Existing synthesis tools can recommend related APIs [13, 35, 36] or compilable snippets [6, 8, 25] for a given natural language query. Some of the tools share a similar workflow with the latter two components in NLI2Code, which first map natural language query to usage patterns and then synthesize local variables. It is difficult to validate generated programs with arbitrary natural language input. Different from existing synthesis tools, NLI2Code first summarizes library functionality into a domain specific language LibNLI and then feeds functional features to our synthesizer. The generated code for each functional feature is validated in NLI2Code.

6   Conclusion

In this paper we have seen the new concept *LibNLI* for reusing libraries. An abstract framework *NLI2Code* is promoted for the construction and usage of LibNLI. From practical perspective, the framework allows user to design an algorithm to promote efficiency for reusing libraries by instantiating the components in the framework. From academic perspective, NLI2Code lays out a design space of building natural language interface for libraries, which would hopefully inspire research in this area.

Acknowledgement. This paper is supported by National Key Research and Development Program of China (Grant No. 2016YFB1000801) and National Natural Science Fund for Distinguished Young Scholars (Grant No. 61525201).

References

1. The Eclipse Foundation. http://www.eclipse.org/
2. IntelliJ IDEA (2019). http://www.jetbrains.com/idea/
3. JetBrains MPS (2019). https://www.jetbrains.com/mps/
4. Allamanis, M., Sutton, C.: Mining idioms from source code. In: Proceedings of the 22nd ACM SIGSOFT International Symposium on Foundations of Software Engineering, pp. 472–483. ACM (2014)
5. Barzilay, O., Treude, C., Zagalsky, A.: Facilitating crowd sourced software engineering via stack overflow. In: Sim, S.E., Gallardo-Valencia, R.E. (eds.) Finding Source Code on the Web for Remix and Reuse, pp. 289–308. Springer, New York (2013). https://doi.org/10.1007/978-1-4614-6596-6_15
6. Buse, R.P., Weimer, W.: Synthesizing API usage examples. In: Proceedings of the 34th International Conference on Software Engineering, pp. 782–792. IEEE Press (2012)
7. Campbell, B.A., Treude, C.: Nlp2Code: code snippet content assist via natural language tasks. In: 2017 IEEE International Conference on Software Maintenance and Evolution (ICSME), pp. 628–632. IEEE (2017)

8. Feng, Y., Martins, R., Wang, Y., Dillig, I., Reps, T.W.: Component-based synthesis for complex apis. ACM SIGPLAN Not. **52**(1), 599–612 (2017)
9. Gabel, M., Su, Z.: A study of the uniqueness of source code. In: Proceedings of the Eighteenth ACM SIGSOFT International Symposium on Foundations of Software Engineering, pp. 147–156. ACM (2010)
10. Galenson, J., Reames, P., Bodik, R., Hartmann, B., Sen, K.: CodeHint: dynamic and interactive synthesis of code snippets. In: Proceedings of the 36th International Conference on Software Engineering, pp. 653–663. ACM (2014)
11. Gu, X., Zhang, H., Zhang, D., Kim, S.: Deep API learning. In: Proceedings of the 2016 24th ACM SIGSOFT International Symposium on Foundations of Software Engineering, pp. 631–642. ACM (2016)
12. Gulwani, S., Polozov, O., Singh, R., et al.: Program synthesis. Found. Trends® Program. Lang. **4**(1–2), 1–119 (2017)
13. Gvero, T., Kuncak, V.: Synthesizing java expressions from free-form queries. ACM SIGPLAN Not. **50**, 416–432 (2015)
14. Gvero, T., Kuncak, V., Kuraj, I., Piskac, R.: Complete completion using types and weights. ACM SIGPLAN Not. **48**, 27–38 (2013)
15. Huang, Q., Xia, X., Xing, Z., Lo, D., Wang, X.: API method recommendation without worrying about the task-API knowledge gap. In: Proceedings of the 33rd ACM/IEEE International Conference on Automated Software Engineering, pp. 293–304. ACM (2018)
16. Jiang, H., Zhang, J., Ren, Z., Zhang, T.: An unsupervised approach for discovering relevant tutorial fragments for APIs. In: Proceedings of the 39th International Conference on Software Engineering, pp. 38–48. IEEE Press (2017)
17. Li, J., Wang, Y., Lyu, M.R., King, I.: Code completion with neural attention and pointer networks. arXiv preprint arXiv:1711.09573 (2017)
18. Little, G., Miller, R.C.: Keyword programming in Java. Autom. Softw. Eng. **16**(1), 37 (2009)
19. Loncaric, C., Ernst, M.D., Torlak, E.: Generalized data structure synthesis. In: 2018 IEEE/ACM 40th International Conference on Software Engineering (ICSE), pp. 958–968. IEEE (2018)
20. Nguyen, T., Rigby, P.C., Nguyen, A.T., Karanfil, M., Nguyen, T.N.: T2API: synthesizing API code usage templates from English texts with statistical translation. In: Proceedings of the 2016 24th ACM SIGSOFT International Symposium on Foundations of Software Engineering, pp. 1013–1017. ACM (2016)
21. Nguyen, T.T., Nguyen, H.A., Pham, N.H., Al-Kofahi, J.M., Nguyen, T.N.: Graph-based mining of multiple object usage patterns. In: Proceedings of the the the 7th Joint Meeting of the European Software Engineering Conference and the ACM SIGSOFT Symposium on the Foundations of Software Engineering, pp. 383–392. ACM (2009)
22. Pel, J., et al.: PrefixSpan: mining sequential patterns by prefix-projected growth. In: Proceedings of 17th IEEE International Conference on Data Engineering (ICDE), Heidelberg, Germany, pp. 215–224 (2001)
23. Perelman, D., Gulwani, S., Ball, T., Grossman, D.: Type-directed completion of partial expressions. ACM SIGPLAN Not. **47**, 275–286 (2012)
24. Rabinovich, M., Stern, M., Klein, D.: Abstract syntax networks for code generation and semantic parsing. arXiv preprint arXiv:1704.07535 (2017)
25. Raghothaman, M., Wei, Y., Hamadi, Y.: Swim: synthesizing what i mean-code search and idiomatic snippet synthesis. In: 2016 IEEE/ACM 38th International Conference on Software Engineering (ICSE), pp. 357–367. IEEE (2016)

26. Raza, M., Gulwani, S., Milic-Frayling, N.: Compositional program synthesis from natural language and examples. In: Twenty-Fourth International Joint Conference on Artificial Intelligence (2015)
27. Robillard, M.P.: What makes APIs hard to learn? Answers from developers. IEEE Softw. **26**(6), 27–34 (2009)
28. Robillard, M.P., Deline, R.: A field study of API learning obstacles. Empirical Softw. Eng. **16**(6), 703–732 (2011)
29. Treude, C., Robillard, M.P.: Augmenting API documentation with insights from stack overflow. In: 2016 IEEE/ACM 38th International Conference on Software Engineering (ICSE), pp. 392–403. IEEE (2016)
30. Treude, C., Robillard, M.P., Dagenais, B.: Extracting development tasks to navigate software documentation. IEEE Trans. Softw. Eng. **41**(6), 565–581 (2015)
31. Treude, C., Sicard, M., Klocke, M., Robillard, M.: TaskNav: task-based navigation of software documentation. In: Proceedings of the 37th International Conference on Software Engineering, vol. 2, pp. 649–652. IEEE Press (2015)
32. Wang, J., Dang, Y., Zhang, H., Chen, K., Xie, T., Zhang, D.: Mining succinct and high-coverage API usage patterns from source code. In: Proceedings of the 10th Working Conference on Mining Software Repositories, pp. 319–328. IEEE Press (2013)
33. Xie, T., Pei, J.: MAPO: mining API usages from open source repositories. In: Proceedings of the 2006 International Workshop on Mining Software Repositories, pp. 54–57. ACM (2006)
34. Yan, X., Han, J.: gSpan: graph-based substructure pattern mining. In: 2002 Proceedings of IEEE International Conference on Data Mining, pp. 721–724. IEEE (2002)
35. Yessenov, K., Kuraj, I., Solar-Lezama, A.: DemoMatch: API discovery from demonstrations. ACM SIGPLAN Not. **52**, 64–78 (2017)
36. Zamanirad, S., Benatallah, B., Barukh, M.C., Casati, F., Rodriguez, C.: Programming bots by synthesizing natural language expressions into API invocations. In: 2017 32nd IEEE/ACM International Conference on Automated Software Engineering (ASE), pp. 832–837. IEEE (2017)

Domain-Specific Software Development

A Double-Edged Sword? Software Reuse and Potential Security Vulnerabilities

Antonios Gkortzis[1](✉) ⓘ, Daniel Feitosa[2] ⓘ, and Diomidis Spinellis[1] ⓘ

[1] Department of Management Science and Technology,
Athens University of Economics and Business, Athens, Greece
{antoniosgkortzis,dds}@aueb.gr
[2] Data Research Centre, University of Groningen, Groningen, The Netherlands
d.feitosa@rug.nl

Abstract. Reuse is a common and often-advocated software development practice. Significant efforts have been invested into facilitating it, leading to advancements such as software forges, package managers, and the widespread integration of open source components into proprietary software systems. Reused software can make a system more secure through its maturity and extended vetting, or increase its vulnerabilities through a larger attack surface or insecure coding practices. To shed more light on this issue, we investigate the relationship between software reuse and potential security vulnerabilities, as assessed through static analysis. We empirically investigated 301 open source projects in a holistic multiple-case methods study. In particular, we examined the distribution of potential vulnerabilities between the native code created by a project's development team and external code reused through dependencies, as well as the correlation between the ratio of reuse and the density of vulnerabilities. The results suggest that the amount of potential vulnerabilities in both native and reused code increases with larger project sizes. We also found a weak-to-moderate correlation between a higher reuse ratio and a lower density of vulnerabilities. Based on these findings it appears that code reuse is neither a frightening werewolf introducing an excessive number of vulnerabilities nor a silver bullet for avoiding them.

Keywords: Software reuse · Security vulnerabilities · Case study

1 Introduction

Code reuse is a widely advocated and adopted practice in software development. A Linux distribution is a great example of software reuse, bundling together several packages to provide the functionality of a modern operating system. In a similar manner, the dominant mobile operating system, Android,[1] is based on a customized Linux kernel and bundles additional open source packages. To

---

[1] https://www.android.com/.

© Springer Nature Switzerland AG 2019
X. Peng et al. (Eds.): ICSR 2019, LNCS 11602, pp. 187–203, 2019.
https://doi.org/10.1007/978-3-030-22888-0_13

develop user applications, the Android platform provides a set of more than 3 million Java libraries from the Maven repository.[2]

Nevertheless, similarly to any other design decision, code reuse has limitations. A prominent side-effect of code reuse is the existence of serious potential security risks. Kula et al. [12] analyzed 4 659 open source software systems and showed that more than 80% of them used outdated external libraries and dependencies, while 69% of the developers they interviewed were unaware of any security risks in their reused code.

As a concrete example, Heartbleed[3] was a severe security vulnerability in the OpenSSL cryptographic software library that allowed any user on the Internet to read arbitrary memory contents. Through this vulnerable version of the library, a malicious user could retrieve secret keys that protected communications, usernames and passwords, personal emails, documents and messages. The bug was detected two years after its introduction in the code. It affected the web servers that were powering 66% of the active web sites at that time [1]. Another, more recent, example is the Equifax incident [2], in which hackers exploited a known vulnerability in a third-party Java library that Equifax knowingly used, and stole personal private information of more than 147 million American citizens. Various initiatives try to battle this problem. GitHub introduced the Security Alert for Vulnerable Dependencies[4] service aiming to increase users' awareness and mitigate the potential security risks. Similarly, any Linux or BSD system by default notifies users for available security updates in vulnerable versions of installed packages and system libraries.

Despite the existence of well-known security mishaps due to software reuse, to the best of our knowledge there is a lack of large-scale studies that investigate how security vulnerabilities are associated with code reuse in software systems. This paper aims to contribute towards this direction by analyzing a large set of open source software systems and comparing the levels of vulnerabilities between the native application source code written by the software development team and external source code introduced through dependencies on third-party libraries. To achieve this, we collected a set of 301 Java projects and compared the native and reused parts of the code with regards to potential security vulnerabilities, which were detected based on static analysis.

The analysis of the produced data revealed a weak-to-moderate inverse correlation between the code reuse ratio and the vulnerability density in open source software systems. This means that software systems with higher reuse ratio tend to have fewer potential vulnerabilities compared to projects where native code is dominant. The main contribution of our work is that, although we observed that the amount of potential vulnerabilities in both native and reused code increases with larger project sizes, a higher reuse ratio is associated with a lower vulnerability density. Additionally, we contribute: (a) the construction process of

---

[2] https://mvnrepository.com/repos/central.

[3] https://nvd.nist.gov/vuln/detail/CVE-2014-0160.

[4] https://help.github.com/articles/about-security-alerts-for-vulnerable-dependencies/.

a dataset that correlates the software reuse ratio of open source Java projects with their potential security vulnerabilities, (b) the aforementioned dataset per se, and (c) a statistical analysis of this dataset. The source code to reproduce the process is available on GitHub[5] and the dataset on Zenodo.[6]

The remainder of the paper is organized as follows. Section 2 presents the related work. Section 3 describes the approach of our study regarding the dataset construction and the analysis tools. Section 4 presents our findings, which we further discuss in Sect. 5. Section 6 presents the limitations of our study and Sect. 7 our conclusions.

2 Related Work

In this section, we present related work. We note that since we could not identify studies that are directly related to ours, we broadened the scope of this section to describe efforts dealing with software defects and vulnerabilities in reused code.

Pashchenko et al. [19] conducted a study on the SAP software ecosystem, investigating how much of the reused code in SAP is affected by known vulnerabilities. The authors, similarly to our study, analyzed the top 200 open source Maven systems that SAP is reusing. Thus, their study is not affected by false positives. However, the nonexistence of known vulnerabilities does not guarantee the absence of any other undetected vulnerabilities. The authors reported that 13% of the direct and transitive libraries that were reused were affected by at least one known vulnerability. In their analysis they excluded none-deployed dependencies (e.g., test dependencies). Regarding vulnerable dependencies Neuhaus et al. [18] investigated the Red Hat Linux (RHEL) distribution and provided empirical evidence that certain packages are correlated to system vulnerabilities.

Shin et al. [23] studied that three software metrics, i.e., complexity, code churn and developer activity, can be used in order to create a prediction model for potentially vulnerable code chunks in RHEL kernel and in Mozilla Firefox. Similarly, Meneely et al. [14] investigated the RHEL kernel and provided empirical evidence that show files modified by more than nine developers or files maintained by independent developer groups are more likely to have vulnerable code compared to files developed by the main core or smaller groups.

Mohagheghi et al. [16] studied historical data of software defects for 12 consequent releases of a large-scale telecom system developed by Ericsson. Their goal was to investigate the impact of reuse on the defect density (defined as defects per lines of code) and the stability of the system (defined as the degree of modification). Their findings showed that reused code components had a lower defect density compared to non-reused ones. Moreover, reused components had a higher stability compared to the non-reused ones.

Additionally, Mitropoulos et al. [15] used FindBugs to statically examine the Maven ecosystem and presented a dataset of the bugs (including security bugs) of more than 17 000 libraries (155 000 considering all their versions). Their

---

[5] https://github.com/AntonisGkortzis/Vulnerabilities-in-Reused-Software.
[6] http://doi.org/10.5281/zenodo.2566055.

dataset can be used to analyze the risk of using outdated libraries that exist in the Maven Central repository. Although, this work does not examine reuse we find it relevant to mention, since among the results, the authors reported a weak correlation between potential security vulnerabilities and the project size.

Concerning the detection of vulnerable reused code, Pham et al. [20] introduced SecureSync, an automatic approach that analyzes existing vulnerabilities, in open source systems and creates models in order to detect suspicious patterns in similar systems. The authors evaluated their approach by analyzing 176 releases of 119 open source projects and identified suspicious code in 51% of them. Practitioners have also made significant contributions in this area. Ponta et al. [21] presented their approach to identify exploitable vulnerabilities based on function call graphs. Recently they made their tool[7] available for detecting known vulnerabilities in Java and Python software systems.

In Table 1, we highlight the main differences of our study compared to related work. In particular, to the best of our knowledge, the study reported in this paper is the first to investigate the association between code reuse and vulnerabilities, as obtained by means of static analysis, in multiple open source systems.

Table 1. Comparison against related work

Study	Context	Focus on security	Number of projects	Source of vulnerabilities	Relate security to reuse
[19]	Open source	Yes	200	Manual analysis	Yes
[16]	Proprietary	No	1	Defect reporting system	Yes
[15]	Open source	Yes	17 505	Static analysis	No
[20]	Open source	Yes	119	Static analysis and clone detection	Yes
[21]	Open source	Yes	500	Static and dynamic analysis	No
[14]	Open Source	Yes	1	Vulnerability reporting system	No
[23]	Open Source	Yes	2	Vulnerability reporting system	Partially
[18]	Open Source	Yes	1	Vulnerability reporting system	Yes
Ours	Open source	Yes	301	Static analysis	Yes

3   Study Design

In this section, we present the protocol of our case study, which was designed according to the guidelines of Runeson et al. [22], and reported based on the Linear Analytic Structure [22].

3.1   Objective and Research Questions

The goal of the study was formulated according to the Goal-Question-Metric (GQM) approach [24], and is described as follows: "*analyze native and reused*

---

[7] https://sap.github.io/vulnerabilityassessmenttool/.

code, for the purpose of evaluation, with respect to the differences in the estimated levels of security, from the point of view of software developers, in the context of open-source software." To fulfill this objective, we have set two research questions (RQs), as follows:

RQ$_1$: What factors can group projects with regards to security vulnerabilities?

RQ$_1$ aims at acquiring an overview of open-source projects with regards to the security vulnerabilities identified through static analysis. This overview allows the provision of demographics for the dataset and the identification of groups of projects with similar features. This information is also useful to support decision-making in software development activities related to reuse, and to drive future research efforts.

RQ$_2$: How is software reuse associated with security vulnerabilities?
  RQ$_{2.1}$: How does native code contribute to the overall amount of vulnerabilities?
  RQ$_{2.2}$: How does reused code contribute to the overall amount of vulnerabilities?

RQ$_2$ aims at investigating an important question associated with software reuse, namely the extent to which reuse influences the security of a project. For that, we exploit static analysis to identify potential vulnerabilities and investigate how native code developed by the project's team and reused code stemming from dependencies on third-party components contribute to the overall estimated security level.

3.2 Cases and Unit of Analysis

To answer the aforementioned research questions, we designed a holistic multiple-case study, i.e., one in which the multiple cases are also the units of analysis [22]. For this study, we chose open source projects as cases and units of analysis. We selected this particular type of study because the case granularity (i.e., project-level) is sufficient, and multiple cases will provide statistical power to the analysis. Moreover, the selected unit of analysis allows answering the set research questions and pinpoint cases that researchers or practitioners may want to investigate in more detail.

The cases were collected from Reaper [17], a subset of the GHTorrent data set [8]. GHTorrent is a large openly-available database of GitHub metadata. Reaper is a curated dataset comprising more than 2 million unique projects. It retrieves information from GHTorrent and filters it on the following criteria: (1) Select only projects that are of the Java, Python, PHP, Ruby, C++, C, or C# programming languages. (2) The project's repositories contain evidence of an engineered software project such as, documentation, testing, and project management. (3) This dataset contains only projects that are publicly accessible, excluding forked and deleted repositories.

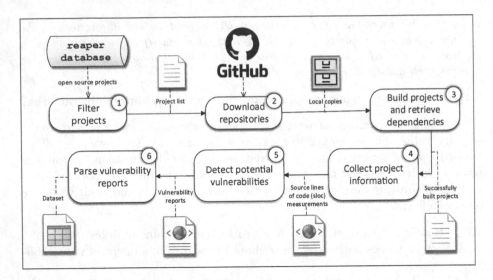

Fig. 1. The dataset construction procedure.

3.3   Variables and Data Collection

To address the research questions, we built a dataset containing two groups of variables for each unit of analysis: (a) project information; and (b) vulnerability information. We built the dataset by following a five-step procedure, which is described in the following paragraphs together with the associated variables. Figure 1 illustrates the data collection. A summary of the recorded variables is presented in Table 2. We note that the complete procedure is automated in a set of scripts available on GitHub.[8]

Step 1: Filter projects. First, we queried the Reaper database [17] and selected the GitHub projects written in Java. We selected Java as a programming language so as to take advantage of automated build support provided by Maven, and the security violations identification capabilities of the SpotBugs[9] tool. Thus, we filtered the projects by selecting only those that were using the Apache Maven automation tool.[10] We applied this filter because this tool is well-known, and it allowed us to automate the build process of multiple projects and retrieve their dependencies. Both operations were necessary for collecting the potential vulnerabilities. Finally, we sorted the projects based on their popularity, by retrieving their *stars* using the GitHub API.[11]

Step 2: Download repositories. Next, using the Git tool, we cloned the top 1000 projects. We selected this amount to improve the representativeness of the sample towards the population and strengthen the statistical analyses.

---

[8] https://github.com/AntonisGkortzis/Vulnerabilities-in-Reused-Software.

[9] https://spotbugs.github.io/.

[10] https://maven.apache.org/.

[11] https://developer.github.com/v3/.

Table 2. List of recorded variables

Variable	Description
Project	Full project name
C_n	Number of native classes
C_r	Number of reused classes
L_n	Number of source lines of code in native classes
L_r	Number of source lines of code in reused classes
V_n	Number of vulnerabilities in native code
V_r	Number of vulnerabilities in reused code
VC_n	Number of potentially vulnerable native classes
VC_r	Number of potentially vulnerable reused classes
VL_n	Number of source lines of code in potentially vulnerable native classes
VL_r	Number of source lines of code in potentially vulnerable reused classes

Step 3: Build projects and retrieve dependencies. With the repositories at hand, we built each project. During the building process, the generated compiled package (i.e., a .jar or .war file) is placed in the local Maven repository (the .m2 directory by default). The dependencies (third party packages or libraries) of each project are also downloaded and placed in the local repository. From the total 1000, we discarded 490 projects that failed to build. For the remaining 510 successful builds, we stored their tree, i.e., the paths to the packages of the project and its dependencies.

Step 4: Collect project information. In this step, we analyzed each project's dependencies' tree and collected the first groups of variables: *project*, C_n, C_r, L_n and L_r. For that, we collected the class files from each package and also used them to retrieve the source lines of code (SLOC), which is estimated based on the number of the statements. We discarded projects that had less than 1000 lines of native code, which led us to a final dataset of 301 projects.

Step 5: Detect potential vulnerabilities. To perform this step we employed static analysis. The benefit of using static analysis for detecting potential security vulnerabilities is the ability to assess a large set of projects without the need of test cases and execution scenarios. Static analyzers can look for patterns in the code base of a system attempting to cover all possible execution paths. Kulenovic et al. [13] studied several static analysis methods for detecting security vulnerabilities. Their findings show that the algorithms used for detecting security vulnerabilities with static analysis are improving constantly, and consequently are increasing the accuracy and the precision of the static analyzers.

We used the static analyzer SpotBugs[12] (v3.1.11) [10,25,27]. This tool considers bug patterns as rules to identify violations of good coding practices [10]. The rules are organized into nine categories, two of them related to security:

---

[12] This is the well-known *FindBugs* tool further developed under a new name.

Security and *Malicious Code.* Moreover, SpotBugs classifies the detected violations into three levels of confidence (low, medium, high) related to the likelihood of their veracity. The tool has already been evaluated in independent studies [6,10] and [4], which reported an average precision of 66%. The studies also reported that the precision can be boosted by ignoring vulnerabilities with a low level of confidence. Nevertheless, there is still a possibility that SpotBugs introduces noise (false positives) to the data collection. However, other studies showed that the detected vulnerabilities are valuable pointers to parts of the system that need to be maintained [3,5,10,11,26,27].

Finally, to further improve the findings of SpotBugs, we included its plugin FindSecBugs,[13] which covers the Open Web Application Security Project (OWASP) top-10 vulnerabilities[14] and several other Common Weaknesses Enumerations (CWEs).[15] CWE is a list of common security weaknesses, maintained by the community, and serves as a common language for classifying vulnerabilities. To detect potential vulnerabilities, SpotBugs requires the path to the compiled Java project and its dependencies. For that, we used the project trees obtained in Step 3. The output of this analysis is a XML file that contains information about the potential vulnerabilities among the native and reused classes.

Step 6: Collect vulnerability information. In this final step, we collected the second groups of variables: V_n, V_r, VC_n, VC_r, VL_n, and VL_r. For that, we parse each SpotBugs' XML report that we generated in the previous step. From these reports we select only the potential security vulnerabilities and we discard all other data. Then, we aggregate the results separately for the native source code and the reused source code.

3.4 Analysis Procedure

To investigate the collected data, we performed various statistical analyses. First, to answer RQ_1, we calculated the descriptive statistics on all collected variables, and used scatter plots and box plots to aid the interpretation of the collected dataset. To answer RQ_2, we first calculated the ratio of reuse Rr and vulnerabilities density Dv as described in (1a) and (1b) below.

$$Rr = \frac{L_r}{L_n + L_r} \ (1a), \quad \text{and} \quad Dv = \frac{V_n + V_r}{L_n + L_r} \ (1b) \tag{1}$$

Next, we used the Pearson correlation [7] to calculate the association between reuse and security vulnerabilities. To further support this analysis, we created scatter plots between the ratio of reuse and the amounts of both native-code and reused-code vulnerabilities. We note that this complete procedure is automated and available online together with all other scripts used in this study.[16]

---

[13] https://find-sec-bugs.github.io/.
[14] https://www.owasp.org/index.php/Top_10-2017_Top_10.
[15] https://cwe.mitre.org/.
[16] https://github.com/AntonisGkortzis/Vulnerabilities-in-Reused-Software.

4   Results

Here, we present the results obtained from the execution of the study design presented in the previous section. In particular, we first present the overall statistics of our dataset. Then we address RQ_1 by obtaining an overview of the built dataset. Next, we examine RQ_2 by analyzing the distribution of vulnerabilities between native and reused code.

Table 3. Dataset size

Variable	Value	Variable	Value
Projects	301	V_n	16 700
Reused dependencies	5 662	V_r	51 744
C_n	288 955	VC_n	7 820
C_r	1 082 995	VC_r	29 140
L_n	8 078 996	VL_n	987 421
L_r	35 279 947	VL_r	3 598 352

4.1 RQ_1 Projects' Overview

In Table 3, we present the overall size of the dataset regarding the variables we presented in Sect. 3. Figure 2 illustrates the distribution of the six variables we presented in Table 2. The Figure comprises six boxplots in a 2×3 matrix. Each column depicts a type of variable (e.g., number of vulnerabilities) and each row the type of code that the variable regards The number of outliers varied for each variable from 6% to 14% (with an average of 11%) of the total amount of projects. For visualization purposes, we omit these outliers in the boxplots.

Table 4. Descriptive statistics

Variable	Minimum	Maximum	Mean	Median	Std. deviation
C_n	3	36 587	960	132	3 641
C_r	4	118 110	3 598	1 715	7 836
L_n	1 002	798 308	26 841	3 710	88 054
L_r	92	2 525 867	117 209	59 679	192 377
V_n	0	2 230	55	5	222
V_r	0	4 175	172	48	351
VC_n	0	801	26	4	88
VC_r	0	2 660	97	28	211

In Fig. 2, we observe that most projects lie in the lowest range of values, a trend that is also visible among all variables. This observation is in line with the descriptive statistics we presented in Table 4, since the mean values are closer to the minimum than to the maximum. Based on these findings, we hypothesize that the number of vulnerabilities in source code increases with the size of the project (measured in SLOC).

We tested this hypothesis by performing independent T-tests. In our first set of tests, we ordered the dataset based on size of native code (L_n) and compared the means between the lower and upper half for: (a) the number of vulnerabilities in native code (V_n) (statistic $= -3.87$, p-value < 0.01) and (b) the number of vulnerabilities in reused code (V_r) (statistic $= -2.26$, p-value $= 0.02$) The results of the tests show a statistical significant difference between the two halves, and that a smaller design size (smaller SLOC) also presents fewer vulnerabilities. Similarly, for the second set of tests, we ordered the dataset based on the size of the reused code (L_r) and compared the means between lower and upper half of the dataset. The results are similar to the first test for both variables.

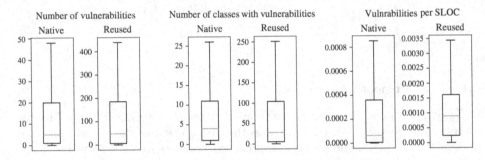

Fig. 2. Boxplot of variables related to vulnerabilities

RQ_1: The independent t-tests provide empirical evidence for the common belief that the number of potential vulnerabilities increases along with the design size (SLOC).

4.2   RQ$_2$ - Association between Reuse and Vulnerabilities

Figure 3 depicts three boxplots that illustrate the distribution of the vulnerability density in the native, reused, and total code respectively. Comparing the vulnerability density in the native code (left boxplot) and the vulnerability density in the reused code (middle boxplot), we observe that the vulnerability density median is similar on both cases. However, there are more projects with higher vulnerability density in native code than in reused code. We also note that the overall density (right boxplot) is similar to the density in reused code compared to the native code. This is due to the fact that the size of reused code

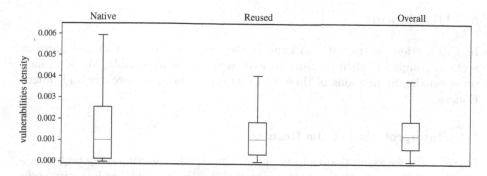

Fig. 3. Boxplots of vulnerability density in native code (left), reused code (center), and overall (right)

is considerably larger than native code, and the normalization procedure is done after the vulnerabilities are combined.

To investigate RQ_2 with regards to the association between the reuse ratio and the vulnerability density, we calculated the Pearson correlation between these variables, which are defined in Sect. 3.4. The result shows a correlation coefficient of -0.18 (p-value < 0.01), indicating a weak inverse correlation between the reuse ratio and the vulnerability density in a project. Figure 4 illustrates the distribution of the vulnerability density in the native code (left scatter plot) and in the reused code (right scatter plot) respectively, with regard to the reuse ratio. Despite the fact that there is more reused code than native, both cases have similar tendency in term of accumulation of vulnerabilities. In particular, there is a clear tendency towards a lower vulnerability density in both native and reused code.

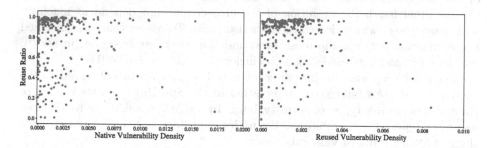

Fig. 4. Scatter plots of vulnerability density in native (left) and reused (right) code

---

RQ_2: The median vulnerability density is similar in both native and reused code. Additionally, the results show a weak inverse correlation between the reuse ratio and the vulnerability density.

---

5   Discussion

In this section, we revisit and explain the findings presented in the previous section, comparing them against related work where applicable. We also elaborate on the implications of these observations to both researchers and practitioners.

5.1   Interpretation of the Results

In summary, we found that the amount of reused code is considerably larger compared to native code. However, the vulnerability density is higher in native code, i.e., it shows a higher count of vulnerabilities per SLOC than reused code. These observations culminate in the fact that the amount of vulnerabilities is mostly associated with the reused code. Viewed simplistically this finding indicates that more reuse leads to more vulnerabilities. However, more reuse is associated with a lower vulnerability density. This result suggests that reused code is mature, and has fewer vulnerabilities. Consequently, if we assume that reused code stands for code that would otherwise have to be written from scratch, the increased reuse of the more mature code may lead to a lower overall density of vulnerabilities. These findings are in line with those of Mohagheghi et al. [16], who performed a comparable study but in a industrial setting and also found a lower defect density (which includes security vulnerabilities) in reused code when compared to native code. Moreover, Mitropoulos et al. [15] found a positive correlation between project size and the amount of vulnerabilities, which also aligns with our findings related to native code.

Regarding the relatively larger amount of reused code, we note that this is understandable due to the nature of our dataset, i.e., with multiple medium-size projects. On one hand, dependencies (e.g., libraries) have a larger impact on the project size as they may introduce a cascade of included dependencies. On the other hand, the evolution of the project may not depend as much on additional reuse, which decreases the reuse ratio. To assess that, we analyzed the correlation between the reuse ratio and the size of native code (in SLOC), and found a moderate association (coefficient $= -0.43$, p-value < 0.01).

The results reported in this paper are based on abstractions observed on the overall dataset. An interesting observation in the SpotBugs reports is type of the most occurring types of security bugs. In Table 5, we list the top-5 most recurrent types of vulnerabilities. We notice that both native and reused code share the same types of vulnerabilities.

5.2   Implications for Researchers and Practitioners

Security assessment of source code is popular among practitioners and researchers. In many cases, this process is executed before every release. In our study, we provided evidence that code reuse has a positive impact on the security of a software system. Our dataset provides information related to reuse ratio and the existence of potential vulnerabilities in 301 projects. Practitioners can

Table 5. Most occurring types of vulnerabilities

Security bugs description	Reported in code
May expose internal representation by returning/incorporating reference to mutable object	Native & Reused
Field is not final but should be	Native & Reused
Field should be package protected	Native & Reused
Method invoked that should be only be invoked inside a *doPrivileged* block	Native & Reused
Classloaders should only be created inside *doPrivileged* block	Native
Field is a mutable collection which should be package protected	Reused

consult the dataset and gain insight on projects of their interest. Software developers can use this information to prioritize bug fixing and assign resources to improve their native code with regards to security. Moreover, practitioners can employ the provided automation scripts to perform a similar analysis on their own code base.

The findings of this study can also benefit researchers. In particular, the provided dataset can be used to investigate research questions different from the ones discussed in this study, e.g., clustering of projects based on one or more of the available variables. Additionally, our proposed approach can be employed to investigate other software quality attributes (e.g., correctness, performance) since SpotBugs can also provide valuable information related to these quality attributes. To examine this aspect, researchers can modify the provided scripts to include bug reports from SpotBugs related to these attributes. Researchers can also reuse our scripts to extend or create their own datasets.

6 Threats to Validity

In this section, we discuss the construct validity, the reliability, and the external validity of our study. Threats to internal validity, are not applicable in this study since it doesn't examine causality. Construct validity examines the relationship between the study's observable object or phenomenon and its research questions. Reliability examines if the study can be replicated and produce the same results. Finally, external validity examines potential threats to generalizing the results of this study to other cases.

Regrading construct validity, we can argue that static analysis can only detect potential security defects and not actually exploitable vulnerabilities. However, these reports are indicators of places that developers should focus when reviewing the code. Furthermore, vulnerabilities reported in the reused code may not all actually affect a project's security, because some vulnerable elements may never be executed by the native code. Moreover, the study can identify only black-box reuse as defined by Heinemann et al. [9]. Black-box reuse requires developers to include a binary version of the dependency, which in our case is a Java package (`jar` or `war` file). White-box reuse is the incorporation of the third-party source code into the native source code. This approach requires clone code-detection like that performed by Heinemann et al. [9], which is out of the scope of this study. Finally, projects were sorted based on their popularity (GitHub stars). This criterion might not be indicative of the usage of these projects.

Concerning reliability, we put our best effort to make this study easy to replicate. The source code, along with detailed instructions, are available in this link.[17] The dataset variable values may vary based on the date of the study. To retrieve the same values researchers should revert the Git repositories to the date of this study (February 10th 2019). To mitigate any reliability risk, two developers were involved and reviewed the process and the actual scripting.

Finally, concerning external validity, we identified two potential risks. Firstly, the project selection was limited to one programming language (Java), and thus generalization of our findings in other languages requires further investigation. Secondly, despite the fact that Maven provided us a straight-forward way of building the projects and easy access to the dependencies, it also limited our dataset. Almost 45% of the initial project selection (1 000) failed to build with Maven or was partially built, and was therefore excluded from the analysis.

7   Conclusion

In this paper, we reported a holistic multiple-case method study with the goal of investigating the association between security vulnerabilities and software reuse in open source projects. In particular, we looked into the distribution of vulner-abilities among native code created by a project's development team and reused code introduced through third-party dependencies, also identifying character-istics of the studied projects. Moreover, we examined the correlation between the ratio of reuse and the density of vulnerabilities. For that, we constructed a dataset with 301 of the most popular projects in the Reaper repository, and collected information regarding the size of both native and external code, as well as vulnerability information obtained from the static analyzer SpotBugs. Unsurprisingly, the results suggest that larger projects are associated with more vulnerabilities in both native and reused code. However, they also show that higher reuse ratio is correlated with a lower overall vulnerability density.

In light of our study design and findings, we envisage several opportunities of future work. On the one hand, it is desirable to extend the provided dataset and incorporate projects from other programming languages and automated build systems, such as Ant, Gradle, npm and pip. The extended dataset could be used for replication and extension studies. The former could mitigate threats to the validity of our study by providing triangulation of data and results. Exten-sion studies could encompass the current or evolved dataset, and explore more in-depth research questions related to, for example, the features of larger and smaller projects, or with more or less external code. On the other hand, the automation scripts shared through this study could be turned into a tool that

---

[17] https://github.com/AntonisGkortzis/Vulnerabilities-in-Reused-Software.

could benefit both practitioners and researchers by providing a workbench for in-house analyses or future studies.

Acknowledgments. We express our appreciation to Paris Avgeriou for reviewing the manuscript and providing us with feedback that improved its quality. The research described has been carried out as part of the CROSSMINER Project, which has received funding from the European Union's Horizon 2020 Research and Innovation Programme under grant agreement No. 732223.

References

1. April 2014 Web Server Survey—Netcraft. https://news.netcraft.com/archives/2014/04/02/april-2014-web-server-survey.html
2. Cybersecurity Incident & Important Consumer Information—Equifax. https://www.equifaxsecurity2017.com/
3. Ayewah, N., Pugh, W.: The Google FindBugs fixit. In: Proceedings of 19th International Symposium on Software Testing and Analysis (ISSTA 2010), pp. 241–252. ACM, Trento (2010). https://doi.org/10.1145/1831708.1831738
4. Ayewah, N., Pugh, W., Morgenthaler, J.D., Penix, J., Zhou, Y.: Evaluating static analysis defect warnings on production software. In: Proceedings of 7th ACM SIGPLAN-SIGSOFT Workshop on Program Analysis for Software Tools and Engineering (PASTE 2007), pp. 1–8. ACM Press, San Diego (2007). https://doi.org/10.1145/1251535.1251536
5. Feitosa, D., Ampatzoglou, A., Avgeriou, P., Chatzigeorgiou, A., Nakagawa, E.: What can violations of good practices tell about the relationship between GoF patterns and run-time quality attributes? Inf. Softw. Technol. (2018). https://doi.org/10.1016/j.infsof.2018.07.014
6. Feitosa, D., Ampatzoglou, A., Avgeriou, P., Nakagawa, E.Y.: Investigating quality trade-offs in open source critical embedded systems. In: Proceedings of 11th International ACM SIGSOFT Conference on the Quality of Software Architectures (QoSA 2015), pp. 113–122. ACM, Montreal (2015). https://doi.org/10.1145/2737182.2737190
7. Field, A.: Discovering Statistics Using IBM SPSS Statistics, 4th edn. SAGE Publications Ltd., Thousand Oaks (2013)
8. Gousios, G., Spinellis, D.: GHTorrent: GitHub's data from a firehose. In: Proceedings of 9th IEEE Working Conference on Mining Software Repositories (MSR 2012), pp. 12–21. IEEE, June 2012. https://doi.org/10.1109/MSR.2012.6224294
9. Heinemann, L., Deissenboeck, F., Gleirscher, M., Hummel, B., Irlbeck, M.: On the extent and nature of software reuse in open source Java projects. In: Schmid, K. (ed.) ICSR 2011. LNCS, vol. 6727, pp. 207–222. Springer, Heidelberg (2011). https://doi.org/10.1007/978-3-642-21347-2_16
10. Hovemeyer, D., Pugh, W.: Finding bugs is easy. ACM SIGPLAN Not. **39**(12), 92–106 (2004). https://doi.org/10.1145/1052883.1052895
11. Khalid, H., Nagappan, M., Hassan, A.E.: Examining the relationship between Find-Bugs warnings and app ratings. IEEE Softw. **33**(4), 34–39 (2016). https://doi.org/10.1109/MS.2015.29
12. Kula, R.G., German, D.M., Ouni, A., Ishio, T., Inoue, K.: Do developers update their library dependencies? Empirical Softw. Eng. **23**(1), 384–417 (2018). https://doi.org/10.1007/s10664-017-9521-5

13. Kulenovic, M., Donko, D.: A survey of static code analysis methods for security vulnerabilities detection. In: Proceedings of 37th International Convention on Information and Communication Technology, Electronics and Microelectronics (MIPRO 2014), pp. 1381–1386, May 2014. https://doi.org/10.1109/MIPRO.2014.6859783

14. Meneely, A., Williams, L.: Secure open source collaboration: an empirical study of Linus' law. In: Proceedings of 16th ACM Conference on Computer and Communications Security, CCS 2009, pp. 453–462. ACM (2009). https://doi.org/10.1145/1653662.1653717

15. Mitropoulos, D., Karakoidas, V., Louridas, P., Gousios, G., Spinellis, D.: The bug catalog of the Maven ecosystem. In: Proceedings of 11th Working Conference on Mining Software Repositories (MSR 2014), pp. 372–375. ACM, Hyderabad (2014). https://doi.org/10.1145/2597073.2597123

16. Mohagheghi, P., Conradi, R., Killi, O.M., Schwarz, H.: An empirical study of software reuse vs. defect-density and stability. In: Proceedings of 26th International Conference on Software Engineering (ICSE 2004), pp. 282–292. IEEE Computer Society, Washington, DC (2004). http://dl.acm.org/citation.cfm?id=998675.999433

17. Munaiah, N., Kroh, S., Cabrey, C., Nagappan, M.: Curating GitHub for engineered software projects. Empirical Softw. Eng. **22**(6), 3219–3253 (2017). https://doi.org/10.1007/s10664-017-9512-6

18. Neuhaus, S., Zimmermann, T.: The beauty and the beast: vulnerabilities in red hat's packages. In: Proceedings of 2009 USENIX Annual Technical Conference (USENIX 2009) (2009)

19. Pashchenko, I., Plate, H., Ponta, S.E., Sabetta, A., Massacci, F.: Vulnerable open source dependencies: counting those that matter. In: Proceedings of 12th ACM/IEEE Internatinal Symposium on Empirical Software Engineering and Measurement (ESEM 2018), pp. 42:1–42:10. ACM, Oulu (2018). https://doi.org/10.1145/3239235.3268920

20. Pham, N.H., Nguyen, T.T., Nguyen, H.A., Wang, X., Nguyen, A.T., Nguyen, T.N.: Detecting recurring and similar software vulnerabilities. In: Proceedings of 32nd ACM/IEEE International Conference on Software Engineering (ICSE 2010), pp. 227–230. ACM, Cape Town (2010). https://doi.org/10.1145/1810295.1810336

21. Ponta, S.E., Plate, H., Sabetta, A.: Beyond metadata: code-centric and usage-based analysis of known vulnerabilities in open-source software. In: Proceedings of 34th IEEE International Conference on Software Maintenance and Evolution (ICSME 2018), September 2018. https://doi.org/10.1109/ICSME.2018.00054

22. Runeson, P., Host, M., Rainer, A., Regnell, B.: Case Study Research in Software Engineering: Guidelines and Examples. Wiley, Hoboken (2012)

23. Shin, Y., Meneely, A., Williams, L., Osborne, J.A.: Evaluating complexity, code churn, and developer activity metrics as indicators of software vulnerabilities, **37**(6), 772–787. https://doi.org/10.1109/TSE.2010.81

24. van Solingen, R., Basili, V., Caldiera, G., Rombach, H.D.: Goal question metric (GQM) approach. In: Encyclopedia of Software Engineering, pp. 528–532. Wiley, Hoboken (2002). https://doi.org/10.1002/0471028959.sof142

25. Tomassi, D.A.: Bugs in the wild: examining the effectiveness of static analyzers at finding real-world bugs. In: Proceedings of 2018 26th ACM Joint Meeting on European Software Engineering Conference on and Symposium on the Foundations of Software Engineering (ESEC/FSE 2018), pp. 980–982. ACM, Lake Buena Vista (2018). https://doi.org/10.1145/3236024.3275439

26. Tripathi, A.K., Gupta, A.: A controlled experiment to evaluate the effectiveness and the efficiency of four static program analysis tools for Java programs. In: Proceedings of 18th Interantional Conference on Evaluation and Assessment in Software Engineering (EASE 2014), pp. 23:1–23:4. ACM, London (2014). https://doi.org/10.1145/2601248.2601288

27. Zheng, J., Williams, L., Nagappan, N., Snipes, W., Hudepohl, J.P., on Vouk, M.A.S.E.I.T.: On the value of static analysis for fault detection in software. IEEE Trans. Softw. Eng. **32**(4), 240–253 (2006). https://doi.org/10.1109/TSE.2006.38

ACO-RR: Ant Colony Optimization Ridge Regression in Reuse of Smart City System

Qiaoyun Yin[1(✉)], Ke Niu[1(✉)], Ning Li[1(✉)], Xueping Peng[2], and Yijie Pan[3]

[1] Computer School, Beijing Information Science and Technology University, Beijing, China
6236609230qq.com, niuke@bistu.edu.cn, ningli.ok@163.com
[2] CAI, FEIT, University of Technology Sydney, Sydney, Australia
xueping.peng@uts.edu.au
[3] Ningbo Institute of Information Technology Application, Ningbo, China
pyj@nbicc.com

Abstract. With the rapid development of artificial intelligence, governments of different countries have been focusing on building smart cities. To build a smart city is a system construction process which not only requires a lot of human and material resources, but also takes a long period of time. Due to the lack of enough human and material resources, it is a key challenge for lots of small and medium-sized cities to develop the intelligent construction, compared with the large cities with abundant resources. Reusing the existing smart city system to assist the intelligent construction of the small and medium-sizes cities is a reasonable way to solve this challenge. Following this idea, we propose a model of Ant Colony Optimization Ridge Regression (ACO-RR), which is a smart city evaluation method based on the ridge regression. The model helps small and medium-sized cities to select and reuse the existing smart city systems according to their personalized characteristics from different successful stories. Furthermore, the proposed model tackles the limitation of ridge parameters' selection affecting the stability and generalization ability, because the parameters of the traditional ridge regression is manually random selected. To evaluate our model performance, we conduct experiments on real-world smart city data set. The experimental results demonstrate that our model outperforms the baseline methods, such as support vector machine and neural network.

Keywords: Smart city system · System reuse ·
Parameter optimization · Ant colony · Ridge regression.

1 Introduction

In recent years, smart city has become the theme of urban development, which is based on information technology and aims at high-quality and happy city life

© Springer Nature Switzerland AG 2019
X. Peng et al. (Eds.): ICSR 2019, LNCS 11602, pp. 204–219, 2019.
https://doi.org/10.1007/978-3-030-22888-0_14

[1]. Smart cities have played a key role in changing different aspects of human life, involving transportation, health, energy and education [2]. The "intellectualization" of various fields in a city is not enough to make a city smart, but considers the mutual relations between various fields in related cities to realize the intellectualization of the city. Therefore, a smart city is regarded as a system or a whole system [3].

Scholars have solved many problems in different fields through different ways of reuse. Paludo [4] proposed the use of patterns to help the software designer to model business processes. Penzenstadler [5] proposed a concrete artefact model for integrated reuse from requirements to technical architecture, which satisfies documentation demands with respect to functionality and the context assumed by the subsystem. Gasparic [6] performed an industrial exploratory case study to analyze the software reuse process of a medium size company which is a technology leader in a niche market. Kaindl [7] presented an integration of business process and software reuse and reusability in the context of developing software supporting business processes. Oumaziz [8] performed an empirical study of duplications in JavaDoc documentation on a corpus of seven famous Java APIs and proposed a simple but efficient automatic reuse mechanism.

Resolving similar problems by multiplexing the same system is important for reducing costs and shortening time [9]. The construction of smart cities is a complicated systematic project. There are many smart cities with high degree of intelligence in China. How can we use the existing experience to effectively avoid the waste of resources and other issues when building a smart city? Reuse of smart city system is a good solution. Recently, such methods have not been put forward in the field of smart cities. But in other fields, similar problems were often solved by reusing methods. Liu [10] improved the modeling efficiency and reliability of complex systems by using model reuse methods in the field of Simulation science. Song [11] proposed an algorithm to solve a multi-objective optimization problem, and introduced an evolutionary scheme that flexibly reused past search experience, further improving the efficiency of the search.

By introducing the reuse of smart city systems into the process of smart city construction, we have solved the problems of resource waste, high manpower and time cost. Cities with different characteristics have different key construction directions for building smart cities. Suitable smart city system should be selected in the reuse of smart city system. The difficult problem in the reuse process is how to choose a suitable system for the needs of the city's construction among the many existing smart city systems. We use the smart city evaluation index system developed by experts according to the characteristics and specific needs of the city to evaluate the smart city. The city with the best evaluation result is the smart one that meets the current its demand. Then we can select the smart city system to realize system reuse in its construction process. For different indicator systems, the ACO-RR algorithm, which we use to evaluate smart cities, can better calculate the weight of each indicator and improve the accuracy of automated evaluation of smart city systems. Then we choose the appropriate reuse parts from existing well-worked smart city system to integrate into the process of intelligent construction.

The remainders are organized as follows. In Sect. 2, we briefly discuss some related work. Then, details about our method are presented in Sect. 3. In Sect. 4, we demonstrate the experimental results conducted on real world public datasets. Finally, we conclude our study and prospect our future work in Sect. 5.

2   Related Work

How to use smart city evaluation system to evaluate the effect of smart city construction and the degree of its development scientifically has been widely concerned by experts and scholars [12]. We can understand the essence of smart city evaluation as ranking and evaluating the level of smart city development [13]. The methods of determining weights in the smart city evaluation process of the existing research include entropy method [14], Analytic Hierarchy Process (AHP) [15], and CRITIC method [16]. The entropy method [14] only calculates the weight from the angle of the index's own information, without considering the influence of the correlation between the indexes on the weight. The Delphi method [17–19] was proposed by Helm and Dark in the 1940s and further developed by Golden and RAND. It first obtains experts' opinions on a certain problem with multiple rounds of communication between an anonymous way, and then sums up the experts' opinions on the results of prediction and evaluation. Delphi with repeated solicitation of opinions has the disadvantage of complex investigation and high resource consumption. When a large number of indicators are needed for evaluation, AHP [15] cannot distinguish the importance of different indicators. CRITIC [20] without specific analysis of the correlation between indicators makes the results of different problems deviate greatly.

Zhang [21] used Principal Component Analysis (PCA) method to rank and analyze the smart cities. However, PCA does not consider the influence of the relationship between independent variables and dependent variables on the accuracy of smart city evaluation results. Many researches begin to use machine learning methods to extract information from data to solve various ranking prediction problems. To approach this challenge, we research machine learning method in other specialties. Aljouie [22] Introduced support vector regression and ridge top regression models to cross-verify the SNP with the highest ranking, and calculated the correlation coefficient between the true and predicted phenotypes. Ran [23] used support vector machine regression to solve the estimation problem of photovoltaic system output. Hong [24] realized power management and solves the problem of load estimation by using support vector regression. Yang [25] solved a difficult problem with the medical field by using Decision Tree model to predict portal vein thrombosis after acute pancreatitis. In the field of smart city evaluation, in 2019, Ma [26] assessed the level of intelligent city construction in 2011–2016 by trained neural network model with smart city data. Compared with resource-rich big cities, the intelligent construction of small and medium-sized cities is a difficult challenge. How to accurately evaluate smart cities, and then help small and medium-sized cities choose smart city systems that meet their own characteristics to assist the city's intelligent construction is particularly important.

Based on the above research, we propose an algorithm ACO-RR. The principle of ACO-RR is based on ridge regression algorithm and ant colony algorithm is used to find the optimal ridge parameters in the process of training model. It solves the influence of multi-collinearity of data onto sorting results and avoids the randomness of manual determination of parameters in traditional ridge regression algorithm. We have proved that ACO-RR algorithm can be used in the task of accurate evaluation of smart cities under different smart city evaluation systems.

3   Proposed ACO-RR Model

3.1   ACO-RR Algorithm Flow

ACO-RR realizes automatic parameter tuning of the model by using group intelligence to find the appropriate ridge parameters. As shown in Fig. 1. Firstly, the solution space is divided, the information concentration and other parameters in each space are initialized, and ants are randomly placed in each space. The second step is to calculate the transition probability of each ant transferring to other space based on the existing information and the information concentration on the path, and determine whether to transfer the ants according to the magnitude of the probability value. In addition, we need to update the information concentration on the path after the ant has transferred. At this time, the search solution space will gradually shrink. We can finally find the optimal solution by repeating the above process. The core of the whole algorithm is the selection of the objective function. The ultimate goal of the algorithm is to make the model learn the intrinsic information reflected by different evaluation index systems, and find out the influencing factors reflecting the evaluation indicators. Therefore, the objective function of the algorithm is set as the accuracy function of the ridge parameter for smart city evaluation.

3.2   Algorithm Principle

The difficulty of ridge regression is how to determine the parameters of the model. But the traditional ridge regression has a certain randomness by manually selecting parameters, which makes the results less accurate. In order to solve this problem, the ant colony algorithm is introduced to optimize the parameters, which improves the robustness of the algorithm and the accuracy of the evaluation. Ant colony algorithm is a simulation optimization algorithm that finds the optimal solution by simulating the ant foraging behavior. It can quickly converge to the optimal solution by using the group wisdom of the ant colony to solve the optimal problem. During the search process, ants continuously release pheromone so that individuals in the ant colony can acquire information of other ants by

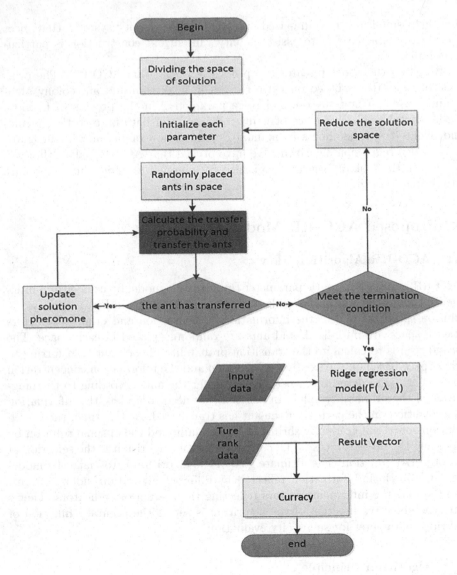

Fig. 1. The main flow chart of the ACO-RR algorithm.

capturing pheromone to realize information transmission. Each ant calculates the transfer probability of the corresponding space according to the pheromone concentration of each transferable space. Then decide which space to transfer to according to the probability values of different spaces. The pheromone of the solution space needs to be updated after the transfer. Repeat the iteration of the above process until the ants no longer transfer. Finally the ant colony will gather near the optimal solution. The ant colony algorithm was originally proposed to solve the discrete optimization problem. While the parameter optimization of ridge regression is a continuous optimization problem. Therefore, the ACO-RR algorithm proposed in this paper is to optimize the parameters in the ridge regression model based on the idea of using ant colony algorithm to solve the extremum of multimodal functions.

Assuming that the optimization problem function is $f(x), x \in [a, b]$. Algorithm divides the domain $[a, b]$ into n subintervals. Equation 1 is the length of the divided interval. Each interval is denoted as $I_1, ..., I_i, ..., I_n$, and Eq. 2 is denoted as solution space i. The middle position of the interval is represented by X_i, which can be calculated by Eq. 3. Ants in ant colony calculate the transition probability value to each interval in the transferable subinterval set according to the pheromone of each interval and the transition cost v from their current position to the next interval. Then select the interval with the largest probability value for transition. Ant will release a certain amount of pheromone in the interval after it moves to the interval.

$$\iota = (a - b)/n \tag{1}$$
$$I_i = [a + (i - 1) * \iota, a + i * \iota] \tag{2}$$
$$X_i = a + (i - 1/2) * \iota \tag{3}$$

Initialize the Position and Interval Pheromone Concentration of Ant Colony. m is the number of ants in the ant colony, n is the number of divided solution spaces. In the first step, all ants are randomly placed in each solution space to complete the initialization of ant colony positions. In addition, the pheromone amount released by each ant at its location is expressed by *const*, and then we can obtain the initial information concentration of each space.

Transferable Set. T_{si} (Transfer set i) is defined as a set of transferable subspaces of ant i as shown in Eq. 4, where k is used to limit the ant transfer range. We take the midpoint position X_i to calculate the corresponding target value $f(X_i)$ and determine whether the current space is the optimal solution space.

$$T_{si} = \begin{cases} \{I_1, ..., I_i, ..., I_{i+k}\}, & 1 \le i \le k \\ \{I_{i-k}, ..., I_i, ..., I_{i+k}\}, & k < i \le n - k \\ \{I_{i-k}, ..., I_i, ..., I_n\}, & n - k < i \le n \end{cases} \tag{4}$$

Ant Colony Transfer. Each ant selects a transferable subspace with a certain limit, and selects the subspace to be transferred by comparing the magnitudes of the spatial transition probabilities. If $f(X_i) - f(X_j) < 0$, the transfer occurs, otherwise the ant does not transfer. Heuristic function is defined as B_{ij} because the transfer cost of solution space i and solution space j is $|f(X_i) - f(X_j)|$. $P_{ij}(t)(s)$ indicates that the ant t is transferred from subinterval I_i to subinterval I_j at the s th iteration as shown in Eq. 6. Where A_j is the pheromone content of interval j at the current moment, and φ is information inspiration. ϕ is the expected heuristic factor.

$$B_{ij} = |f(X_i) - f(X_j)| \tag{5}$$

$$P_{ij}(t)(s) = \begin{cases} 0, & otherwise \\ \dfrac{A_j^{\varphi}(s)B_{il}^{\phi}}{\sum_{l \in T_{si}} A_l^{\varphi}(s)B_{il}^{\phi}}, & j \in T_{si} \end{cases} \tag{6}$$

Pheromone Update. The information increment of ant colony corresponding to subinterval j after completing one transfer is $\triangledown A_j^t(s)$. If ant t transfers from I_i to I_j, ant t will release a certain amount of pheromone $\triangledown A_j^t(s)$ on I_j in the process of iteration s, c_1 is a normal number. While all ants complete one transfer, the algorithm updates the information concentration of all subintervals as shown in formula 8. Where χ is the pheromone volatilization factor, and $A_j(s)$ represents the information concentration of current interval j.

$$A_j^t(s) = c_1(f(x_i) - f(x_j)) \tag{7}$$
$$A_j(s+1) = (1-\chi)A_j(s) + \triangledown A_j(s) \tag{8}$$

Narrow Solution Space. After several times of ant colony transfer, all ants will concentrate in the interval near the maximum value, and there are no ants in other intervals. These ant - containing intervals are taken out as new solution spaces. Then the above steps are repeated until the refined space is small enough. We found that the position where the ant stayed at this time was the position of the required optimal solution.

The core of smart city system reuse is to use the evaluation results to help small and medium-sized cities that need smart city construction to choose a suitable smart city system. Therefore, the accuracy of evaluation results is the key issue.

4   Experiments

According to the given evaluation index system, we established ACO-RR model to evaluate the smart city, and verified the accuracy of the model through a number of experiments. Compared with the experimental results of other algorithms, we found that ACO-RR had higher accuracy and stronger stability. The experiment consisted of three parts: in order to verify whether the algorithm always has high accuracy for smart city evaluation under different index systems, the first part of the experiment is a comparative experiment based on three different smart city evaluation systems in 2013, 2014 and 2015 respectively. The second part of the experiment mainly considers the influence of different data samples on the accuracy of the algorithm. In addition, we use the third part of experiments to verify the change trend of algorithm accuracy with the change of sample size.

4.1   Experimental Data

Our experimental data come from the evaluation report on the development level of China's smart cities issued by the Chinese Academy of Social Sciences and Other Smart City Research Center in 2013, 2014 and 2015. The extraction of data in the report were collected in the following four ways: Literature review, Network surveys, Telephone surveys and Technical inspections. Since the smart city data in recent years have not been published, we used the smart city data sets of 2013, 2014 and 2015 as the experimental data of different evaluation index systems. For example, in the field of e-government, the index system in 2013 considers the application level of government website construction. In 2014, more attention was paid to the level of government collaboration. In 2015, the government's online service level has become a key point. Through the experiments of comparison, it was found that ACO-RR algorithm was more suitable for solving the problem of smart city evaluation with different evaluation index systems. Sample 1 is the smart city data of 2013, sample 2 is the smart city data of 2014, and sample 3 is the smart city data of 2015.

Partial sample data of the experiment are shown in Table 1. The focus of this paper is not on the construction of the index system, we will not describe the construction and composition of the evaluation index system. Because the corresponding smart city evaluation index systems in the smart city development level evaluation reports of different years are different, the published three-year city data and the evaluation index system of corresponding years are used for subsequent experiments. Before the experiment, the data need to be standardized in order to eliminate the influence caused by different dimensions of different indexes.

4.2   Experimental Methods and Processes

Experimental Methods

Decision Tree. Decision Tree is a common class of machine learning methods. First, we select the optimal partitioning attribute at the splitting node, and use the value of this attribute to partition the sample to generate many new splitting nodes. Then, we repeat the above process of each new splitting node, and finally generate a Decision Tree with strong generalization ability. In the experimental part, the Decision Tree model was applied to solve the regression prediction problem by dividing the feature space into several units with specific output. Each partition checked the values of all the features in the current set and chose the best value as the segmentation point according to the criterion of minimum square error.

SVR. Support Vector Machine is proposed for the principle of structural risk minimization, which overcomes the disadvantages of traditional models caused by the principle of empirical risk minimization and has strong generalization ability. Owing to the regression problem of smart city evaluation problem, we

Table 1. Partial Sample Data

Indx	Wuxi	Pudong	Ningbo	Shanghai	Hangzhou	Beijing
Index1	71.4	102.9	80.85	89.25	78.75	71.4
Index2	94.5	94.5	63	73.5	94.5	73.5
Index3	36.75	31.5	21	31.5	26.25	21
Index4	157.5	126	147	126	105	157.5
Index5	36.75	21	36.75	52.5	42	21
Index6	96.6	86.1	96.6	92.4	84	94.5
Index7	84	47.25	73.5	73.5	68.25	73.5
Index8	47.25	36.75	47.2	21	31.5	21
Index9	42	105	73.5	42	42	52.5
Index10	77.7	81.9	54.6	56.7	46.2	100.8
Index11	52.5	94.5	42	94.5	84	105
Index12	105	52.5	81.9	79.8	77.7	75.6
Index13	42	84	42	63	105	42
Index14	105	126	126	115.5	115.5	126
Index15	105	63	105	63	73.5	84
Index16	73.5	73.5	84	63	73.5	63

applied the method of SVR to make empirical analysis. The goal of SVR is to find a regression hyperplane to minimize the distance from all sample data to the plane. Given training samples $D = (X_1^{\cdot}, Y_1), (X_2, Y_2), ..., (X_n, Y_n)$, model will learn an $f(x)$ as close as possible to Y. Assuming that there is a maximum ϵ deviation between $f(x)$ and Y that we can tolerate, the loss is calculated when the absolute value of the difference between $f(x)$ and Y is greater than ϵ. This is equivalent to building a spacing band with a width of 2ϵ with $f(x)$ as the center. The training sample will be considered to be the predicted correct sample if it falls within this interval band.

Neural Network. Neural network is essentially a neural network with error back propagation. It consists of an input layer, an output layer and an implicit layer, wherein the implicit layer may have more than one layer. The learning process of neural networks with different hidden layers is similar. Firstly, the connection weights of each hierarchical structure in the network are initialized, and the training sample data is selected to calculate the mean square deviation of the final output data and the actual data through the hierarchical structure of the network to determine whether the next sample needs to be selected to continue iteration. Then reverse error propagation is carried out to further correct the error. The initial weights of each layer of the neural network are randomly generated, and the slow training speed of the network leads to the local minimum problem.

Experimental Processes. The experimental data were standardized by the specific gravity method. According to the results of literature research, we selected Decision Tree [27] and SVR [22,23] algorithms that had achieved good results in other fields, and neural network [26] algorithms used in the field of smart city evaluation as the comparison algorithms to verify the effectiveness of ACO-RR in this paper.

In the first part, we conducted three groups of experiments by using Decision Tree, SVR, neural network and ACO-RR on three different samples. In each group of experiment, the data were first divided into training sets and test sets. The model trained by the training sets was used to evaluate smart cities in the test sets. Pearson correlation coefficient between the evaluation results vector of the model and the actual ranking result vector of the city was calculated as the accuracy of the model. In order to prevent possible differences caused by data sets, the same training set and test set were used to train their models respectively with four algorithms in the intra-group experiments, and the trained models were used to evaluate smart cities. In this part, there were a total of 12 experiments in three groups. The first group consisted of experiments 1-1, 1-2, 1-3, and 1-4. The four experiments were based on sample 1 using Decision Tree, SVR, and neural network. Sample 1 was used as experimental data in the four experiments, and then Decision Tree, SVR, and neural network and ACO-RR algorithms were respectively used for comparative experiments. The second set of experiments consisted of experiments 1-5, 1-6, 1-7, 1-8, the four experiments in this group used sample 2 as experimental data to compare the effectiveness of the four algorithms. The third group consisted of experiments 1-9, 1-10, 1-11, 1-12. Similarly, these four experiments were comparative experiments of four algorithms based on sample 3.

The second part of the experiment consisted of four groups of 16 experiments. First, we randomly divided sample 3 into four times to obtain four sets of test sets and training set samples of the same scale, and the data sets obtained by the four divisions were represented by D1, D2, D3, and D4. We used the above four algorithm training models to evaluate the smart city, and finally calculated the accuracy of each model separately. The first set of experiments consisted of experiments 2-1, 2-2, 2-3, and 2-4. The four experiments were based on the data set D1 using Decision Trees, SVR, neural networks, and ACO-RR algorithms for comparison experiments. The difference between the three sets of experiments and the first set of experiments was only that the data sets were different. The second set of experiments was based on the comparative experiment of the data set D2 through four algorithms, and the third and fourth sets were based on the data sets D3 and D4 respectively.

The third part of the experiment consisted of 12 groups of 48 experiments. In each of the 12 sets of experiments, we conducted four experiments using the above four algorithms to train the model and evaluate the smart city. Throughout the third part of the experiment, we gradually increased the number of data samples in the training set to observe the change trend of accuracy rate of different algorithms with the change of data sample size.

4.3   Experimental Results and Analysis

We used the third-party package in Python to construct the model of comparative experiments, and set the default parameter value to the parameter value of the model. We added the network layer and adjusted the number of neurons and other parameters to optimize the neural network model. For decision tree, overfitting is prevented by changing the number and depth of the tree. The parameters of SVR model such as C value set to 1.0, cache size value set to 200, degree value set to 3, epsilon value set to 0.1, kernel value set to RBF. For the ridge regression parameters of ACO-RR algorithm, we find that the parameters of the model established under different index systems are Different. For example, the ridge parameter under sample 1 is 0.65, while that under sample 2 is 0.33. In fact, ACO-RR algorithm can quickly and effectively realize intelligent city evaluation because the algorithm can automatically find such differences.

The accuracy of the results of all experiments was shown in Table 2. We measured the accuracy of the evaluation results of the algorithm model by calculating the Pearson correlation coefficient between the two vectors. The more big the Pearson correlation coefficient value, the more close between the evaluation results of the model and the real ranking of the city, which also showed the higher the accuracy of the algorithm. The comparison results of algorithm accuracy under different index systems were shown in Fig. 2. The left-to-right bar chart in the figure showed the accuracy of Decision Tree, SVR, neural network and ACO-RR algorithm in evaluating smart cities based on different evaluation systems respectively. It is not difficult to find that the Pearson correlation coefficient of ACO-RR algorithm is always the highest compared with the other three algorithms, which further illustrates the applicability of this calculation in the field of smart city evaluation. In the second part of the experiment, the results obtained by different division methods of data are shown in Fig. 3. The figure shows that the accuracy of SVR, neural network and Decision Tree algorithms are greatly affected by the difference of samples under different sample data with the same data size. The accuracy of ACO-RR algorithm is basically stable, and the experimental results show that the stability of the algorithm is higher than that of the other three algorithms.

Table 2. Algorithm accuracy under different index systems

Year	Decision Tree	SVR	Neural_network	ACO-RR
2013	0.96	0.87	0.87	0.99
2014	0.97	0.92	0.89	0.99
2015	0.98	0.97	0.96	0.99

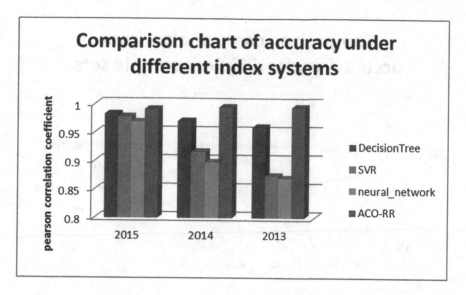

Fig. 2. Comparison chart of accuracy under different index systems

The experimental results in the third part are shown in Fig. 4. No matter how the sample size changes, the accuracy rate obtained by ACO-RR algorithm is always higher than that of the other three algorithms. Furthermore, it proves that ACO-RR algorithm has high accuracy in the evaluation of smart cities. From the curve trend in the figure, we find that the accuracy of all algorithms has been improved and gradually converge with the increasing sample size. However, ACO-RR always has the highest accuracy rate, which indicates that the algorithm is more suitable for solving smart city evaluation problems.

Through the above experimental results, we come to the conclusion that SVR, Decision Tree and neural network algorithms are highly sensitive to data sets. When the data sets change, the accuracy of the model changes greatly. Neural network is actually an optimization method of local search in which the weights in the network are gradually adjusted along the direction of local improvement. It is suitable for solving a complex nonlinear problem. In fact, the distribution characteristics of smart city evaluation index data are not suitable for evaluation by neural network. Because the network often learns too many sample details to make the learned model unable to reflect the rules contained in the sample. In fact, network based on data distribution characteristic of smart city evaluation index usually learn too many sample details, resulting in that learned model cannot reflect the rule contained in the samples. Therefore, neural networks are not suitable for the evaluation of smart cities. However, the support vector machine algorithm mainly determines whether the output data of the model is close to the actual data by dividing the region band. As the errors in the region band can be accepted, the evaluation accuracy cannot reach higher accuracy. The low accuracy of decision trees is mainly due to the fact that a small change

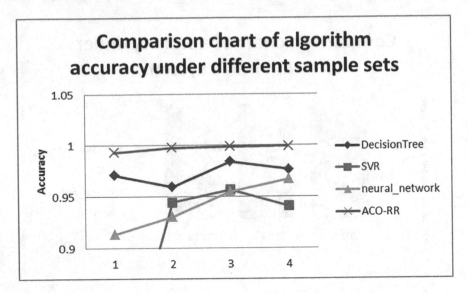

Fig. 3. Comparison chart of algorithm accuracy under different sample sets

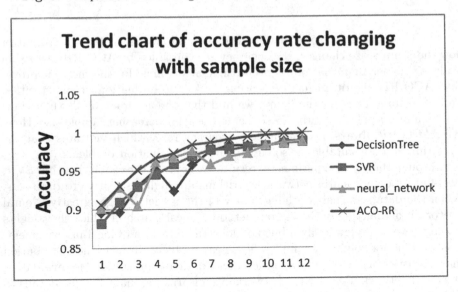

Fig. 4. Trend chart of accuracy rate changing with sample size

in the data may lead to the generation of a completely different tree, and the decision trees are easily over-fitted by dividing with features as nodes.

Through many groups of experimental results, it is proved that ACO-RR algorithm not only has higher accuracy but also has stronger applicability and stability in solving the problem of smart city evaluation. In the early stage of the construction of a smart city, we can use ACO-RR algorithm to evaluate the existing smart city under the index system formulated by experts that conforms to the city's own characteristics. According to the evaluation results, an appropriate smart city system is selected and applied to the construction of smart cities. By reusing the smart city system, the problem of insufficient resources in small and medium-sized cities is solved to a certain extent. Meanwhile, a large amount of manpower and material resources are saved, and the construction efficiency is further improved.

5   Conclusion

The algorithm proposed in this paper uses the regularization of ridge regression to solve the multicollinearity problem of data, and introduces the optimization of ant colony algorithm to solve the randomness problem of artificial parameters. We have proved that ACO-RR algorithm can always capture the changes of information and maintain high accuracy despite the changes in the index system. When a small and medium-sized city is ready to build a smart city, the first step is to use the evaluation system given by the city experts to evaluate the existing smart city combined with the algorithm in this paper, then select the corresponding smart city system according to the smart city with the highest degree of intelligence, and finally reuse the smart city system in the construction process. This not only solves the problem of waste of resources in the construction of smart cities, reduces the development time and labor costs, but also further improves the reliability and efficiency.

In the experiment, different intelligent city index systems were used for model training, and the results show that ACO-RR algorithm is more suitable for smart city evaluation than other algorithms no matter how the smart city index system change. Other experimental results of smart city evaluation under different data samples show that the proposed algorithm is more stable than other algorithms. In addition, through a variety of comparison algorithms, it can be proved that ACO-RR algorithm can improve the accuracy of evaluation results for smart cities. Therefore, with the continuous expansion and rapid development of smart cities, we can try to evaluate smart cities with this algorithm. After choosing the right smart city system, our next step will be to solve the problem of how to use the system to build a new smart city. In addition, we will focus on the study of whether some comprehensive evaluation models can solve the evaluation of smart city. With the gradual acceleration of the development of smart cities, the diversity of data will be further considered when evaluating smart cities in the future.

Acknowledgment. This paper is supported by the National Key R & D Program of China (No. 2018YFB1004100), the Beijing Education Commission Research Project of China(No. KM201911232004) and the National Natural Science Foundation of China (No. 61672105).

References

1. Pan, J.G., Lin, Y.F., Chuang, S.Y., Kao, Y.C.: From governance to service-smart city evaluations in Taiwan. In: International Joint Conference on Service Sciences, no. 74, pp. 334–337 (2011)
2. Hashem, I.A.T., Chang, V., Anuar, N.B., et al.: The role of big data in smart city. Int. J. Inf. Manag. **36**(5), 748–758 (2016)
3. Osman-Shahat, M.A.: A novel big data analytics framework for smart cities. Future Gener. Comput. Syst. **91**, 620–633 (2019)
4. Paludo, M., Burnett, R., Jamhour, E.: Patterns leveraging analysis reuse of business processes. In: Frakes, W.B. (ed.) ICSR 2000. LNCS, vol. 1844, pp. 353–368. Springer, Heidelberg (2000). https://doi.org/10.1007/978-3-540-44995-9_21
5. Penzenstadler, B., Koss, D.: High confidence subsystem modelling for reuse. In: Mei, H. (ed.) ICSR 2008. LNCS, vol. 5030, pp. 52–63. Springer, Heidelberg (2008). https://doi.org/10.1007/978-3-540-68073-4_5
6. Gasparic, M., Janes, A., Sillitti, A., Succi, G.: An analysis of a project reuse approach in an industrial setting. In: Schaefer, I., Stamelos, I. (eds.) ICSR 2015. LNCS, vol. 8919, pp. 164–171. Springer, Cham (2014). https://doi.org/10.1007/978-3-319-14130-5_12
7. Kaindl, H., Popp, R., Hoch, R., Zeidler, C.: Reuse vs. reusability of software supporting business processes. In: Kapitsaki, G.M., Santana de Almeida, E. (eds.) ICSR 2016. LNCS, vol. 9679, pp. 138–145. Springer, Cham (2016). https://doi.org/10.1007/978-3-319-35122-3_10
8. Oumaziz, M.A., Charpentier, A., Falleri, J.-R., Blanc, X.: Documentation reuse: hot or not? An empirical study. In: Botterweck, G., Werner, C. (eds.) ICSR 2017. LNCS, vol. 10221, pp. 12–27. Springer, Cham (2017). https://doi.org/10.1007/978-3-319-56856-0_2
9. Yao, Y., Liu, M., Du, J., et al.: Design of a machine tool control system for function reconfiguration and reuse in network environment. Rob. Comput.-Integr. Manuf. **56**, 117–126 (2019)
10. Liu, Y., Zhang, L., LaiLi, Y.J.: Study on model reuse for complex system simulation. Sci. Sin. (2018)
11. Song, S., Gao, S., Chen, X., et al.: AIMOES: archive information assisted multi-objective evolutionary strategy for Ab initio protein structure prediction. Knowl.-Based Syst. **146**, 58–72 (2018)
12. Luo, S.L., Xia, H.X.: Reflections on the evaluation of smart cities from the perspective of capability maturity. Sci. Res. Manag. **s1** (2018)
13. Gu, D.D., Qiao, W.: Research on the construction of evaluation index system for smart cities in China. Future Dev. **35**(10), 79–83 (2012)
14. Liu, W.Y., Wang, H.L., Liu, K.G., Zhou, X.X.: Applying the combination model of entropy weight and TOPSIS to construct the evaluation system of smart city - taking Beijing, Tianjin and Shanghai as an example to explore. Mod. City Res. **1**, 31–36 (2015)
15. Qi, J.Q., Ba, Y.Q.: Smart city construction evaluation system study based on the specialists method and analytic hierarchy process method. In: International Conference on Smart City and Systems Engineering, no. 115, pp. 149–152 (2016)
16. Liu, Y.L., Cao, W.J.: Application of CRITIC-GREY comprehensive evaluation method in quality evaluation of medical work. China Health Stat. **33**(6), 991–993 (2016)

17. Wu, C.Z., Ma, L.L., Zhang, B.G., Hong, Z.Z.: Study on indicators choosing for navigation safety assessment of three gorges reservoir areas based on Delphi method. In: Asia-Pacific Conference on Information Processing, pp. 282–285 (2009)
18. Zeng, G., Li, H.: Method and Application of Modern Epidemiology, pp. 250–259. Joint Press of Beijing Medical University and Beijing Xiehe Medical University, Beijing (1994)
19. Hu, C.P., Yang, J.: Delphi method in building a government performance indicators system to the township government-as an example. J. Shaanxi Inst. Adm. **4**(21), 12–15 (2007)
20. Diakoulaki, D., Mavrotas, G., Papayannakis, L.: Determining objective weights in multiple criteria problems : the critic method. Comput. Oper. Res. **22**(3), 763–770 (1995)
21. Zhang, N., Sheng, W.: Research on the development of intelligent cities based on principal component analysis and entropy method. J. Urban Sci. **03**, 30–335 (2018)
22. Aljouie, A., Roshan, U.: Prediction of continuous phenotypes in mouse, fly, and rice genome wide association studies with support vector regression SNPs and ridge regression classifier. In: IEEE International Conference on Machine Learning and Applications (2016)
23. Ran, L.I., Guang-Min, L.I.: Photovoltaic power generation output forecasting based on support vector machine regression technique. Electr. Power (02) (2008)
24. Hong, W.C.: Electric load forecasting by support vector model. Appl. Math. Model. **33**(5), 2444–2454 (2009)
25. Yang, F., Kun, G., Jian, H.: Predicting the incidence of portosplenomesenteric vein thrombosis in patients with acute pancreatitis using classification and regression tree (CART) algorithm. J. Crit. Care **39**, 124–130 (2017)
26. Ma, Q.T., Shang, G.Y., Jiao, X.X.: Research on evaluation of smart city construction level based on BP neural network. Pract. Underst. Math. **48**(14), 64–72 (2018)
27. Ramezankhani, R., Sajjadi, N., Nezakati, R.E., et al.: Application of decision tree for prediction of cutaneous leishmaniasis incidence based on environmental and topographic factors in Isfahan Province. Geospatial Health **13**(1), 664 (2018)

An Improved Approach for Complex Activity Recognition in Smart Homes

Nirmalya Thakur[✉] and Chia Y. Han

Department of Electrical Engineering and Computer Science,
University of Cincinnati, Cincinnati, OH 45221-0030, USA
thakurna@mail.uc.edu, han@ucmail.uc.edu

Abstract. The essence of intelligent assistive technologies in smart homes can be outlined as their ability to enhance the user experience in many ways. A way to accomplish this goal is to make such systems aware and knowledgeable about user interactions in the context of the given environment. In the context of smart homes, the ability of such intelligent systems to understand and analyze human behavior in the context of Activities of Daily Living is very essential. Modern day software-based solutions for development of such intelligent systems, should not only be able to sense human movements through Internet of Things based technologies but they should also be able to analyze these components of user interactions in a manner that facilitates optimal utilization of system resources, increases software productivity, improves system interoperability, reduces development and maintenance costs and allows both internal and external reusability of the solutions. Therefore, this paper discusses a study on the 'Complex Activity Recognition Algorithm' [1] and proposes a systematic approach to improve this algorithm for better performance and system optimization. The improved version of this algorithm has been tested on several activities and the results obtained uphold the relevance for implementation of the same in different real-time environments.

Keywords: Activity recognition · Smart homes · Time complexity ·
Software reuse · Activities of Daily Living · System interoperability

1 Introduction

To sustain this ever-increasing world's population, advanced urban development policies equipped with sound infrastructures and modern technologies, such as smart homes are necessary to create better living experiences in day to day lives of people. In the future of smart homes and smart cities, users are expected to interact with systems and robots alike, on a regular basis [2]. To ensure that communications between users and such systems result in good user experiences and increased acceptance of technology by its users, the future intelligent systems would have to analyze much more than user response data collected from touch and speech-based interactions [3]. Specifically, the analysis of human behavior would allow to understand multimodal aspects of user interactions to foster human-technology partnerships [4].

© Springer Nature Switzerland AG 2019
X. Peng et al. (Eds.): ICSR 2019, LNCS 11602, pp. 220–231, 2019.
https://doi.org/10.1007/978-3-030-22888-0_15

Human behavior in smart homes is primarily composed of activities which broadly encompasses interaction with different context parameters to achieve an end goal or objective. While the nature of activities performed by a user in the domain of a smart home can be diverse, Activities of Daily Living (ADLs) are an integral component of these user interactions and represent the daily routine tasks performed by a user [4].

These ADLs can be broadly classified in the following categories [4]:

- Personal Hygiene: Refers to activities like showering, grooming etc.
- Dressing: Refers to activities that involve changing clothes, putting on new clothes and similar tasks.
- Eating: This refers to eating different meals during the course of the day and as per ones eating habits.
- Maintaining continence: This primarily comprises the activity of using a restroom.
- Mobility: This involves the activities of moving around from one place to another as per the requirement.

Activity recognition is a complex process and involves intricate analysis of all the actions and tasks performed by a user on the context parameters at that given point of time. Each ADL has more than one action or task performed by the user. For instance, the ADL of 'eating food' may involve several tasks like sitting down at the table, picking up a spoon and so on. Again, these ADLs and their associated sub tasks are dependent on the environment variables or in other words – context parameters [4].

For instance, in the above scenario, if the chair is missing or if the user has any disorders which limit their ability to sit down, the user might remain in a standing position while completing the rest of the steps to complete eating the food. In other words, activity recognition is not only concerned with analysis of these macro interaction components associated with the given activity being performed by the user, but it also involves analysis of the context parameters that influence these actions or tasks. These small actions or tasks are called atomic activities and the context variables on which they are performed are called context parameters. Together these atomic activities and context parameters constitute a complex activity [1].

There may be various ways in which a user performs these ADLs, for instance the user can perform one ADL at a time, i.e., completing one ADL and then moving on to the next. Such relationship between ADLs is called sequential. Similarly, while performing an ADL, the user can also start off with another ADL and then come back later to complete this ADL. Such relationship between ADLs is called interleaving. Figure 1 shows the different ADLs and illustrates the different relationships based on the nature in which they can be performed [5].

The future of smart homes would involve interconnected and interoperable software systems in an Internet of Things (IoT)-based environment that can cater to the needs of users in a multifaceted way. These software systems would be working in association with the future of intelligent systems and robotics technologies to create better living experiences for its users.

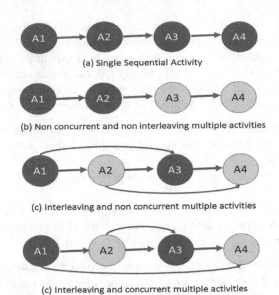

(a) Single Sequential Activity

(b) Non concurrent and non interleaving multiple activities

(c) Interleaving and non concurrent multiple activities

(c) Interleaving and concurrent multiple activities

Fig. 1. Different kinds of relationships that may exist between complex activities and Activities of Daily Living.

Thus, it is essential that these software systems function in a way that involves less operation time so that the existing resources may be reused by other systems. These tools should also incorporate lesser development and running costs to further increase software productivity, foster system interoperability's and improve software reusability, to ensure better user experiences in the context of ADLs.

Recent works [4, 10–15] have used several machine learning, computer vision and data mining technologies to analyze varied relationships in ADLs. However, these systems have a number of limitations, which include (1) the systems require large amount of data for their training and it is quite often difficult to generate so much training data to facilitate proper training of these systems, (2) these tools are not highly accurate for recognition and analysis of different relationships between ADLs as shown in Fig. 1, and (3) these methodologies involve significant amount of operation times which affects their functionality in real-time scenarios.

In view of all these limitations, this paper proposes a study on the 'Complex Activity Recognition Algorithm' [1] and discusses a state of art approach for improvement of the operation time of this algorithm for recognition of ADLs in a Smart Home environment. A couple of recent researches in this field have been used to propose this work. First, is the Complex Activity Recognition Algorithm (CAR-ALGO), proposed by Saguna et al. [1] that uses probability theory-based reasoning principles for complex activity recognition. The second is a four-layered hierarchical model proposed by Ma [7] that uses computer vision to analyze human behavior.

For discussing the effectiveness of this proposed approach, this improved version of CARALGO, has been implemented on complex activities from the UK Domestic Appliance Level Electricity Dataset (UK DALE) [8]. The UK DALE dataset consists of information which describes the nature in which various electrical appliances were used with a time resolution of 6 s involving 109 appliances in 5 smart homes. This data was collected in Southern England, UK from 2012–2015. A related work [9] on this dataset has been used to infer about the associated complex activities from this appliance usage data. The work is presented as follows. Section 2 provides an overview of the recent works in this field following a similar approach. Section 3 discusses the proposed improvement on CARALGO and Sect. 4 presents some of the preliminary results obtained. Section 5 concludes the paper with an overview of the future scope of work.

2 Literature Review

Most of the research in the field of activity centric computing can broadly be divided into two categories – information-based approaches and information-driven approaches. Information-based models for the most part make use of ontologies to infer about human movements and associated activities. Azkune et al. [10] proposed a multilayered system to study human activities in a smart home environment. The design comprised of various layers which were related with understanding of the information collected from IoT-based sensors and analysis of this information to infer details about the task performed by the user. Riboni et al. [11] did not use ontologies to infer about the task being performed, but used ontologies to improve the result obtained from their activity recognition approach. Their work had a knowledge base which had details of different actions or tasks performed by the user and by using a host of reasoning principles and probability theory concepts, they were able to analyze the user's behavior and the associated activity. Nevatia et al. [12] developed an approach to infer about user behavior based on both recorded and real time video data.

Information driven methods for activity analysis have mostly involved using various machine learning and data analysis methods. In the work done by Kasteren et al. [13] different activities were represented using different states of a Hidden Markov Model (HMM). The model analyzed the data coming from IoT-based sensors and using the HMM approach, it was able to infer the activity being performed by the user. Cheng et al. [14] developed a multi layered framework for activity recognition. The framework had three layers with multiple functionalities in each layer. The framework was able to analyze both individual and group activities. Skocir et al. [15] used Artificial Neural Networks (ANN) for activity recognition in a simulated smart home environment. In addition to other activities, the model was able to infer about entry and exit events in a smart home based on data collected from sensors.

A four layered hierarchical framework for activity recognition was recently proposed by Ma [7]. This helps to analyze both individual as well as social interaction behavior based on motion capture data. The first layer of this framework provides information about movement data, based on gait orientation of the user. It also uses the RGB data and infers about the objects and features surrounding the user at that given point of time. The second layer analyzes this motion data and classifies it as Type 1 or Type 2 behavior. Type 1 stands for behavior which relates to the upper body movements and Type 2 stands for behavior which relates to the lower body movements. Interactions with the objects in the environment as well as with other users are also analyzed in this layer. The third layer studies the sequence of these movements for both Type -1 and Type -2 behavior. The fourth layer studies the social interaction components and analyzes the same in terms of Type -1 and Type – 2 movements and their associated data (Fig. 2).

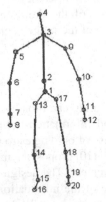

num	Definition	num	Definition
1	Hip Center	11	Wrist Right
2	Spine	12	Hand Right
3	Shoulder Center	13	Hip Left
4	Head	14	Knew Left
5	Shoulder Left	15	Ankle Left
6	Elbow Left	16	Foot Left
7	Wrist Left	17	Hip Right
8	Hand Left	18	Knew Right
9	Shoulder Right	19	Ankle Right
10	Elbow Right	20	Foot Right

Fig. 2. Motion tracking information involving joint points that may be obtained from Microsoft Kinect Sensors [5].

As per the Complex Activity Recognition Algorithm (CARALGO) [1], the series of tasks that are associated with a given activity at hand are called atomic activities (Ati) and the associated objects or environment parameters on which these activities are performed are called context attributes (Cti), together they make up the complex activity. CARALGO also defines the concept of start atomic activities (AtS), start context attributes (CtS), end atomic activities (AtE) and end context attributes (CtE). The start atomic activities refer to those atomic activities which are associated with the start of the given complex activity being performed by the user. The context parameters on which they occur are called start context attributes.

Similarly, the atomic activities that are associated with the end of the complex activity are called end atomic activities and their associated context attributes are called end context attributes. The concept of core atomic activities (γAt) and core context attributes (ρCt) is also explained in CARALGO.

The core atomic activities are those atomic activities which are highly important for successful completion of the given complex activity and have the highest weights associated with them. The context parameters on which these core atomic activities occur are called core context attributes. As per CARALGO [1], every atomic activity and its associated context attribute is associated with a weight which is determined based on probabilistic reasoning principles. Every complex activity is also associated with a threshold function, which is a function of the weights associated with the atomic activities and their associated context attributes. The final weight of the complex activity should be more than the value of this threshold function to infer successful activity completion. In the event, when the final weight is less than the threshold function value, then CARALGO infers that the complex activity was not completed, even though it might have been started. Even though a number of these approaches were able to accurately analyze human activities, but it is essential to improve the system performance and optimization, in terms of reducing the time complexity of operation of the associated algorithms. This forms as the main motivation for this work for suggesting an improvement to CARALGO.

3 Proposed Approach

CARALGO [1] performs a complete analysis of all the atomic activities and context attributes associated with a complex activity. It uses a loop (referenced by a loop counter variable 'i') that starts from the first atomic activity or start atomic activity and analyzes its associated context attribute. As the user continues to perform different atomic activities on different context attributes, it continues checking whether any of those match with the definition of the core atomic activities and core context attributes for that given complex activity. The looping condition runs 'n' times, till the last atomic activity or end atomic activity and its associated context attribute and then performs the condition checks to determine if the complex activity was successfully performed. Here 'n' is the number of atomic activities associated to the given complex activity.

There are two conditions that are checked by CARALGO. First, it checks whether the atomic activities and context attributes performed by the user aligned with the definition of the core atomic activities and core context attributes for that given complex activity. Performing the core atomic activities and their associated core context attributes is the minimum condition to complete a given complex activity as per CARALGO.

Then, it checks if the weight of the atomic activities and their associated context attributes exceed the value of the threshold function. The threshold function determines its value based on the weight of the core atomic activities and their associated core context attributes. For an activity to be successfully performed, the weight associated with its atomic activities and context attributes should exceed the value of this threshold function. The pseudo code describing this working mechanism of CAR-ALGO is represented as follows:

1. A loop, referenced by a loop counter variable, 'i', runs from AtS to AtE – 'n' times, incrementing itself by one each time
   a. for each Ati: check for γAt
   b. for each Cti: check for ρCt
   c. record all the γAt being performed
   d. record all the ρCt being performed
2. Check if all γAt were performed
3. Check if all ρCt were performed
4. Calculate the total weight of all Ati
5. Calculate the total weight of all Cti
6. Check for Threshold condition – to determine activity completion

   where i = loop counter variable

AtS = start atomic activity
AtE = end atomic activity
CtS = start context attribute
CtE = end context attribute
Ati = ith Atomic activity
Cti = ith Context Attribute
n = number of atomic activities associated with the given complex activity
γAt = core atomic activity
ρCt = core context attribute.

The major complex activities from the UK DALE dataset as shown in Fig. 3, were analyzed through CARALGO. To ensure that the volume of this paper is within reasonable limits, analysis of one of the complex activities – 'Watching TV' is being presented next.

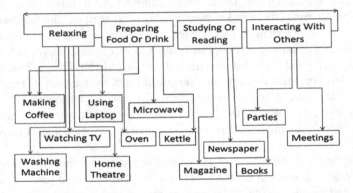

Fig. 3. An overview of the major complex activities from the UK DALE dataset [16].

Table 1. Analysis by CARALGO for the complex activity of 'Watching TV'.

Complex Activity WCAtk (WT Atk) - WT (0.55)	
Weight of Atomic Activities WtAti	At1: Walking towards TV (0.15) At2: Turning on the TV (0.30) At3: Fetching the remote control (0.25) At4: Sitting Down (0.08) At5: Tuning Proper Channel (0.12) At6: Adjusting Display and Audio (0.10)
Weight of Context Attributes WtCti	Ct1: Entertainment Area (0.15) Ct2: Presence of TV (0.30) Ct3: Remote Control Available (0.25) Ct4: Sitting Area (0.08) Ct5: Channel Present (0.12) Ct6: Settings working (0.10)
Core γAt and ρCt	At2, At3 and Ct2, Ct3
Start AtS and CtS	At1 and Ct1
End AtE and CtE	At6 and Ct6

As observed from Table 1, the atomic activities associated to this complex activity of 'Watching TV' are At1: Walking towards TV, At2: Turning on the TV, At3: Fetching the remote control, At4: Sitting Down, At5: Tuning Proper Channel, At6: Adjusting Display and Audio and their associated context attributes are Ct1: Entertainment Area, Ct2: Presence of TV, Ct3: Remote Control Available, Ct4: Sitting Area, Ct5: Channel Present, Ct6: Settings working.

The weights associated with these atomic activities are At1: 0.15, At2: 0.30, At3: 0.25, At4: 0.08, At5: 0.12, At6: 0.10 and the weights associated to the context attributes are Ct1: 0.15, Ct2: 0.30, Ct3: 0.25, Ct4: 0.08, Ct5: 0.12, Ct6: 0.10. The start atomic activity and its associated context attribute is At1: Walking towards TV and Ct1: Entertainment Area. The end atomic activity and its associated context attribute is At6: Adjusting Display and Audio and Ct6: Settings working. The core atomic activities are At2: Turning on the TV and At3: Fetching the remote control. The context attributes associated to these core atomic activities are Ct2: Presence of TV and Ct3: Remote Control Available. As At2 and At3 have the highest weights so they are considered as the core atomic activities and their associated context attributes are considered as the core context attributes for this complex activity of 'Watching TV'.

CARALGO runs a loop that goes from At1 to At6 checking for the occurrence of the core atomic activities to check for the minimum condition of having successfully completed this complex activity. However, as can be observed from Table 1, that the core atomic activities and their associated core context attributes occur in the first half of the list of atomic activities associated with this complex activity. According to [6], activity is a sequential process and the nature of completion of each step determines the nature of completion of the next. Using this principle, we posit that the specific order in which the atomic activities are performed are essential for successfully completing any given complex activity.

For instance, in this given example of 'Watching TV', there is no way that the user can perform At5 and At6 and then perform At2 and At3. Another interesting observation, that comes out from this detailed study of CARALGO, is that the core atomic activities and their associated core context attributes are very important and significant for any given complex activity, so they are generally performed towards the beginning of the complex activity.

As can be observed from this example of 'Watching TV', the core atomic activities and their associated core context attributes occur in the first half of the list of atomic activities and context attributes associated with this complex activity. Thus, instead of running the loop in the CARALGO algorithm, to check for core atomic and core context attributes, till the end atomic activity, the same could be run till the first half of the list of atomic activities associated with this complex activity. This is further illustrated in the pseudo code below.

1. A loop runs from 1st Ati to $n/2^{th}$ Ati – incrementing itself by one each time
   a. for each Ati: check for γAt
   b. for each Cti: check for ρCt
   c. record the core Ati being performed
   d. record the core Cti being performed
2. Check if all γAt were performed

3. Check if all ρCt were performed
4. Calculate the total weight of all Ati
5. Calculate the total weight of all Cti
6. Check for Threshold condition – to determine activity completion

Relating this pseudo code to this example presented in Table 1, the algorithm would run from the first atomic activity till the third atomic activity to check for the occurrence of core atomic activities and their associated core context attributes. As At2 and At3 are the core atomic activities so by running till the third atomic activity, the algorithm would have automatically identified the same and it would not have to unnecessarily check At4, At5 and At6 to see if those atomic activities also belong to the list of core atomic activities or otherwise. This ensures that the algorithm still performs the same function but in less operation time. This is further explained in the following section.

4 Results and Discussion

As discussed in the previous section, the actual CARALGO algorithm can be considered as a loop running from 1 to n where each iteration of the loop involves comparing the atomic activity that occurred in that iteration, with the list of core atomic activities for that complex activity, to see if it matches with any. In a simpler manner it can be represented as a for loop (although any other looping construct would also be equally fine) as shown below:

```
for (i = 1; i<=n; i++)
{
Compare Ati with γAt
Compare Cti with ρCt
}
```

The time complexity of the above is $O(n)$, where n represents the total number of atomic activities associated with the complex activity.

In a similar manner, this proposed approach to reduce the operation time of CARALGO, can be considered as a loop that goes from 1 to n/2, instead of n, as shown below

```
for (i = 1; i<=n/2; i++)
{
Compare Ati with core Ati
Compare Cti with core Cti
}
```

The time complexity of the above is $O(n/2)$, where n represents the total number of atomic activities associated with the complex activity.

As can be observed from this discussion that this proposed improvement over CARALGO, which has a time complexity of O(n/2) would execute in half the amount of time as compared to the actual CARALGO algorithm, without failing to perform any of the associated functionalities that CARALGO implements.

The complex activity discussed here, 'Watching TV', involves 6 atomic activities and 6 context attributes. However, during this study on the UK DALE dataset, it was observed that several complex activities were way too complicated and involved a lot more actions or tasks required for completion, where this method of activity analysis proved to be useful. A recent work [17] in this field helps to analyze the different ways by which a complex activity can be performed by a user which is as follows:

$$U = xC0 + xC1 + xC2 + \ldots\ldots.xCx = 2^x \tag{1}$$

$$V = (x-p)C0 + (x-p)C1 + (x-p)C2 + .. + (x-p)C(x-p) = 2^{(x-p)} \tag{2}$$

$$W = 2^x - 2^{(x-p)} = 2^{(x-p)}.(2^p - 1) \tag{3}$$

where

U: total number of ways a user may interface with a given complex activity. This includes successful completions as well as false starts

V: total number of ways by which a user may successfully complete the given complex activity

W: total number of ways by which a user may never be able to successfully complete the given complex activity

x: total number of atomic activities

y: total number of context attributes

p: total number of core atomic activities

q: total number of core context attributes

Here 'C' stands for the notation of combination in mathematics.

In any given IoT based environment, performing a complex activity would involve accomplishing several tasks and sub-tasks. Although the formulae above, helps to analyze complex activities and the associated atomic activities and context attributes better; but in a realistic scenario it would involve high computational cost and time, which is not desirable. Therefore, this proposed improvement of CARALGO is also expected to address the limitations of the work in [17] for complex activity recognition and analysis, in a way that ensures low time complexity, improves system interoperability, reduces development and maintenance costs and allows both internal and external reusability of the solutions.

This approach can therefore be considered be considered for real-time implementation. Some potential applications of this improved version of CARALGO may involve smart home activity recognition systems, patient behavior monitoring in hospitals, behavior monitoring in rehabilitation centers, activity recognition and monitoring in elderly homes etc. Such an improvement in the operation time of CARALGO would reduce both computational time as well as memory requirements for its implementation. This would increase software productivity, reduce maintenance costs and foster optimal utilization of system resources in an IoT-based setting.

5 Conclusion and Future Work

This paper presents a detailed study on the 'Complex Activity Recognition Algorithm' (CARALGO) [1] and discusses an approach to reduce the time complexity of the same. The modified version of CARALGO, with a reduced time complexity, without any limitations in its functionalities has been tested on several complex activities from the UK DALE dataset [8]. The results are presented and discussed for one of the complex activities – 'Watching TV'.

To the best knowledge of the authors, no similar work has been done in this field yet, which features a similar approach. The preliminary results presented prove that this modification in CARALGO would significantly reduce its operation time as compared to the actual version of CARALGO. As of the study completed on this approach, this modified version of CARALGO has been tested on several complex activities from the UK DALE dataset [8] and the results obtained uphold the relevance for its practical implementation. Future work would involve implementation of this algorithm on complex activities from other user interaction datasets as well as real-time implementation of the same in smart and connected IoT-based environments.

References

1. Saguna, S., Zaslavsky, A., Chakraborty, D.: Building activity definitions to recognize complex activities using an online activity toolkit. In: IEEE 13th International Conference on Mobile Data Management, pp. 344–347, August 2012
2. United Nation: World Urbanization Prospect (2014). http://dl.acm.org/citation.cfm?id=308574.308676
3. Davies, N., Siewiorek, D.P., Sukthankar, R.: Activity-based computing. Pervasive Comput. IEEE **7**, 20–21 (2008)
4. Kaptelinin, V., Nardi, B.: Activity Theory in HCI Fundamentals and Reflections. Morgan and Claypool Publishers (2012). ISBN 9781608457045, eISBN 9781608457052
5. Chakraborty, S.: A study on Context Driven Human Activity Recognition Framework" – Masters thesis at University of Cincinnati (2015). http://rave.ohiolink.edu/etdc/view?acc_num=ucin1439308572
6. Tao, G., Zhanqing, W., Xianping, T., Hung Keng, P., Jian, L.: epSICAR: an emerging patterns based approach to sequential, interleaved and concurrent activity recognition. In: IEEE International Conference on Pervasive Computing and Communications, pp. 1–9 (2009)
7. Ma, T.: A framework for modeling and capturing social interactions. Ph.D. dissertation, University of Cincinnati, December 2014
8. Jack, K., William, K.: The UK-DALE dataset, domestic appliance-level electricity demand and whole-house demand from five UK homes. Sci. Data **2**, 150007 (2015)
9. Yassine, A., Singh, S., Alamri, A.: Mining human activity patterns from smart home big data for health care applications. In: IEEE Special Section on Advances of Multisensory Services and Technologies for Healthcare in Smart Cities, June 2017

10. Azkune, G., Almeida, A., López-de-Ipiña, D., Chen, L.: Extending knowledge driven activity models through data-driven learning techniques. Expert Syst. Appl. **42** (2015). https://doi.org/10.1016/j.eswa.2014.11.063
11. Riboni, D., Bettini, C.: Context-aware activity recognition through a combination of ontological and statistical reasoning. In: Zhang, D., Portmann, M., Tan, A.-H., Indulska, J. (eds.) UIC 2009. LNCS, vol. 5585, pp. 39–53. Springer, Heidelberg (2009). https://doi.org/10.1007/978-3-642-02830-4_5
12. Nevatia, R., Hobbs, J., Bolles, B.: An ontology for video event representation. In: Proceedings of the 2004 Conference on Computer Vision and Pattern Recognition Workshop, CVPRW 2004, vol. 7, p. 119. IEEE Computer Society, Washington, DC (2004)
13. van Kasteren, T., Noulas, A., Englebienne, G., Kröse, B.: Accurate activity recognition in a home setting. In: Proceedings of the 10th International Conference on Ubiquitous Computing, UbiComp 2008, pp. 1–9. ACM, Seoul, Korea (2008)
14. Cheng, Z., Qin, L., Huang, Q., Jiang, S., Yan, S., Tian, Q.: Human group activity analysis with fusion of motion and appearance information. In: Proceedings of the 19th ACM International Conference on Multimedia, pp. 1401–1404, Scottsdale, Arizona, USA, 28 November–01 December 2011
15. Skocir, P., Krivic, P., Tomeljak, M., Kusek, M., Jezic, G.: Activity detection in smart home environment. In: Proceedings of the 20th International Conference on Knowledge Based and Intelligent Information and Engineering Systems, 5–7 September 2016
16. Thakur, N., Han, C.Y.: A complex activity based emotion recognition algorithm for affect aware systems. In: Proceedings of the IEEE-CCWC 2018 Conference, 08–10 January 2018, Las Vegas, USA (2018)
17. Thakur, N., Han, C.Y.: A context-driven complex activity framework for smart home. In: Proceedings of the 9th Annual Information Technology, Electronics and Mobile Communication Conference (IEMCON) 2018, Vancouver, Canada, 1–3 November 2018. https://ieeexplore.ieee.org/document/8615079

Examining the Reusability of Smart Home Applications: A Case Study on Eclipse Smart Home

Paraskevi Smiari[1(✉)], Stamatia Bibi[1], and Daniel Feitosa[2]

[1] Department of Informatics and Telecommunications Engineering,
University of Western Macedonia, Kozani, Greece
{psmiari, sbibi}@uowm.gr
[2] Data Research Centre, University of Groningen, Groningen, The Netherlands
d.feitosa@rug.nl

Abstract. Smart Homes consist of a plethora of IoT devices most of which developed by different manufacturers. To handle the diversity of IoT devices within the context of Smart Home automation, literature has suggested the use of frameworks. In this paper we argue that developers can benefit from such frameworks as a solution to build flexible and easily extendable systems by reusing their components. For this purpose, we explore the reuse opportunities that can be offered by Eclipse Smart Home (ESH) framework. In particular, we performed a case study and analyzed 107 packages from the ESH framework that offered 240 reusable components to the OpenHab application. We investigated (a) which types of functionality are mostly facilitated for reuse (b) which types of reuse are mostly adopted and what is the integration effort required (c) what is the quality of the reused components and compared them to the components built from scratch. The results of the case study suggest that: the main functionality reused is the one related to Interface Adapters and the main type of reuse is Variable Type. Regarding the effort for integrating the reused components it can range from 38 lines of code to 1421 lines of code. Moreover, the quality of the reused components is slightly improved compared to the rest of the components built from scratch.

Keywords: Smart Home · IoT applications · Reusability · Effort estimation · Flexibility · Extendibility

1 Introduction

Since the last decade, the emerging paradigm of the Internet of Things (IoT) dominates the Smart City [15] landscape, offering a range of citizen services [34] that include among others, healthcare, education, energy consumption, and home automation. According to ABI[1], the research of the realization of the Smart City concept should start from the Smart Home. At the moment the Smart Home revenue amounts at 69,551

---

[1] https://www.smartcitiesworld.net/special-reports/special-reports/why-the-smart-city-could-increasingly-start-at-home.

© Springer Nature Switzerland AG 2019
X. Peng et al. (Eds.): ICSR 2019, LNCS 11602, pp. 232–247, 2019.
https://doi.org/10.1007/978-3-030-22888-0_16

million dollars and is expected to present an annual growth of 20.3%, while the penetration of Smart Home technologies in households is still in its infancy. By 2019, 9.5% of households have already adopted Smart Home technologies, a percentage that is expected to hit 22.1% by 2023[2]. IoT devices are the key concept in Smart Homes to manage energy, security, lighting and appliances [1]. Smart Homes consist of a plethora of IoT devices (i.e., sensors and meters) that need to cooperate and are mostly developed by different manufacturers, as well as designed and implemented with heterogeneous technologies. Therefore, Smart Home applications need to be flexible so as to manipulate the individuality of each device [12], and also extendable so as to integrate new devices [28].

To handle this inherit diversity of IoT devices within the context of Smart Home automation, literature has suggested the use of frameworks that are based on highly modularized software building blocks [11, 12, 25]. In these frameworks, despite the fact that they are very large and complex, one can identify a core set of concepts (i.e. Devices and Controllers) which can enable reuse. Therefore, developers can benefit from such frameworks as a solution to build flexible and easily extendable systems by reusing their components. Currently there are several available Open Source Software frameworks[3] with big support from the community that can facilitate reuse. The main challenges that an engineer confronts while reusing components from one of these frameworks are summarized as follows:

(a) Select the *type of functionality to reuse.* The functionalities offered by Smart Home frameworks can be classified based on the requirement that they implement. For example, a component can be related to a core Smart Home purpose (i.e., a Device) and therefore increase its potential reuse or can implement specific details (i.e., Visualization Graphs) and decrease its potential reuse.

(b) Plan the *type of reuse* and the *effort* required for integrating the reused components. The *type of reuse* can vary from simply using components as they are, to implementing new functionalities on the reused components for integrating them. In the last case it is important to have an approximation of the *effort* required to integrate the reused component, which can be measured as the time required to apply the changes or the amount of new lines of code added.

(c) Ensure that the *quality of the reusable components* does not compromise the overall quality of the application. For this purpose, it is important to examine the quality aspects that are important for Smart Home applications and make sure that they do not present quality differences with the rest of the application developed from scratch.

In this study we explore how the aforementioned challenges are confronted when reusing components from the popular Eclipse Smart Home (ESH) framework that is used as the 'source' application. ESH was selected because it is frequently used in research [19, 21, 33], has a strong support from industrial players like Bosch and QIVICON, and is often reused for building commercial products (e.g., Mixtile Hub,

---

[2] https://www.statista.com/outlook/279/100/smart-home/worldwide.

[3] https://www.eclipse.org/smarthome/, https://www.openhab.org/, https://www.home-assistant.io/.

Coqon). As a 'target' application, we employ the OpenHab project, which is based on ESH. OpenHab takes advantage of the abstraction level that ESH provides and offers a holistic platform that supports different devices under one design. As part of this study we analyzed 107 packages from the ESH framework, which offers 240 reusable components to OpenHab. Our results showed that the main functionality reused is the one related to Interface Adapters, the main type of reuse is Variable Type and the effort for integrating the reused components can range from 38 lines of code to 1421 lines of code. Moreover, the quality of the reused components is slightly improved in comparison to the rest of the components built from scratch; however, without presenting a statistically significant difference.

The rest of this paper is organized as follows. Section 2 discusses the related work. Section 3 describes the case study design whereas Sect. 4 presents the results obtained from the case study. Finally, Sect. 5 discusses the results and addresses the threats to validity of this study and Sect. 6 concludes the paper and presents ideas for future work.

2 Related Work

Software reuse is a widely known and used technique for the creation of a new software product that is based on the adoption of existing software components [30]. Among the major benefits offered by software reuse is the minimization of the cost and the effort required to develop an application [13]. Several studies [26, 31] mention that increased productivity along with cost reduction is among the main objectives of software reuse. This is achieved through placing emphasis on identifying and integrating reusable components instead of designing and implementing new functionalities from scratch [6, 16]. Another benefit of software reuse is the improvement of software system flexibility [10, 31]. According to Jatain et al., [10] development based on components increases significantly the system flexibility. This is achieved through the separation of the stable parts of systems from the specification of their composition [10]. Software reuse is also related to the increased quality of the final product [26] in the sense that the reuse of software components that are already tested and validated, increases the probability of developing applications of increased quality [26].

Discovering the reusable software is a challenge itself as it is important to efficiently prioritize candidate assets for reuse and select the most appropriate ones [2]. Research has focused on data mining techniques [22, 32] for identifying reusable assets by taking into consideration several software quality metrics. Evaluating reusable components through a set of metrics and predicting whether or not are qualified as reusable [17] is very important when it comes to discovering reusable software. Moreover, clustering techniques for identifying components of similar functionality and reusability have been thoroughly discussed by Jatain et al. in [10].

Another major challenge that arises when it comes to the reusability of the software is adapting the components that are being reused into the new environment that is being developed [27]. It is often required to parameterize the reusable components in order to integrate them in the existing environment [9, 18]. Refactoring in a component that is being reused, or in the project that reuses it, can have the opposite effect and can be time consuming, especially if the new environment is demanding [5]. Therefore, it is important to place special emphasis on carefully planning the integration of the reusable artifact into the new application [7].

To the best of our knowledge, the practice of software reuse in the IoT development process has not been explored so far, despite the numerous benefits that it offers. In this study we go beyond current literature by examining the software reuse potentials for building home automation IoT applications. In particular, we investigate to which level the aforementioned reuse goals are achieved and explore the challenges of reuse that are related to the quality of the reused components and the effort required to integrate the components to the new environment.

3 Case Study Design and Evaluation

In this section, we present the design of the case study performed to assess the reusability potentials of IoT frameworks. We report the details of this case study based on the guidelines of Runeson et al. [24]. In Sect. 3.1, we present the research objectives of the study. In Sects. 3.2 and 3.3, we describe the two applications that participate in this study and the data collection processes. Finally, we provide an overview of the data analysis process in Sect. 3.4.

3.1 Research Objectives and Questions

The overall goal of this case study is to *examine the reuse potentials for IoT home automation application frameworks* in terms of (a) the *type of functionality* of the component that is being reused (b) the level of *customization* required for integrating the reused component and (c) the *quality* of the final product. To ease the design and reporting of the case study, we split the aforementioned goal into five research questions, based on the analysis perspectives that we introduced in Sect. 1, as follows:

RQ1: Which types of functionality offer the most components in the context of IoT home automation application reuse?

This research question aims at identifying the types of functionalities that offer the larger pool of components. The classification scheme adopted to assess the types of the functionalities offered by the reused components was inspired from the concept of "clean architecture" [14]. The discipline of Clean Architecture defines four core types of functionalities namely, the Enterprise Business Rules, the Application Business Rules, the Interface Adapters, and the Frameworks & Drivers [14]. The analysis in this question will provide an overall view of the number of the reused components offered by each type of functionality.

RQ2: Which types of reuse offer the most components in the context of IoT home automation application reuse?

This research question aims at identifying the *types of reuse* that are mostly adopted in the context of IoT applications. We consider three types of reuse, Variable type reuse, Static method or Constant value reuse, and Implementation of interface or parent class (see Sect. 3.3). The analysis in this question will provide an overall view of which types of reuse is expected to be adopted.

RQ3: What is the level of customization required to integrate the reused components?

This research question explores the effort required to integrate a reused component in the new project. The integration effort, in our case, is measured as the lines of code for implementing new functionalities related to the reused artifacts (see analytically in Sect. 4). The output of this research question will provide insights on the level of changes required for each type of functionality reused.

RQ4: What is the quality of the reused components with respect to the functionalities offered?

This research question investigates the quality of the reused components by assessing four indices of the QMOOD model [3], *Reusability, Flexibility, Extendibility* and *Functionality*. We selected these quality aspects as two of them (Reusability and Functionality) are highly related to the reusability of the new application [4, 20], while the other two (Flexibility and Extendibility) are appointed as important quality aspects of IoT applications [28]. The result of this research question will be an analysis of the quality of the reused components per type of functionality offered.

RQ5: Is there a difference between the quality of the components developed with reuse and the quality of the components developed from scratch and how is this reflected to the different types of the functionalities offered?

This research question compares the quality of the components developed with reuse and the quality of the components developed from scratch, by assessing the four indices of the QMOOD model [3]: *Reusability, Flexibility, Extendibility* and *Functionality*. The result of this research question will provide insights on whether reuse of components in IoT application development is expected to bring quality benefits. As a second step, we will diversify between the quality of components built with and without reuse with respect to the offered functionalities.

3.2   Case Selection

This section presents the details of the two projects that were selected for examining the reuse potentials in IoT applications. The first part of this section presents the context of the Eclipse Smart Home application, which is considered as the 'source' of the reusable components. The second part of this section presents the context of OpenHab 2, which is considered as the 'target' of the reusable components.

Eclipse Smart Home

The **Eclipse Smart Home (ESH)** project is an open source framework for developing home automation IoT applications[4] that have a strong focus on heterogeneous environments. It is comprised of a set of OSGi bundles that support the integration of different protocols and standards. ESH was launched in 2014 and it is part of the

---

[4] https://www.eclipse.org/smarthome/, https://iot.eclipse.org/.

Eclipse IoT, which comprises four projects providing open source implementations of IoT protocols, services and frameworks. The community of ESH is composed of over 179 active contributors, while more than six companies have adopted this framework for developing on top IoT applications. Currently, the project has been forked over 829 times and has a history of four releases.

In this study, we explored ESH, version ref-0.10.0 as the 'source' that provides the reusable components for building IoT applications on top. Currently, ESH provides all the benefits of an open source project, such as a big support from the community and cost efficiency which renders it a primary choice when it comes to reusing components for building IoT solutions. Additionally, ESH is consistently used for empirical research the last years in the context of building automations [19], monitoring environments for smart and secure homes [21, 33], and from the perspective of user interface [29]. Table 1 presents the summary statistics of the two projects adopted in this study.

OpenHab2

The **O**pen **H**ome **A**utomation **B**us (OpenHab) is an open source, technology agnostic home automation platform launched on February 2010. The platform has been actively maintained in the last 9 years and it is a solution built upon the ESH framework. The founders of OpenHab, afterwards, donated the core framework of the application to the Eclipse Foundation so as to benefit from the rigid intellectual property management and clear contribution processes that Eclipse provides. For the purposes of this study, we use the latest version of OpenHab 2^5 (v2.4). The functionalities offered by OpenHab 2 are split into two projects: OpenHab Core and OpenHab AddOns. The OpenHab Core is the repository in which all the core framework bundles are implemented, whereas OpenHab AddOns is a repository that contains all the bindings and services. Bindings are responsible for integrating physical hardware, external systems, and web services in OpenHab.

Table 1. Eclipse Smart Home and OpenHab projects.

Project	Packages	Nof. classes	LoC	Releases
Eclipse S. Home	107	2197	363.735	4
Eclipse S. Home (r)*	47	240	139.174	4
OpenHab	147	3384	394.788	5
OpenHab (wr)**	140	704	259.661	5

* Statistics of the Eclipse S. Home packages, classes, etc. being reused
** Statistics of the OpenHab packages, classes, built with reuse

---
5 https://www.openhab.org/.

In this case study, OpenHab is the 'target' of the reused components and will serve as a sample to explore the benefits acquired from reuse with respect to the different types of functionalities reused. We selected to explore the level of reuse performed in the context of the development of OpenHab because: (a) it is a fully functional and 'open' platform that can be considered as an end-product instead of a framework (that is the case of Eclipse Smart Home); (b) it is open source, which allows as to fully explore all the types of reuse potentials; (c) it is very popular, counting almost 30,000 members, supporting the interface of over 1,500 IoT devices and gadgets; and (d) it can be considered as a representative of closed-source commercial projects (e.g., Mixtile, Qivicon) that are based on Eclipse Smart Home Framework to implement end-product solutions.

3.3   Data Collection

In order to answer the research questions of this study we followed the process summarized in the next steps:

Step1: We calculated the **Actual Reuse** of each component of ESH, using the information reported in the Maven[6] repository. We isolated the packages that are being reused, mapped these packages to the related OpenHab packages and counted the *Number of Components* that each ESH package offers and the *Lines of Code* offered to OpenHab.

Step2: The second step was to classify the **Type of Functionality** offered from ESH reused packages into the four categories of Clean Architecture, Enterprise Business Rules, Application Business Rules, Interface Adapters, and Frameworks & Drivers. For this purpose, we extracted the semantics behind every ESH class. For example, the class Thing represents everything that can be physically added to the system. It is one of the core classes in ESH and part of the core architecture which makes it an Entity and, therefore, part of the Enterprise Business Rules. In Table 2 we provide the keywords used to classify each class into one of the four categories of functionalities.

Step3: As a next step we classified the **Type of Reuse** in one of the following classes: Variable type reuse, Static method or Constant value reuse, and Implementation of interface or parent class. By *Variable type* reuse we mean an instantiation of a new object from the reused class that has not been subject to changes. *Static method or constant value reuse* refers to the utilization of a parameter or function of a reused class that has not been subject to changes. *Implementation of interface, or parent class* refers to the extension of the reused class by adding new functionalities or implementing existing definitions.

Step 4: Next, we recorded the **New Lines of Code** developed for integrating the reused components. For this purpose, we counted the lines of code developed in the case of *Implementation of interface, or parent class* type of reuse, considering that in the other two types of reuse no changes have been performed, since in the cases

---

[6] https://mvnrepository.com/.

were OpenHab adds new functionalities in an ESH class always occurs from the inheritance of a class.

Step 5: As a final step we recorded the *Quality* of the Components participating in the reuse process by calculating the metrics defined by Bansiya et al. for assessing the *Functionality*, the *Extendibility*, the *Reusability,* and the *Flexibility* [3]. We calculated these four quality metrics for the Reused (R) components coming from ESH and for the components developed With Reuse in the OpenHab project. To have a holistic view of the quality obtained with and without reuse, we also calculated the Quality of the Components developed Without Reuse (WR). Table 2 presents the metrics considered within the scope of this study and their description.

Table 2. Design metrics

Type	Metric	Description
Reuse metrics	Development with reuse	Shows if a component has been built with reuse (Yes/No)
	Type of functionality	Enterprise Business Rules (keyword = Thing) Application Business Rules (keyword = Configuration) Interface Adapters (keyword = Handler) Frameworks & Drivers (keyword = SiteMap)
	Type of reuse	Variable Type Static method call or Constant value Implementation of Interface or Parent class
	Number of components (NoC)	Number of components reused (each component corresponds to one class)
	Total reuse of components (TRC)	Total number of times a component is reused in OpenHab
Effort metrics	New lines of code	Lines of code added by OpenHab
	Lines of code reused	Lines of code provided by reusable components of ESH
Quality metrics	Functionality	$0.12 * CAM + 0.22 * NOP + 0.22 * CIS + 0.22 * DSC + 0.22 * NOH$
	Extendibility	$0.5 * ANA - 0.5 * DCC + 0.5 * MFA + 0.5 * NOP$
	Reusability	$-0.25 * DCC + 0.25 * CAM + 0.5 * CIS + 0.5 * DSC$
	Flexibility	$0.25 * DAM - 0.25 * DCC + 0.5 * MOA + 0.5 * NOP$

CAM = Cohesion Among Methods of Class, NOP = Number of Polymorphic Methods, CIS = Class Interface Size, DSC = Design Size in Classes, NOH = Number of Hierarchies, ANA = Average Number of Ancestors, DCC = Direct Class Coupling, MFA = Measure of Functional Abstraction, DAM = Data Access Metric, MOA = Measure of Aggregation [3]

3.4   Data Analysis

The data analysis of this case study includes the calculation of the frequency and descriptive statistics, and the application of Analysis of Variance (ANOVA).

For *RQ1,* we provide the frequency statistics of the total number of components and packages offered by ESH with respect to their *Type of Functionality*. Additionally, ANOVA is performed to identify whether the *Number of Components* offered by the different *Types of Functionality* varies significantly.

Concerning *RQ2,* we discuss the frequency with which the different *Types of Reuse* are implemented by providing the relevant pie chart.

For addressing RQ_3 the descriptive statistics (min, max, mean, st.dev) are presented for the offered *Type of Functionality* and the *Lines of Code* required for integrating the reused components. In this case, ANOVA is performed to identify whether different types of functionality offer components that present *significant* differences in the effort required for their integration.

In *RQ4,* we perform ANOVA to identify whether there are significant differences in the quality *(Extendibility, Flexibility, Reusability, Functionality)* of the provided components for the different *Types of Functionality*. The descriptive statistics are also presented.

Similarly, in *RQ5,* we perform ANOVA to identify whether there are significant differences in the quality *(Extendibility, Flexibility, Reusability, Functionality)* of the packages developed with reuse and the packages developed without reuse. In this case, the grouping variable is the *Development with Reuse.*

4   Results

In this section, we present and interpret the results of this case study, organized by research question, and based on the data analysis presented in Sect. 3.4.

RQ1 – Which types of functionality offer the most components in the context of IoT home automation application reuse?

Table 3 presents the summary statistics for the four types of functionality offered by ESH, ranked by the frequency of the reused components (see RF - column 5). It can be observed that the highest number of components (see CR – column 4) offer functionality related to Frameworks & Drivers and Interface Adapters. In terms of the highest reuse frequency per functionality type components (see RF – column 5), we observed that the maximum percentage is recorded for two functionality types: Application Business Rules and Frameworks & Drivers. On the other hand, the least reused components offer functionality related to Enterprise Business Rules.

Table 3. Reuse per type of functionality

Type of functionality	TP	TC	PR	CR	RF
Application Business Rules	22	214	16	53	0.25
Frameworks & Drivers	42	567	26	97	0.17
Interface Adapters	38	1224	25	81	0.07
Enterprise Business Rules	5	192	1	9	0.05

TP: Total number of packages in ESH per functionality type.
TC: Total number of components per functionality type.
PR: Number of packages of ESH reused by OpenHab per functionality type.
CR: Number of components of ESH reused by OpenHab per functionality type.
RF: Reuse Frequency = CR/TC

To investigate if the aforementioned differences are statistically significant, we performed an Analysis of Variance (ANOVA), which suggested that there are not significant differences in the reusable components of the different types of functionality (F: 2.276, sig: 0.087).

RQ2 – Which types of reuse offer the most components in the context of IoT home automation application reuse?

Concerning RQ2, we discuss the frequency of the different Types of Reuse (see Fig. 1). The results of the pie chart suggested that most of the reused components are used directly as Variable types or Calls to static methods/constant values. However, the implementation of new functionality was required in 24.2% of the reused components. It seems that in the majority of the cases reuse is performed without any changes of integration effort. This can be interpreted intuitively since, as mentioned in RQ1, the majority of the reused components offer core functionality (i.e., Application Business rules and Enterprise Business Rules), which are the least likely to require changes.

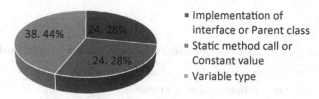

- Implementation of interface or Parent class
- Static method call or Constant value
- Variable type

Fig. 1. Pie Chart (Frequency of usage types)

RQ3 – What is the level of customization required to integrate the reused components?

To investigate the effort required for the integration of the components with respect to the different types of reused functionality, we calculated the descriptive statistics and performed ANOVA for the variable *New Lines of Code,* but only for the cases where the reuse type is Implementation of interface/parent class. In Table 4 we present the summary statistics of the effort required to integrate the components of different functionality types. The first column shows the value of ***TRC*** variable that indicates accumulatively the total number of the times that the components of different functionality types have been reused. It can be observed in Table 4 that the type of functionality that requires the greatest effort on average is Interface Adapters. This result can be interpreted intuitively since Interface and Adapters components are responsible for integrating and supporting a wide range of smart devices, a fact that requires certain code for the customization of the generic components being reused.

Table 4. Effort required to integrate the reused components per type of functionality.

Type of functionality	TRC	Mean	Std. Dev	Min	Max
Enterprise Business Rules	1	72.00	–	72	72
Application Business Rules	9	208.44	95.06	94	387
Interface Adapters	357	237.37	221.29	42	1421
Frameworks & Drivers	144	155.23	85.02	38	662

To investigate if the aforementioned differences are statistically significant, we performed an ANOVA (F: 10.140, Sig: < 0.001), which showed a significant difference between groups in OpenHab with respect to the effort required when it comes to their integration.

RQ4 – What is the quality of the reused components with respect to the functionalities offered?

In Table 5 we present the results of the quality of the reused components provided by ESH.

Table 5. Quality of the ESH and OpenHab components per type of functionality offered.

Type of functionality	Quality	ESH	OpenHab
Enterprise Business Rules	Reusability	15.71	6.22
	Flexibility	0.07	0.25
	Functionality	5.67	3.02
	Extendibility	0.60	0.1
Application Business Rules	Reusability	10.19	90.73
	Flexibility	0.15	1.00
	Functionality	3.28	42.06
	Extendibility	0.32	1.51
Interface Adapters	Reusability	12.16	12.28
	Flexibility	0.37	0.26
	Functionality	3.43	6.19
	Extendibility	0.30	0.50
Frameworks & Drivers	Reusability	9.65	11.67
	Flexibility	0.13	0.28
	Functionality	2.93	5.57
	Extendibility	0.09	0.34

For this research question, we examined *Reusability, Flexibility, Functionality, and Extendibility* with respect to the offered functionalities. In terms of *Reusability,* the differences are small, with the exception of Enterprise Business Rules, which is observed to have a higher mean value in comparison to the other functionality types. Additionally, the results of ANOVA calculated between groups (F: 0.196, Sig: 0.899) confirmed that there is no significant difference between groups. In terms of *Flexibility*, the differences are also small, with the exception of Interface Adapters having higher mean value in *Flexibility* than the other types of functionality. After the calculation of ANOVA, the results (F: 0.532, Sig: 0.663) do not suggest the existence of significant differences. In terms of *Functionality*, we observed one noticeable distinction about Enterprise Business Rules, having a somewhat higher mean value, although only one package can be described with that functionality. The results of ANOVA (F: 0.345, Sig: 0.793) did not suggest the existence of significant differences. Concluding with *Extendibility*, the differences are negligible, and Enterprise Business Rules display the highest mean value, while the results of ANOVA calculated between groups (F: 1.953, Sig: 0.135) did not suggest the existence of significant differences.

In Table 5 we also present the results of the quality of the components developed with reuse in OpenHab. In terms of *Reusability* we observed difference in the mean values with higher being the Application Business Rules. Additionally, the results of ANOVA calculated between groups (F: 2.620, Sig: 0.05) suggested the existence of significant differences. In terms of *Flexibility* the difference between the mean values across packages offering different functionality types is very small, a fact that is also confirmed by the calculation of ANOVA (F: 0.155, Sig: 0.927). Furthermore, in terms of *Functionality* the results show that there is no significant difference, ANOVA (F: 2.285, Sig: 0.082), between functionality types with Application Business Rules having the highest mean value. Concluding with *Extendibility* we can observe that Application Business Rules and Interface Adapters have the highest mean values though there isn't a statistically significant difference between functionality types ANOVA (F: 1.428, Sig: 0.237).

RQ5 – Is there a difference between the quality of the components developed with reuse and the quality of the components developed from scratch and how is this reflected to the different types of the functionalities offered?

In Table 6 we compared the quality of the OpenHab packages that were developed with reuse (140 packages) to those developed without reuse (7 packages). In terms of *Reusability* there is a difference between components developed with reuse and components developed from scratch. We observed that components developed with reuse have a significantly higher value, as confirmed by the calculation of ANOVA (F: 6.096, Sig: 0.015). In terms of *Flexibility* the packages developed with reuse showed higher values. From the calculation of ANOVA (F: 5.224, Sig: 0.024), we noticed a significant difference between groups. In terms of *Functionality*, we observed a substantial difference, in which the components developed with reuse show a greater average value with the ANOVA (F: 6.194, Sig: 0.014) confirming the significant difference. The final quality metric we explored is Extendibility, which did not show differences between the two groups, although components developed from scratch showed a higher value. After the calculation of ANOVA (F: 0.419, Sig: 0.519).

Table 6. OpenHab per quality type

Developed with reuse	Reusability	Flexibility	Functionality	Extendibility
No	2.00	0.14	0.89	0.57
Yes	15.74	0.26	7.69	0.48

5 Discussion

The results of this paper revealed that the top two types of component functionality that are more likely to be reused in the context of Smart Home application development are: *Application Business Rules and Interface Adapters*. *Application Business Rules* and *Enterprise Business Rules* types of functionality are the least likely to require integration effort as they are usually implemented as Variable type or Static method call/constant value. On the other hand, components implementing Interface Adapters are the ones that require significantly more effort to be integrated in the new application (on average, 234 Lines of Code). Regarding the quality of the reused components, it is observed that there are no significant differences between the components offering different types of functionality. Finally, regarding the difference between the quality of the packages build with reuse and the packages built without reuse we observe that there are significant differences in terms of *Functionality, Reusability and Flexibility*, showing that software reuse can lead to increased quality of the application.

The results of this study provide useful information and guidance to **practitioners** on planning the reuse of components in the context of Smart Home application development. In particular, some general conclusions that we reached from this case study are:

- Engineers of IoT, Smart Home applications can greatly benefit from reusing a core set of general purpose components, which in our case are the *Enterprise Business Rules* and the *Applications Business Rules*. These components, in their majority, can be reused as is without requiring any integration effort.
- The reuse of components offering functionality related to *Interface Adapters* can also be beneficial, since this type of functionality offered the most reused components. However, reusing components related to Interface and Adapters required certain integration efforts for implementing or extending the classes reused.
- In terms of the four examined quality characteristics, components of type Interface Adapters seem to present the highest potentials of being reused. This can be interpreted intuitively, as these types of components should be hardware-agnostic and abstract the details of the Application Business Rules.

Based on the results of this case study, we encourage **researchers** to:

- Further explore the reuse of components in the context of IoT application development for Smart Home automation by examining other Open Source projects (e.g., Home Assistant). Researchers can investigate whether the same type of components, as appointed by this study, have been systematically reused. The results of this study can also guide researchers in assessing the appropriateness of the reused components.

- Introduce a process for systematic, planned reuse of IoT components. Such a process would define clear procedures for: (a) identifying and sorting the reusable components, (b) integrating the reused components into the new applications, and (c) maintaining these components.

To conclude this section, we refer to the *threats to validity* of this case study [24]. A possible threat to *construct validity* is related to the metrics that are used to answer our research questions. Regarding the effort metrics, we believe that the new lines of code are indicators of the effort required to integrate the reused components. This metric has been also adopted in [8] and [23] for assessing the reuse effort. Nevertheless, we acknowledge that there are other metrics that can also be used. For the quality assessment of the reused components, we have used QMOOD, which is an established quality model that has been rigorously validated [3]. However, we acknowledge that other quality models could lead to variations in the observed results. With regard to *reliability*, we acknowledge potential researchers' bias during the data collection due to the manual classification of components into types of functionality performed by the first author. To mitigate reliability threats the second and third author validated the results. Finally, we acknowledge that the *external validity*, is threatened by the fact that the entire data set is taken from one single reuse case between Eclipse Smart Home and OpenHab. However, we believe that the results can be generalize in the context of reuse of Smart Home automation frameworks since the majority of applications are built from modular blocks that can be easily classified in the functionality types employed in this study [14]. Threats to *internal validity* are not discussed in this paper, as we did not seek to identify causal relations in this study.

6 Conclusions

In this paper, we explored the reuse opportunities stemming from the popular Eclipse Smart Home framework for building home automation IoT applications. We performed a case study and investigated the types of functionality that can be reused, the effort required for integrating the reused components and whether or not such reuse leads to quality benefits. We analyzed 107 packages from the ESH framework and 240 reused components from the OpenHab application. The results of this case study suggest that: the main reused functionality is related to Interface Adapters; the main type of reuse is Variable Type; and the effort for integrating the reused components can range from 38 lines of code to 1421 lines of code. The quality of the reused components is slightly higher compared to components built from scratch. As future work we intend to further explore reuse opportunities within home automation IoT frameworks by examining other open source frameworks (e.g., Home Assistant), retrieving candidate components, and comparing them.

Acknowledgement. This research was co-funded by the European Union and Greek national funds through the Operational Program Competitiveness, Entrepreneurship, and Innovation, grant number T1EDK-04873.

References

1. Alam, M.R., Reaz, M.B.I., Ali, M.A.M.: A review of smart homes—past, present, and future. IEEE Trans. Syst. Man Cybern. Part C (Appl. Rev.) **42**(6), 1190–1203 (2012)
2. Ayala, C., Hauge, Ø., Conradi, R., Franch, X., Li, J.: Selection of third party software in Off-The-Shelf-based software development—an interview study with industrial practitioners. J. Syst. Softw. **84**(4), 620–637 (2011)
3. Bansiya, J., Davis, C.G.: A hierarchical model for object-oriented design quality assessment. IEEE Trans. Softw. Eng. **28**(1), 4–17 (2002)
4. Benni, B., Mosser, S., Moha, N., Riveill, M.: A delta-oriented approach to support the safe reuse of black-box code rewriters. In: Capilla, R., Gallina, B., Cetina, C. (eds.) ICSR 2018. LNCS, vol. 10826, pp. 164–180. Springer, Cham (2018). https://doi.org/10.1007/978-3-319-90421-4_11
5. Brereton, P., Budgen, D.: Component-based systems: a classification of issues. Computer **33**(11), 54–62 (2000)
6. Caldiera, G., Basili, V.R.: Identifying and qualifying reusable software components. Computer **24**(2), 61–70 (1991)
7. Crnkovic, I., Larsson, M.: Challenges of component-based development. J. Syst. Softw. **61**(3), 201–212 (2002)
8. Gui, G., Scott, P.D.: Coupling and cohesion measures for evaluation of component reusability. In: Proceedings of the 2006 International Workshop on Mining Software Repositories, pp. 18–21. ACM (2006)
9. Gupta, A., Cruzes, D., Shull, F., Conradi, R., Rønneberg, H., Landre, E.: An examination of change profiles in reusable and non-reusable software systems. J. Softw. Maint. Evol. Res. Pract. **22**(5), 359–380 (2010)
10. Jatain, A., Nagpal, A., Gaur, D.: Agglomerative hierarchical approach for clustering components of similar reusability. Int. J. Comput. Appl. **68**(2), 33–37 (2013)
11. Kamilaris, A., Trifa, V., Pitsillides, A.: HomeWeb: an application framework for Web-based smart homes. In: 2011 18th International Conference on IEEE Telecommunications (ICT), pp. 134–139 (2011)
12. Kim, J.E., Boulos, G., Yackovich, J., Barth, T., Beckel, C., Mosse, D.: Seamless integration of heterogeneous devices and access control in smart homes. In: 2012 8th International Conference on IEEE Intelligent Environments (IE), pp. 206–213 (2012)
13. Ma, S., Yang, H., Shi, M.: Developing a creative travel management system based on software reuse and abstraction techniques. In: 2017 IEEE 41st Annual Computer Software and Applications Conference (COMPSAC), vol. 2, pp. 419–424. IEEE (2017)
14. Martin, R.C.: Clean Architecture: A Craftsman's Guide to Software Structure and Design. Prentice Hall Press, Upper Saddle River (2017)
15. Mehmood, Y., Ahmad, F., Yaqoob, I., Adnane, A., Imran, M., Guizani, S.: Internet-of-things-based smart cities: recent advances and challenges. IEEE Commun. Mag. **55**(9), 16–24 (2017)
16. Ostertag, E., Hendler, J., Prieto-Díaz, R., Braun, C.: Computing similarity in a reuse library system: an AI-based approach. ACM Trans. Softw. Eng. Methodol. **1**(3), 205–228 (1992)

17. Padhy, N., Singh, R.P., Satapathy, S.C.: Software reusability metrics estimation: algorithms, models and optimization techniques. Comput. Electr. Eng. **69**, 653–668 (2018)
18. Pacheco, C.L., Garcia, I.A., Calvo-Manzano, J.A., Arcilla, M.: A proposed model for reuse of software requirements in requirements catalog. J. Softw. Evol. Process **27**(1), 1–21 (2015)
19. Panwar, A., Singh, A., Kumawat, R., Jaidka, S., Garg, K. Eyrie smart home automation using Internet of Things. In: 2017 Computing Conference, pp. 1368–1370. IEEE (2017)
20. Paschali, M.-E., Ampatzoglou, A., Bibi, S., Chatzigeorgiou, A., Stamelos, I.: A case study on the availability of open-source components for game development. In: Kapitsaki, G.M., Santana de Almeida, E. (eds.) ICSR 2016. LNCS, vol. 9679, pp. 149–164. Springer, Cham (2016). https://doi.org/10.1007/978-3-319-35122-3_11
21. Perera, C., McCormick, C., Bandara, A.K., Price, B.A., Nuseibeh, B.: Privacy-by-design framework for assessing internet of things applications and platforms. In: Proceedings of the 6th International Conference on the Internet of Things, pp. 83–92. ACM (2016)
22. Prakash, B.A., Ashoka, D.V., Aradhya, V.M.: Application of data mining techniques for software reuse process. Procedia Technol. **4**, 384–389 (2012)
23. Prieto-Diaz, R., Freeman, P.: Classifying software for reusability. IEEE Softw. **4**(1), 6 (1987)
24. Runeson, P., Höst, M.: Guidelines for conducting and reporting case study research in software engineering. Empirical Softw. Eng. **14**(2), 131 (2009)
25. Serna, M.A., Sreenan, C.J., Fedor, S.: A visual programming framework for wireless sensor networks in smart home applications. In: 2015 IEEE Tenth International Conference on Intelligent Sensors, Sensor Networks and Information Processing (ISSNIP), pp. 1–6 (2015)
26. Sharma, A., Grover, P.S., Kumar, R.: Reusability assessment for software components. ACM SIGSOFT Softw. Eng. Notes **34**(2), 1–6 (2009)
27. Singh, S., Singh, S., Singh, G.: Reusability of the software. Int. J. Comput. Appl. **7**(14), 38–41 (2010)
28. Smiari, P., Bibi, S.: A smart city application modeling framework: a case study on re-engineering a smart retail platform. In: 2018 44th Euromicro Conference on Software Engineering and Advanced Applications (SEAA), pp. 111–118. IEEE (2018)
29. Smirek, L., Zimmermann, G., Beigl, M.: Just a smart home or your smart home–a framework for personalized user interfaces based on eclipse smart home and universal remote console. Procedia Comput. Sci. **98**, 107–116 (2016)
30. Vale, T., Crnkovic, I., De Almeida, E.S., Neto, P.A.D.M.S., Cavalcanti, Y.C., de Lemos Meira, S.R.: Twenty-eight years of component-based software engineering. J. Syst. Softw. **111**, 128–148 (2016)
31. Varadan, R., Channabasavaiah, K., Simpson, S., Holley, K., Allam, A.: Increasing business flexibility and SOA adoption through effective SOA governance. IBM Syst. J. **47**(3), 473–488 (2008)
32. Wangoo, D.P., Singh, A.: A classification based predictive cost model for measuring reusability level of open source software (2018)
33. Wen, X., Wang, Y.: Design of smart home environment monitoring system based on raspberry Pi. In: 2018 Chinese Control and Decision Conference (CCDC), pp. 4259–4263. IEEE (2018)
34. Zanella, A., Bui, N., Castellani, A., Vangelista, L., Zorzi, M.: Internet of things for smart cities. IEEE Internet Things J. **1**(1), 22–32 (2014)

Post Papers

"Reuse on Steroids": Reuse of Code, Compliance Tools, and Clearing Results

Arun Azhakesan[1] and Frances Paulisch[2(✉)]

[1] Development Center, Siemens Healthcare Private Ltd., Bangalore, India
Arun.Azhakesan@siemens-healthineers.com
[2] Development Center, Siemens Healthcare GmbH, Forchheim, Germany
Frances.Paulisch@siemens-healthineers.com

Abstract. This short paper summarizes our industrial experience with applying an open-source based approach not only for development but also for the license compliance activities. We use and actively participate in the various communities using open-source based license compliance tools. When we use open-source components in our products, we share the license clearing reports of those across the company so that they can be reused where applicable. Thus, we reuse not only the code, but also apply reuse to the license compliance tools as well as to the clearing results. As is commonly known, the amount of open-source used throughout the world is large and growing. We hope that by sharing our experiences that the global software engineering community is more aware of these more novel aspects of open source and not only focus on the reuse of the components themselves

Keywords: Open source · License compliance · Open source software license clearing · Compliance clearing tools

Background. As with many other companies, our products include third-party software components (commercial or open-source). Taking advantage of using such components requires that one has a suitable license compliance process established and that this is supported by appropriate tools. The OpenChain (https://www.openchainproject.org) standard describes some of the basic organizational elements. This talk describes our experience with using open-source based approaches to handle the license compliance aspects.

The Problem. In order to ensure that one does the license compliance correctly, one must have the transparency on what OSS components are used and how they are used. And one must know what licenses are used in those components so that one can meet the associated license obligations. The problem is how to do this in an efficient way and one that can keep up to the high pace of innovation in the software community.

Our Approach. A core idea of our approach is that we do not only reuse the components themselves, but also apply "reuse" by using open-source tools to support the license clearing and then also make those license clearing reports available across the company in a reusable form in a central repository. Especially with the growing amount of open source used and the fast pace of modern software development lifecycles, it is

© Springer Nature Switzerland AG 2019
X. Peng et al. (Eds.): ICSR 2019, LNCS 11602, pp. 251–252, 2019.
https://doi.org/10.1007/978-3-030-22888-0

important to be able to reuse the license clearing reports when the components are used in the same context.

In contrast to using commercial tools for this process, we chose explicitly to use an open-source based approach. The main tools we use for license clearing and component management are FOSSology and SW360. FOSSology [1] is a Linux Foundation project used as the basis for our license scanning service. It has a very precise license scanning facility that allows us to identify licenses, not only at the main license level, but deep licenses, as well as copyright and other relevant information. SW360 is a project hosted by the Eclipse Foundation. It serves as our central software component repository and provides the necessary transparency needed to manage our license compliance (e.g. status of clearing reports).

An important aspect of our approach is that we do not only "take" from the open-source community but we use standard formats like SPDX (a common way to share metadata on software licenses driven by the Linux Foundation). Furthermore, we actively participate in the compliance community activities e.g. the new Automated Compliance Tooling (ACT) activities of the Linux Foundation and activities presented at a forum organized by a German BITKOM [2] Forum. The main tools we use, Fossology and SW360, are not the only ones in this space – there are a number of other ones such as Quartermaster, OSS Review Toolkit as well as ScanCode, Tern, and ClearlyDefined. Also, the Software Heritage project could play an important part of the OSS ecosystem as a central source code repository. It is our impression that the various communities strive to establish a healthy ecosystem and have links to each other rather than compete – for that it helps that they all have an open-source mindset.

In summary, we have found the open source mindset to match well to reuse - not only for code but also for license compliance tools, their clearing results and, in future, even more. Be aware that there is an ecosystem of "ready for prime time" open-source based tools available to use today to help ensure that you do not simply reuse the code but also take appropriate care of the license compliance activities.

References

1. Jaeger, M.C., Fendt, O., Gobeille, R., Huber, M., Najjar, J., Stewart, K., Weber, S., Würl, A.: The FOSSology project: 10 years of license scanning. Int. Free Open Source Softw. Law Rev. **9**(1)
2. Forum Open Source 2018 - BITKOM 2018. https://www.bitkom.org/Themen/Technologien-Software/Open-Source/Forum-Open-Source-2018.html

Sustainable Software Reuse in Complex Industrial Software Ecosystem: The Practice in CFETSIT

Yixiao Li[1][✉], Zhubin Chuan[1], Tong Wu[1], Yijian Wu[2], Xin Peng[2], and Gang Zhang[2,3]

[1] CFETS Information Technology (Shanghai) Co., Ltd., Shanghai 201203, China
{liyixiao_zh,chuanzhubin_zh,wutong}@chinamoney.com.cn
[2] School of Computer Science, Fudan University, Shanghai 201203, China
{wuyijian,pengxin}@fudan.edu.cn
[3] Emergent Design Inc., Shanghai 200090, China
gangz@emergentdesign.cn

Background. CFETS Information Technology (Shanghai) Co., Ltd. (CFETS-IT) is a company fully invested by China Foreign Exchange Trade System (CFETS). The company is dedicated to software development, operation and maintenance, and information services for the establishment of a global trading platform and pricing center for RMB and related financial products. Software products of the company are mainly sophisticated financial software systems. The products form up complex software ecosystem covering the monetary financial business domain. General-purpose components and frameworks have been developed over the past two decades. Software reuse requirements and opportunities emerge as the software ecosystem grows. Therefore, the company seek systematic and sustainable software reuse and software assets management to improve software quality and productivity.

Problem. Systematic and sustainable reuse of hundreds of millions lines of source code and all software assets becomes more and more challenging due to the growing amount of software assets, the complex composition of the development teams, and the continuous evolution of all software products. (1) *Managing growing source code assets.* One obvious problem is code clones and provenance. While large amount of source code is precious resource for reuse, uncontrolled code clones may cause many problems such as defect propagation and licence violations, and bring severe difficulty in quality management. It is essential to detect code clones and to discover possible provenance of code for sustainable code reuse. (2) *Managing complexity and instability of development teams.* Software reuse can only be properly practiced by proper teams. However, teams are usually unstable in an IT company like CFETSIT. Moreover, in most projects, both in-house developers and outsourced teams are involved, bringing complexity to the team composition. It is important to ensure proper software reuse training and monitoring for building up sustainable development forces. (3) *Managing continuous evolution of products.* It is more and more difficult to maintain systematic software reuse while all products continuously evolve in parallel. Archi-

© Springer Nature Switzerland AG 2019
X. Peng et al. (Eds.): ICSR 2019, LNCS 11602, pp. 253–255, 2019.
https://doi.org/10.1007/978-3-030-22888-0

tectural design may be overlooked and the system integrity decays. Static code analysis tools are used for source code check but low accuracy makes it inefficient for the developers to reuse of previous fix solutions. Therefore, sustainable reuse of architectural assets and historical solutions is difficult under the circumstance of continuous evolution.

Practice. Aiming at systematic and sustainable software reuse in the enterprise's software ecosystem, CFETSIT deploys a big code platform, designed and implemented by the software engineering team of Fudan University, that acts as a fundamental facility to manage enterprise software assets. The platform mainly consists of three layers, namely *Data Layer*, *Analysis Layer*, and *Application Service Layer*. The *Data Layer* consists of services that are designed to register software projects and keep track of their changes. Source code updates are monitored by automatic detections of commits to the code repository. Source code in open-source projects are also managed so that code provenance analysis in a wider range is feasible. The *Analysis Layer* consists of multiple stand-alone code analysis facilities, such as code clone detection, code differencing, code style check and defects detection. Analysis facilities are implemented as loosely coupled services that work as plugins to a well-designed architecture. They can be newly developed services or existing software engineering tools as well. All analysis results (also generally called *issues*) are stored under a unique basic data structure, with extensions of information specific to each analysis tool. Moreover, analysis results are aligned in terms of the location (i.e., file, method, and lines) of the source code, by a dedicated alignment service. The purpose of the alignment is to keep track of the *same* detected issues to minimize manual tracking efforts. The *Application Service Layer* provides services that serve individuals in the development team, including code recommendation, issue tracking, code searching, early warnings for code defects and design flaws, and many more.

While the platform is still on its way to maturity, we have practised some capabilities of the platform on several projects in the company and see promising early results. (1) *Clone Detection, Monitoring, and Management:* Code clones are detected within and across all projects in the software ecosystem. Cloned code are visible to programmers and managers. Similarity-based code provenance analysis is also enabled for evaluating code reuse practices. (2) *Issue Tracking:* The results produced by static code analysis tools are collected and aligned between versions. False alarms or neglectable information may be suppressed. Developers are able to focus on the issues that indeed need attention and reuse development knowledge. (3) *Developer Profiling:* Developers' performance on source code production and defect production is collected and analyzed so that sustainable development forces can be achieved. (4) *Early Warnings and Repairing Assistances:* Fixes to issues of the same type or similar defective source code usually undergo similar fixes, which are recommended to developers for reuse. Developers writing error-prone code get early warnings with examples of code fixes in the history.

Conclusion. Systematic and sustainable software reuse is essential for companies like CFETSIT, whose software projects are highly domain-specific and software development involves multiple in-house and outsourced teams. The big code platform shows a promising way to manage and reuse software assets, and to exploit value from code big data for quality software and high productivity.

Author Index

Printed in the United States
by Book masters

Printed in the United States
By Bookmasters